TESTIMONIALS

"Zen Gardner does an adventurous thing and a right thing and an exciting thing: he knocks down the wall between between consciousness and the world, without diminishing the heights to which consciousness can rise. Think about that. And read what he writes, because he's also updating original Zen to make it relevant to today and tomorrow. He shreds the illusory barrier between wisdom of the past and life as it is this minute."

Jon Rappoport

"My dear Friend and Brother Zen Gardner has an absolutely Magical and Divine touch to his words. He is one of our times' greatest and most important writers and philosophers."

Ole Dammegård

"'You Are The Awakening' - the title spells it out exactly. Zen's inspirational writings let knowledge seekers understand they are not alone as the great cycle unfolds, memories return and we begin to shake off the shackles of suppression. Zen's book is history in the making. Generations to come will be able to look back and see how it all unfolded."

Steve (Philosophers Stone / Phoenix is Risen)

"Zen's work is potent and powerful. He truly has his mind and heart tuned to the many facets of the awakening."

Sharron Rose, Producer of The Last Avatar

"Zen Gardner's collected works blow the lid off the lie that we are powerless against the many conspiracies that hold the world at large in physical, economic and spiritual bondage. If Paul Revere were re-incarnated for a digital, globally connected and enlightened generation such as ours, his midnight ride might feel a lot like a breakneck gallop through Zen's mind."

Dylan Charles, Editor of WakingTimes.com

You Are The Awakening

Zen Gardner

You Are The Awakening

*Lovingly dedicated to a
magnificent butterfly named Elle,
without whom this would
never have been possible.*

*May the wings of love bear you up
to new heights and vistas
you never thought possible.*

"Enlightenment is a destructive process. It has nothing to do with becoming better or being happier. Enlightenment is the crumbling away of untruth. It's seeing through the facade of pretense and the complete eradication of everything we imagined to be true."

\- Adyashanti

Introduction

This first book of a series is a compilation of updated articles regarding the awakening to a more fully conscious awareness of who we are and why we are here. I've selected my more appropriate essays to help empower and encourage anyone who is on this wonderful path of realizing our infinite potential, highlighting the fact that any change we seek in the world around us begins with each of us individually.

We cannot expect the true reality we know in our hearts to come to fruition without full conscious awareness on an individual basis. Otherwise, any effort to reform or transmute the world of suffering around us will only reinforce the same constructs and limited understanding that created it.

The dynamics of the awakening are much different from the programmed approach of this world we were born into. In order to tap into the limitless source of our full potential we have to step aside from the severely limited ways of thinking we are accustomed to and apply entirely new seemingly unstructured principles. The only way to find these dynamic forces awaiting us is by letting go of our previous notions, even so-called logic in many cases, as well as a host of reflexive mind sets and emotional responses. These only cloud the heart from realizing itself in our lives.

I liken this awakening process to unhooking a type of velcro attachment to our souls one hook and loop at a time. The process is continual, but as we free ourselves we grow more awake and aware and hence empowered to pursue this process which in turn inevitably leads to a changed worldview and detached yet empowered lifestyle, as well as feeling compelled to help inspire the same in others. This happens via accessing information, inner realizations and taking action on what we have come to learn. Synchronistic thoughts and events begin to manifest more frequently and as we take these cues seriously and put them into effect, a glorious new life blossoms in the rich soil of our hearts.

The articles are arranged in sections but each one is a stand alone entry so they can be read in sequence or individually. It's meant to serve as a sort of empowerment handbook you can easily reference in full, by section or by particular article anytime you'd like to help encourage all those embarking on this wonderful journey.

May these words inspire and empower you.

Much love, Zen

www.zengardner.com

Table of Contents

PART 2

Navigating Our Changing World

PART 3

Language, Beliefs and Other Hazards

PART 4

Take Action

Part 1 -
The Awakening

An Introduction to Awakening

The waking up process is a very personal experience. Once we become aware of the existence of a fabricated world we thought to be real and that our true nature is anything but what we've been told, there's no turning back.

It may appear to be a lonely path, but we are by no means alone in this awakening. It is happening in all walks of life.

Whether a banker, corporate employee or lay wanderer wakes up to the scam being perpetrated on humanity and pulls out of the matrix, or a normal taxpaying worker realizes they're contributing to a military industrial machine hell bent on control and world domination, we're all the same.

And those are just surface issues compared to the deliberate suppression of man's innate spiritual nature, whether we call it social liberty or the freedom to create and manifest as we truly are.

Triggers for Awakening

There are many such triggers that wake people up. Once someone realizes such things as how the world was scammed on 9/11 and that the powers that be are willing to perpetrate such atrocities to promote their agenda, the digging begins. When we realize we're seemingly at the complete mercy of parasitic central bankers more than willing to not only implode the world's economy, but finance both sides of any conflict for personal gain and control and that our governments are complicit in this scheme, we start to grasp the enormity of what befalls us.

That we have rapidly evolved into an advanced militarized surveillance police state is driving many to ask some hard questions – and the answers can be startling and difficult to swallow, especially when we realize they have cut off all avenues of recourse.

Another major issue is that it's more evident by the day that our very health is under attack, again by complicit government and multinational corporations pushing GMOs, adulterated food, vaccines, pharmaceuticals, atmospheric aerosols and the like, all of which have been proven to be extremely hazardous to humanity.

Yet they push harder by the day, mandating program after destructive program. Meanwhile, natural and organic farming and foods, as well as natural supplements, are under intense attack by these very same perpetrators.

The truth about these issues are many including massive planet harming programs such as fracking, electrosmog, and the geoengineering assault on humanity that are driving a major perceptual paradigm shift amongst all walks of life as we delve more deeply into who is doing all this and why.

There Is No "They" – Oh Really?

This is often the final breakthrough point for many people. As the true picture starts to crystallize, the horrific realization that the "powers that be" are fundamentally a clandestine cabal with front men comes into focus. These are powerful minions, more interested in weakening and subjugating humanity via health degradation, dumbed down education, mindless "bread and circus" government controlled media, depraved violence and sex oriented entertainment, and a draconian militarized police crackdown.

The ugly truth then comes to the fore.

It can be staggering. If you take just 9/11 and other false flag events and realize they were staged to bring about this Orwellian police state where the citizens are now terrorist suspects, it can be very difficult to swallow.

A quick perusal of history soon follows, where people soon realize these same false flag/false enemy tactics were used to justify almost every war, leading to such totalitarian states as Stalinist Russia, Communist China and Nazi Germany, each of which descended into horrific pogroms, decimating their own populations of anyone potentially daring to question the new regime.

It's not all black and white. There are of course good people working for bad people, powers and programs, wittingly and unwittingly. Many are trying to change and improve our existing structure. Many good people are performing wonderful services within this societal program thinking it can be changed constructively. What we're addressing are the overarching deceitful and destructive powers and mechanisms at play that are attempting to bring humanity into a weakened subservient role to some sort of worldwide fascist control state, eliminating personal and national sovereignty in order to support and obey a very few powerful self-appointed elites.

And it's coming on fast.

This becomes evident as anyone pursues almost any avenue we're discussing here. To realize this massive program is being orchestrated by some form of "they" soon becomes obvious. The reality of the conspiracy that JFK so eloquently pointed out before he was surgically removed from office via assassination hits squarely home. Please listen to his entire speech on line.

We Have to Find Out for Ourselves

An essential element to a true awakening is investigating and learning for ourselves. One of the main control mechanisms has been teaching humanity to only trust what they've been told by these same agendized so-called authorities. How many times have you heard, "If 9/11 was an 'inside job', surely it would have been on CNN. If something was really wrong surely someone would have said something."

Well, a lot of people have and continue to speak out. And what's the response? Anything contrary to the official narrative is "outlandish conspiracy theories", and result in the subsequent elimination, demonization and marginalization of any form of questioning or healthy criticism.

Waking up from that media and education entrancement is another shocker. Could they do such a thing? Could we really be facing such a totalitarian crackdown? And why?

When I was young there were over 60 media companies vying for audiences. Real investigative reporting, although it's always been tampered with or suppressed, was still available. Today 6 mega corporations own all of the media. The very same corporations that co-own much of the corporate military industrial infrastructure. Conspiracy is not a stretch – of course these power brokers would twist information to suit their intentions. The word conspiracy has been stigmatized for a reason – don't ask questions or there will be consequences.

All of this will take some serious researching, most likely in places people have never dared to look before. And this is good. Don't let anyone tell you what the truth is, find out for yourself and be convinced in your own mind and heart. That's a new phenomenon for most, as odd as that may seem, but stepping outside the propaganda mainstream is a must. And is oh so refreshing.

The Shock Does Wear Off – And Don't Worry, We're in this Together

There are so many interconnected "rabbit holes" of similarly repressed, twisted or hidden areas of information that it can be staggering. Once we realize we've been lied to about any one of these serious issues, we begin to question everything. And that is extremely healthy. You may not find support for your new found perspective from those around you, but there are millions who are sharing your experience. Thanks to the internet you can find others undergoing the same transformation quite readily and derive a lot of encouragement and support.

Battling through the naysaying of close friends and loved ones seems to act like a chrysalis, much like the cocoon a metamorphosing butterfly has to struggle to escape. And as we know, that is exactly what drives the blood into the wings of the birthing creation that will soon bear the beautiful new awakened soul to glorious new heights and vistas.

One thing that won't wear off is your absolute disdain for what is being perpetrated on our fellow humans. As the expression goes, "If you're not angry, you're not paying attention." If you knew your home was under attack and malevolent forces were coming for you and your children, you would do anything in your power to protect your family. That soon becomes an innate awareness regarding the current toxic social and physical world we're experiencing and the need for a conscious response.

Awakening Your Spirituality

This goes hand in hand with anyone experiencing this consciousness shift. If things here are so massively manipulated, what lies beyond all of this? What are we being kept from? Why do I sense I am so much more? Where does God or Love or human kindness come in? And for so many with some form of religious or spiritual background, the question always arises, "Is this some form of spiritual warfare?"

These are very important questions to pursue. There must be meaning in all of this. "Certainly all of humanity is not as wicked as these psychopathic control freaks." Yes, that's true. Unfortunately, the aggressor often rules the day in this hierarchy of control our world has adopted for millennia. History bears this out.

The beauty of gaining a new spiritual perspective is that it puts these influences in their place. We discover new ways to perceive our true indomitable nature which gives tremendous peace and confidence in spite of what we're currently faced with. This sense of profound conscious awareness and spirituality only grows as our pursuit for truth, in love, gains momentum.

Awake, But Never Alone

A sense of isolation following the initial awakening is natural. It's foreign to everything we've been taught, with implications that can be mind-boggling as well as heart breaking as those close to us do not share our newfound awareness. However, we are very much connected and sharing a profound common experience. Knowing we are not alone is very important to keep in mind.

Building community also becomes a priority, where we can contribute to the healing of the planet at every level possible. Whether it's activist or spiritual associations this is very important. It may only be on-line at first, that's fine. Find kindred spirits and empowering and informative websites and blogs and even attend or even create meet up events in your area on some of these subjects of concern.

This awakening of consciousness is transpiring at an accelerating pace, and it's something to be very encouraged about. Once you get past the shock of what you've "found out", it becomes easier, but it will drastically alter your life.

Enjoy it, be empowered by it, and take action accordingly. Trust your heart.

The darkness cannot put out the Light no matter how hard they try.

You Are the Battlefield

There's no looking for crowd validation. There's no waiting for outside redemption. There's no collective bargaining to rely on.

The awakening is you. Only you.

That's what all this ruckus is about. The battle for your spirit and soul. And that's the boat each of us is in. There is nothing more important in this life for you, or me, than waking up. Once that's straightened out the rest will follow.

How we perceive the world around us creates and reinforces the world around us. Once we become conscious and aware that this existing matrix we're witnessing is an arbitrary creation manipulated by power-crazed puppeteers, however you perceive them, that is when the change happens. And the Universe will tell you what to do from there.

That's what to respond to. Nothing else. That's your job. That's my job. Don't shirk it when it happens.

Enjoy Your Earthly Suit, But Rediscover Who You Truly Are

Like me, you are sitting inside, or somewhat near anyway, the body you chose to be in. We're looking through and freely operating these amazing biological machines on a fabulous planet. And, "Wow, there appears to be a whole lot of other beings like me walking around. Where am I? What am I here for? And what am I supposed to do?"

That's exactly our predicament. And what immediately sets in once we arrive? As young children we have this abandon as we experience this incredible place and all of its feelings, sights and sounds. We screech with delight, sing made up songs, swing our arms around wildly and run in place. We just express.

Then what happens? We start to conform to what we're seeing, as well as what we're being told. We become more regimented and are herded into classrooms and categories. We start feeling social pressures and are then handed this fundamental doctrine of insecurity where fear and scarcity become our main drivers. Your purpose in life now is to "fit in and get a job" so you won't run out of money or food.

Your internal, conscious response? "This is strange. Everything's a problem here. Sure didn't feel that way when I arrived."

The Illusory Attachment Trap

The main trick of the illusory world around us is to make us think we're somehow attached to it, and therefore dependent, and that we need to conform to this world we're viewing. We tend to judge by the standards we're exposed to, and act accordingly. We base our lives and actions around these perceived behavior patterns, which in turn gradually dull the voice of conscious awareness.

You might have noticed how blind people, such as entertainers Ray Charles and Stevie Wonder, gesticulate totally freely, rocking their heads while singing or talking, and have wildly free facial expressions, almost as if they're disturbed or unnatural in some way.

Obviously they're not. But it strikes you. They're free from visual conformity. They don't know how everyone else acts. They're free to physically express their emotions without having to conform to the suppressed, fearful conformist nature of our hung up society. They don't know you don't rock back and forth, shake your head and smile so broad your face almost cracks. How liberating.

And that principle can be applied across the board.

We judge so much by how we think it will measure up to the world around us rather than just express what we're thinking and feeling openly. Whether with close friends and family, our peer group, or the message we pick up in public or from the media, we're being programmed. Programmed to not respond to obvious needs, but to strange, shallow self-serving impulses. Just like everyone else.

You can say that's just natural, but it's not. It's induced behavior from a manipulated and self-regulating created collective. Natural for the matrix, but not for a conscious human being, especially when the crowd is clearly going the wrong way. But who's looking when you're sleep walking?

The Cost of Vicarious Living and Beyond

In the end most humans end up living a vicarious life, acting out the projection they think they're supposed to live up to. That's bondage. The yardstick is acceptance rather than truth or conscience. This is heavily reinforced through education, the media and the existing paradigm they've succeeded in creating. It appears to be the only option out there...but only to the unawakened.

But there's a price to pay.

Everything. Waking up costs everything. So what? What are you saving up for? Aren't you paying that price anyway even if you're not waking up? Life always costs everything. You'll leave here eventually, like me, and the cost will be your life.

How did you spend it? Consciously, or trying to conform, and using that to hide behind to justify living as a comfortable, selfish, lazy brain donor to the system you're too afraid to buck?

That's the battlefield. You. Me. It goes no further. What we see playing out in the world is a bunch of you's and me's deciding if they'll live consciously and truly respond to that still, small voice within them, or not. The sad reality is almost every one of them has been duped into being fixated on what all the other "me's" are doing in order to keep up with the projected reality. It's like a school of fish feverishly clinging together in response to a perceived predator.

The only thing is, for conscious, spiritual reality there is no predator. That's the secret. We are eternal consciousness having an experience.

The way to solve these problems is to re-create the perceived reality through conscious awareness and conscious actions.

When You Get the Call, Take It

We, individually, have to change first. We have to commit to consciousness, get free of entanglements and live a conscious life. The rest has little meaning until we get out of the matrix ourselves.

If each of us would get that message the phony world structure would crumble in a minute. Every soldier would drop his weapon and go home. Every politician would wake up as if out of a dream and go be with his family. Every soldier and policeman would lay down his gun, take off his uniform, and go help someone in need, smiling and greeting people on his way.

It's you. It's me. Your personal world and experience is the only one you'll ever know. Don't bite off more than you can chew at the start, but get started. Just let consciousness be your guide. But act on it.

And don't fret too much about what it is you're supposed to do. You'll know it when you see it. It comes in the form of little things, little decisions, the rest follows. Learn to listen to that voice and act accordingly and it gets louder and louder.

Just walk away from what you know to be wrong, and do what you know to be right. It's not that hard once you start.

And again, once you get your boat in motion, the rudder will take effect.

"A journey of a thousand miles begins with a single step."

- Lao Tzu

The Tipping Point Is Here - And It's All About You

There's no question about it. We're there. And I'm not just talking about the globalist takeover bid they're hastily and clumsily trying to execute.

The awakening is erupting.

Many feel lost and afraid right now all across the spectrum of humanity. This deliberate creation of chaos is designed to do just that. However, parallel and simultaneous to their psychotic designs is a massive arousal of the human spirit, spurred on by an arising of conscious awareness and a deep sense of growing personal realization and empowerment.

Most may not recognize these rising seemingly confusing energetic changes as being the creative process at work, but it is. Awakening is first of all a destructive process, eliminating everything that is unreal and inhibitive of personal development and progress. These two dynamics work concurrently.

When you stand back and observe with washened eyes you'll see it, and it brings great peace in the midst of these stormy times.

What Price Awakening?

Being awake comes with a price, and it may have been upped a bit or even a lot lately. You're being worked on. Letting go and getting the most out of challenging circumstances and conditions is vital to growth. Don't fight it, whatever you do.

It's very sad to see unawakened humanity being tossed to and fro without a clue as to what is really going on.

But even that is an "engineered" shake up designed by Universe to help every one of us come to our senses and transcend this false reality. Millions are flocking to alternative news sources to try to make sense of what's going on, and they're stumbling on realities they never considered before.

And that's a wonderful thing. It will cause a lot of pain to make the realizations they're being presented with but again, that's alright.

Truth comes with a cost – the end of the lies and illusions they had previously based their entire lives on. And it's an ongoing process.

Many will be forced to enter the "dark night of the soul" whether they want to or not. I can tell you from personal experience that it's a hell of a lot easier and quicker if you elect to let yourself go through it, and in many ways the sooner you do, if you haven't already, the better.

What Do We Do?

So what should we do? If we know the truth, we're responsible not only to share it passionately, but also to live it. This is where it gets even more uncomfortable, but it must be done. The hour is late and the times we are living in are dire. There's no alternative any more.

We have to rise to the occasion. It's virtually us or them, life or death, truth or lies, freedom or slavery – for not just ourselves but our loved ones, progeny and the entire human race. That's what makes this the opportunity of a lifetime, and our marvelous creative Universe is there to meet you if you dare walk the path.

In fact, you'll even meet your true self, what you've been looking and longing for your whole life!

The Tipping Point

There are many remarkable signs that to me are clear signals that the tide is not just turning, but the tide of humanity awakening is rising quickly. What we do from here is supremely important as we have a growing array of opportunities for active participation unfolding before us. And there will be more, but waiting to start somewhere is not an option.

The time to activate is now. Let anything that hinders this fall away from your life, whatever the cost. The call for our inner warriors to rise could not be any clearer.

You'll see these manifestations of the tipping point we've reached everywhere if you look. People's tones are changing, minds are tossed about but exploring new perspectives, truths are being outed like never before. It's an amazing time. Don't stare at the machinations of the powers that shouldn't be, they're designed to distract and disempower. This is crucial.

And don't think Gaia is going to take all this lying down either. We're talking about a massive energetic change we have the privilege to be a part of. Remember, nature bats last.

Fed Up? Good!

Many are getting fed up with false flags, mass shootings, war drums, complete media bullshit and the fear riddled blo-viations of the psychopaths in the news. That's actually good, and one of the main symptoms of what I'm addressing here. You're fed up – you've had enough. So turn it off. Just get the essentials from the independent and alternative news to keep an eye on things then turn it off. Draw on empowering sources that feed your soul and inspire your heart and draw close to supportive loved ones.

Take the exploration of self you're no doubt being present-ed with and see where it takes you.

That's the primary battle at hand. We need to become who we truly are if we're to finish this out the way we should, could, can and will. But don't dwell on your own damn ass all day either. Activate and proliferate the truth and build com-munity and bonds of love with those you're being called to be with. We all need this support and strength, and environments where we can be our authentic selves and grow into the full stature of awakened, empowered souls.

Enjoy the ride, but don't buck at the pain and sacrifices when they present themselves. They're small fry compared to the glorious new world being birthed in the hearts of our beloved mankind.

Love always,

Zen

Personal Notes:

You Are Not Alone

Why a sense of isolation often engulfs and disempowers many of us is peculiar. We have mothers, fathers, friends, family and even new heartfelt alliances all around us yet we still feel this yearning.

Are we searching for a greater, more truly connected family?

I tend to think so. All evidence points to the fact that we are not who we have been told we are. We are each part of something so much greater and grander than we ever imagined.

And we search for that greater connectivity.

We're Alive

The link ups between all of us on planet earth are way more "spooky" and profound than we've been led to believe. We simply find each other as we continue our search. That's how it works. Like the wondrous mycelium network crawling through the ground to hook up with itself, we organic, conscious beings sent to this planet are finding each other through a very wonderful, organic process. We're alive, we're growing, and we're even protected, buried as if in the heart of mother earth's warm and succulent soil.

Totally contrary to the fear ridden narrative we're being handed here on the surface, we are actually quite safe in the bosom of love itself. This is what you sense in your heart of hearts and can have complete confidence in.

That's innate empowerment. And the place from which we should all operate.

Underlying and Overarching Love

This is the true nature of existence. The fear based projection we're witnessing in today's societal construct is an illusion. It appears real, but it's not. It hits your screen and gets activated only if you buy into it. As the expression goes, fear is "false evidence appearing real." We simply need to live outside of that false reality.

When you "wake up" this is apparent. Your life takes on new dimensions as your true spirit gets released. This is the time to make new, conscious decisions as to the course of your life and act on them. As well as make new friends and relationships from all quarters that you never imagined possible, but suddenly become completely natural as they unfold before you.

A wonder-full experience.

It feels like a magnificent gift when it happens but it's really only a re-discovery that was buried by a plethora of outside influences. Once you see these external projections for what they are and pierce through the veil of deceit it all becomes extremely clear. And it's marvelous.

Suddenly everything comes into perspective and life begins anew. This is where the birth of realization happens and we see everything has an underlying message of love and empowerment.

When you know you've hit pay dirt you just know it. It's experiential and no one can deny that to you.

The Next Step

Move on, with confidence and courage. The barrage of denial and discreditation will always be there. Brush it aside. You're living on a planet of mainly unawakened beings. You'll find your way to others like yourself but never bend to societal pressures to conform to the norm. The "whirled" out here is still finding its footing, but is still steeped in the maws of desperate manipulators who want things their way and are playing on every pre-programmed string they can to do so.

This is why it's important to identify their every action for what it is. We awakened don't want to fall into any of their mind twisting, subversive trickery. That's the motive for everything they do, no matter the well meaning dupes they enlist in their programs. Ours is to stay above it and operate consciously.

This will bring about the greatest good and ultimate positive outcome.

But it won't come without a price. Too much has been invested by these dark forces to attempt to quash our awakening for them not to use their machinations. No worries, it never compares to conscious awareness, we just have to learn to utilize it in great, well-foundationed confidence.

Use great wisdom in the days to come. Find your true family first and foremost, but prepare against the storm nonetheless.

And always remember, we are ultimately living in the bosom of love.

Hooks, Hoops and Letting It Go

I love the expression, "What if they had a war and nobody came?" I feel the same about the matrix and the awakening.

What if the matrix of control over this world had nowhere to manifest?

Our idea of self is contrived. It's broadcast at us from birth and reinforced by the world around us. It's on this false, heavily reinforced self-screen on which they are able to project their manipulated worldview. We cooperate, believe their paradigm to be the only one, and help pass it on to succeeding generations.

All the while asleep to the True reality within and without us.

Bugs on the Windshield

We use our egos like a windshield. The trouble is, it often keeps us from fully experiencing true reality. Imagine there was no windshield. You are spirit and not material. Those bugs would pass right through your field of vision, and you, instead of creating their artificial reality on the screen of your life outlook.

Which is exactly what happens. Your reality, what you see and perceive in life, becomes the crap stuck on your windshield with less and less of the true picture getting through to you.

It's the same with consciousness. When you wake up you realize you have nothing to defend, nothing to fear, nothing to strive for. You find out you're already complete and connected to everything. No one can take your freedom because you are freedom. You realize this whole game of life that's been meticulously laid out for us is built upon implanted wants and perceived needs based on, amongst other things, a false sense of scarcity, and the impulse to strive to get what you are told you need.

None of this has to be. It's all based on ignorance and the whims of a predator race that feeds off of the sleeping worker aphids they've co-created and manipulated.

Sad, but true.

Hooks and Hoops

That's all Velcro is. Now if those little hooks were straightened out or the hoops cut, nothing would stick to the hoops, would it? Picture our manipulated idea of self and the outside world as these bent attitudes and deformed ideas of reality. You can get "strung along" by just about anything. And when it sticks, your hooks and hoops feel useful and you start accumulating stuff. You grow and start to appear as though you are what is sticking to you.

Everyone else is mimicking the same thing, so you feel justified and even comforted. In fact you even look for stuff to stick to you.

This is happening on several levels. People sit and watch TV and stringy Velcro balls are flying at them in all dimensions and they can't even see most of them. They just come away with more crap clinging to their minds, hearts and spirits and hardly notice.

The only reason this stuff sticks is because they're "hooked". Somehow, somewhere, you and I were programmed with these hooks and hoops that attach to stuff.

Detaching

Letting go of this mindset is not an overnight thing, but your wake can be. It takes time to realize all the ways we've been programmed and the vast quantity of disinformation and wrong mechanisms we've been given. The beautiful thing is it's actually a very simple process to get free. You just have to listen to your inner consciousness and dig into real and true information.

Then do what your awakened consciousness tells you to do.

That's the "catch". Unless you put what you've learned to be true into action you'll be just another stillborn spiritual baby. That's not what you want. Just get started one response at a time and it all just kicks in.

What makes it difficult is that waking up is cross-grain to society. The matrix is built to search out and smother dissent. It doesn't like to be exposed, so it will activate all kinds of machinations to stop you; fear, guilt, humiliation, doubt, retribution, peer pressure, financial worries, and ultimately governmental threatenings.

It's nothing new. That's how they run everybody's lives. But when you start speaking up as well as changing your life according to what you've learned to be true, you'll see fantastic confirmations. But you'll also see some weird stuff come up.

My advice is to just let it pass. Operate from a detached sense of conscious awareness and you won't have to put the windshield back up..it's all a lie to get you to do that.

The Spider and the Fly

The central spider concept is a real one. Nasty forces are behind this Matrix web. The beauty of it is once you "get it" the Matrix loses its power over you. True Universal Consciousness, of which we are part, is beyond these lower level matrices and paradigms.

However, those unaware are subject to many influences. I don't fully understand the dynamics by any means, but those trapped in this web of deceit and control are not just subject to psychological, social, political and economic manipulation, but spiritual manipulation as well.

The worst of which is religion, but this has also morphed by manipulated "new age" dynamics into a new, updated disguise. There's much to beware of.

True spirituality is diametrically opposed to organized religion, doctrines, or beliefs of any kind. Oddly enough, those entrapments feed off of this hunger for spirituality and then build their elaborate hierarchical structures to control and contain it.

It's really a case of mistaken identity. So many adhere to their religious beliefs based on very real spiritual experiences, but these are hijacked by those seeking control, not truth and freedom. This is where people need to be open to new ways to understand their spirituality outside of the constructs of religion and set belief systems.

Warning – Cling-Ons Are Real

The warning, though, is this. Beware the cling-ons...the real ones. Whatever you want to call these negative, parasitic socio-political "conventionals" and even inter-dimensional influences. "Cling-ons" is simply appropriate because that's exactly what they do while implying the sci-fi aliens many are familiar with. But the "hooks and hoops" need to be in place for the cling-ons to be effective. That's where conscious awareness comes in, realizing you are in complete control.

You've seen dark and mean people who appear to be periodically powered by something outside themselves. This is real. And we'll be seeing more and more of this in the days to come.

It happens to people who invite these influences in, consciously or subconsciously. They either like the lusty lives they get into as a result, the psychopathic control over others, or their propensity for violating others that gives them a sense of power.

It often manifests in outright Satanism or extreme religiosity or "drive to get ahead" or some such self-righteous exercise. Sexual deviance and child abuse "naturally" run rampant amongst these people.

Stay far away from anyone prone to these influences. Trust your instincts.

This is why we need to wake people up. The ignorant can not only be easily manipulated by the matrix, but they can get "jumped" by weird things going around. As I've often said, these types of things are manifesting more and more as the Matrix falls apart and we're bombarded with these vibrational changes.

This shouldn't put fear into anyone, but we do need a healthy respect for the quickly evolving battleground we are in and aware of its many challenges and influences.

Letting Go

That's the key. Detaching from everything. We are the only ones who let anything have power over us. It happens when we're ignorant of the truth and base our thoughts or actions on misconceptions, misled perceptions and outright lies.

It happens when we're tense, overly left brained about something, in a hurry, or many other "reasons". All of this is to be vigilantly monitored and avoided.

It happens when we try to defend ourselves and any sense of "who we are". It happens when belief replaces knowledge and experience. It happens when we don't respond to what

Love tells us to do. It happens when we're attached to some outcome and miss the opportunities and prompts that are showing us a better way.

This Velcro effect is a tough one, it keeps growing back and catches so many. When we get set in our minds that something needs to be a certain way, or we need to be in a certain place, or at a certain time when it's actually arbitrary, or think our goals of any sort are "set in stone", we're setting ourselves up for trouble. That applies even more so to "beliefs".

What if the Universe opens another door? We're not free to enter it in that mindset. Our mind's made up. In fact, in that state of mind we can't even see the new door that's opened, for any one of the reasons listed above.

In those states we're "unconscious" and subject to the influences swirling about us.

Synchronicity for Fun and Prophet

My definition of personal freedom is when we're free to follow life's signs and live in synchronicity. This for me is a daily adventure and constant check for me whether I'm in the moment now, or somewhere else.

The wonderful thing is, following synchronicity is fun. Wrong turns become right turns. Delays become adventures. Red lights become free time...free to enjoy the scenery and look for something we might need to see.

Carl Jung defined synchronicity as the "acausal connecting principle" that links mind and matter. It manifests as uncanny yet meaningful coincidences and serendipities. Since we're all interconnected in a flowing field of information it makes perfect sense we should be able to see this inter-connectivity at work, and the more conscious we become and learn to fully live in the moment, the more we'll see.

So keep an eye out for synchronicities—they're extremely powerful experiences and really enhance your life.

This is a great time be alive..but not a good time to be asleep.

So keep the wake up rolling–if folks don't listen now, they'll remember what you said real soon.

Keep it loving.

The Beginning Is Near

We have free will, a majestic gift of choice coupled with conscious awareness at a level that seems to be unique to creation. All of creation has its own vibrational attributes, but humanity has been gifted in a very special way. Whether we utilize this gift consciously or not appears to be the dilemma we're faced with.

Yet we seek an escape from this life, a place of refuge. Quite ironic when you consider the inborn sense of wonder and adventure we're each endowed with at birth.

Or is it a sense of knowing that something more real and wonderful exists?

There's much talk about portals, energy vortices, jump locations and wormholes. Where we're trying to go to is a fundamental issue. The point is, how and where do we find a place of transition to other circumstances? Is it activism? Is it our personal way of perceiving reality?

Or both? And perhaps other factors?

Do we already have access to this other reality? Has escape always been the default position in this accosted world resulting in religion and sequestered lives driven by survival and an engineered sense of scarcity? Is this what has happened with the stand and fight mentality?

Does Humanity Get What It "Deserves"?

This is a huge question. Not just the karma issue, but the even deeper innate mechanics of the Universe. If Universe is perfect in every way, everything we're experiencing is "justified".

Has humanity allowed itself, yes allowed itself, to be so degraded that its very decrepit condition invites and encourages predators?

To continue the analogy, are the parasites and viruses "going for the whole enchilada"?

This is pretty serious stuff to consider, especially in the light of society being a reflection or reinforcement of anything imposed upon it.

The question remains; does a dying body politic invite the very influences it eschews?

The Universe is Reflective

What we impose comes back. What we are willing to receive is another factor. But just imagine we're abutted and infused with a huge energetic field, ready to do our bidding. An extremely empowering notion. No matter what is living in this force field is considered fair game for such a Universal force. As an independent resource we should revel in such an idea.

Most profoundly, this "field" reflects our intentions and desires.

Now picture a human race that is enthralled with its own survival, under similarly subjected conditions. But they're under attack. Where will they place themselves in the scheme of things? Will they realize their condition, or relinquish their autonomy for something that seems to save them while in fact they are abusing and devouring them?

Taking It Lying Down Is a Choice

A dead or dying organism invites parasites of all kinds. This is the current state of our world. As perverted, drugged down and immune deficient humanity glides into their brave new world of somatization, we see the growth of the totalitarian police state.

We're inviting it. By our acquiesced degradation.

A dead animal, or human, decays at an accelerating pace. Parasitic organisms move swiftly to devour and do away with the dead corpse, which is true in the plant kingdom as well. It's natural.

However the degradation of ethical and spiritual aspects of human culture, an unnatural degradation, is also inviting dissolution. As we lay down, we accept the seemingly inevitable. A terrible vortex in which to find our collective selves, but we are there apparently, circling the drain.

Our Aliveness is the Key

An alive, resilient body is not a target for disease. The dead and dying are. The overall diseased "body politic" of today is a sitting duck for control and manipulation. Ours is to keep alive and activating.

As synchronicity has it, as I was pondering these thoughts, I walked past a dead animal under a tree by the roadside. It was infested with hungry insects devouring the food. The next day all that was there was the fur. They work fast once the subject has succumbed.

Will humanity succumb? It doesn't look good from a macro perspective. But I know individually the awakening is creating health and wellness at an enormous rate. Will it be in time?

It's up to us.

Be alive. Be active.

You are in charge. Use your majesty of free will.

Bridging the Reality Gap

Have you ever wondered why people can't make the leap to real awareness of what's going on?

How can world conditions not completely startle someone into thinking clearly? Why do so few people seem to care about the dangers of the unreported radiation levels and toxic debris washing across the Pacific? Why are GMOs and EMFs sideline issues? How is it no one but local residents raise the alarm about the horrific effects of the Gulf oil spill and the poisonous seafood landing on American dinner tables and the disastrous effects of fracking, never mind the proliferating radiation levels?

As the Orwellian American police state sweeps into place, the economy crumbles, and their faultless leader languishes on his latest vacation, Americans are actually celebrating their entry into a brave new police state with minimal awareness of the true dangers already dissolving their health, wealth and chances for survival in an engineered conflagration of mythic proportions that is already descending on their heads. Buried, blindfolded heads, I might add.

Sensory Overload and the Ostrich Effect

As the gap between reality and manipulated public perception grows, it may just be too big of a leap for many at this point. Having been dumbed down and unresponsive for so long, it's too much for them to take in, never mind respond to. Or so they've been conditioned to think.

Sad, but again, that's the projected reality that many unconsciously adopt.

"Hey, why wake up when everything's such a bummer if you do?" That's the underlying mentality. The thing is, this is a conditioned response. Overload and recoil. And it's been going on a long, long time.

Why? Like the dumbing down effect of not just the manipulated media but fluoride and heavy metal aerosols and adulterated food, this continual conditioning eventually suppresses natural responses. When the real alert presents itself, the subject will not be able to react and protect himself, never mind mount a coordinated response.

Why all the dramatic end of the world sci-fi movies? Why the emphasis on violence and horror and graphic, destructive wars? Why does the news major on the bad events of the day?

Why the combative gladiator sports, emphasis on technology instead of humanity, and the mind-numbing crass consumerism and hyper-sexualization of society?

This is deliberate social engineering, and that's the elephant in the living room.

Continual conditioning.

It's all engineered..and that's the last thing most people want to realize. And it usually is the last thing for those who refuse to see it sooner.

The Power of Cognitive Dissonance

The world has become essentially schizophrenic in outlook. Being told one thing while the exact opposite is happening before their eyes for so long, the "dissonance" created by this conflict causes humanity to either shut down or accept a carefully synthesized solution.

America is the perfect example. Fighting for freedom and liberty they commit genocide and destroy nation after nation. To supposedly protect their liberties the government has overturned all of the basic rights originally afforded via the Bill of Rights and the Constitution, however rigged it was.

Yet the populace sits and takes it. Why?

It's too big of a leap.

If it turned out they've been so completely conned by a massive manipulated agenda they may just completely break down. And subconsciously the horror of that reality is therefore a "No. I'd rather pass on in my numb, however ill-founded false reality."

Yes. Even if all of this manipulation were true they're at the point they'd rather not know.

I'll Take Conscious Reality

"Why all the negativity?" is what you'll hear a lot of the time when you bring these things up. The answer is that what we're trying to make known isn't negative, it's ignorance that's negative. Truth is empowering, no matter how awful it may be sometimes. And at this point in history the more you learn the more negative it may seem, with the Controllers' agenda in full, final-phase swing.

But so what. Keep learning and you'll have that breakthrough into the wonders their veil has been hiding. The infinite well of our source of empowerment awaits. The purpose of life is to rediscover who we truly are, and that wonderful awakening makes everything else pale in comparison. Our mission then becomes to inform and empower, share and encourage.

The same one it has always been.

That it's taking this kind of extreme compression to awaken the slumbering masses is really no surprise, and ultimately a gift from the Universe to help people back into the real world.....that of conscious loving awareness.

Awaken from slumber, one and all. Make the choice to do it now. That's always the best time to awaken.

And once you find out, get your butt in gear telling others any way you can.

The storm is coming....in fact, it's clearly already here.

Spread the word, under any conditions.

Personal Notes:

Are We Alone? Or Strategically Placed

I continue to hear from so many people who feel isolated and alone during this awakening and massive paradigm shift taking place around the globe.

Spouses can't wake up partners to the truth; family members and close friends think you've gone wonky, while the mainstream matrix mouthpieces keep up their barrage of derision and even threats against anyone who dares to look past the range of their narrow, confining blinders.

We all experience this phenomenon and the isolation that seems to accompany the wake up.

Here's a hugely happy thought. If we're an organic, cosmically influenced body of crystalline receivers and broadcasters in an alive and amazing all-knowing Universe, perhaps we're exactly where we're each supposed to be.

In fact, we're probably carefully distributed to create a world-wide grid of truth.

In other words, once again, there's no mistake with synchronicity.

Oh, Look At All the Lonely People…All Connected

Are we all truly strategically positioned for the best possible effect on the cosmos and the awakening?

Resonates with me, as trippy as it may seem. Why not?

We're each generators, nodes, transmitters, relays, conduits and vessels of light, truth and love. The ultimate power of positive transformation. And we may be just where we're supposed to be, lonely or not. So take heart.

So the loneliness is from what? Perhaps devised separateness, a systematically broken down and compartmentalized imposed society of induced helpless creatures supposedly awaiting the touch of a distant god or some romantic "other" to free them? All based on conceptual lies of separateness.

They do try, don't they?

Yes we need emotional and physical bonding, but within a constructive framework. The purpose of the imposed matrix is to break us down to negative, destructively entropic self-degrading emotions and responses, fight or flight left brain reactions, and self-flagellating flailing about in the mystic. And then bonding to their "idols" of confusion and materialistic insanity for so-called security.

Wrong. Clearly wrong. Don't let anybody fall for it.

Be...and Broadcast Where You Are

This is perhaps a revolutionary idea, but nothing that's not already in place. I contend that to not realize this concept is to decrease the intensity and effectiveness of our power grid. Immensely.

Realizing who, what and all we are is tantamount to spiritual strength. And effect.

Those of you who've awakened to this realization of the importance of "now consciousness" know what I'm talking about. That humanity has been distracted from this knowledge and understanding through false teaching, amusements and entertainment is one of history's greatest lies and tragedies for humankind.

We can't all be physically together, except in a very large concept, although it is clearly a time to connect locally, contrary to their imposed paradigm of separation. The truth warriors with whom we each communicate are often in far flung locations and operate in their own personal nexus but there are many others nearby to each one of us.

But in the grid? We are already one.

Turn It Up and Shine! We are One and Now

Who knows, as hardly any of us are completely mobile and ready to join up and live with other truth advocates. But we can get in touch. Some are making the move and if that's what we're supposed to do we'll do it.

We'll each keep evolving according to conscious unraveling. It's a little freaky to try to conceptualize but I at least just wanted to relieve some angst for those worrying about this feeling.

We are where we're supposed to be….at any time, in any place. But changes do happen.

Fear not. I hope you enjoyed the ride through potential realization but I sincerely feel now is the time to step out and find others near you.

Whether alone or connected, spread the truth. We each make a huge difference in more ways than we know. So keep on.

Being Alone Together

There is much suffering today. Most of it is spiritually derived, no matter how physically challenging it may be.

So many are distressed and feeling there's no way out of this quagmire they're being confronted with. Even for those of us spiritually predisposed and somewhat prepared it's the same story. We're literally at war. Not just of head and heart bashing confrontations, but one of carefully contrived attrition. A starvation of confirming information that reaffirms the simple realities we would otherwise thrive on and be empowered by.

And there's a big batch of inserted confusion to throw us off to boot.

How they've managed to close off obvious truths from the common mind is almost surreal. But there is even something more going on. The bombardment is continually more persistent. The nature of the constructed and controlled world we live in is more malicious by the day. We must be aware of this escalation, while not dwelling unnecessarily on the negative.

Live Past What We're Up Against

The purpose of their tactics is to separate us from our potential; from our fundamental reference points, from loved ones, and from our innate sense of reality. It's a deliberate corrosion of our connectivity.

You can hear this disconnection occasionally in your own mind when a sense of isolation kicks in. It can come out of the mouths of those close to us who are being buffeted and confused and express heavy doubts and discouragement. It's definitely in the increasingly insane news we're having to endure as society descends into dystopia.

Nothing seems to make sense. The danger comes when we interpret these disjointed events and Orwellian newspeak as if something is wrong with us personally.

Turning inward in this fashion can be a very deep trap, when in fact the opposite is true. It has nothing to do with us; this is a spiritual onslaught we're facing from outside forces seeking to turn us about-face and upside down.

The daily news gives a taste of this warped reality; whether it's police brutality, the totalitarian clampdown by governments, staged cyber attacks in order to censor, staged terrorism, or the media mind flips that accost our senses. The objective is to continually subdue humanity into an ever diminutive sense of significance.

It's an out and out war on our lives, and more importantly, our consciousness.

We Are Never Alone

Knowing we're in this together and experiencing the same thing is all important. We know divide and conquer is their M.O., but when it gets personal and hits close to home the principles we're familiar with seem to fade into the dust of mental and moral confusion. Emotions and attachments rise as personal issues come to the surface to further obscure our perspectives.

If this happens to you do not let it throw you. Look for centered awareness, but don't be afraid to seek advice from those you trust, or solace from loved ones, and remember fundamental truths you are familiar with. Hold them dearly. It's not an easy time by any means and we need to stick together in every way possible.

All important is knowing we are each experiencing the same onslaught, and that what we're being handed is a total lie. It's nothing more than a massive fabricated distraction of planned debilitation of their opposition. Also known as us.

Stand strong, even when you're feeling weak. This all comes and goes in waves. Let it pass.

We Knew This Was Coming

We've known this was coming for some time. None of us are above this. We each have our strengths and weaknesses, we each have our calling to truth.

Some things can knock you out before you know it – loved ones falling under the spell, personal plans being derailed, seemingly psychotic breaks with previous modes of understanding, unexpected twists in the matrix around you. Or a full on combination.

Other symptoms are more predictable when times are not as confusing, but there are clearly many ways we're being accosted more than ever at this point and it can get difficult.

These waves of confusion have been expected. And they're here.

When our personal frames of reference take a beating, either individually or via those we love, it's a very challenging time. I find myself rewinding previous lessons I've learned and playing them back like medicine in order to endure many situations. As stated before, we're sailing unchartered seas and there is no precedent for what we're experiencing.

We can take this two ways – as a beating down, or as a powerful lift under our wings of conscious awareness.

Embracing Each Other – The Power of Tenderness and Understanding

There are no pat answers to any or every situation. We're all learning and growing and that's how it should be, and is. What strikes me is the realization of how we need to stick together more than ever as the storm presses on. I've heard from many people how much it's helped them to get some feedback via comments on my website or emails from compassionate acquaintances.

These can make or break us at times.

When we're being laid low and feeling disabled and discouraged it is usually a very personal thing. We tend to make the mistake of looking inward. There may be lessons to be learned, but on the battlefield anything that is crippling is immediately suspect as far as I'm concerned. The issues are too prescient.

We simply have to see these instruments of debilitation as they are in a time of war. And learn from, ignore and/or dispel them.

Shared Camaraderie

Often, we all find out, there are wonderful personal lessons to be learned, but when the barrage of self-doubt and confusion persists we know something much more nefarious is afoot. Shared camaraderie during these times is becoming more and more important. In conjunction with a deep determination to push on through this madness.

We all of course wish we were "stronger", but really the right kind of weaknesses are some of our greatest strengths. Compassion in sharing an honest heart to heart with other spiritual people is so very powerful. Many face serious opposition in their family situations where they feel alone in their conscious awakening. That can be a gnawing source of discouragement. Despite obstacles, so many have been waking up at a steady pace the past several years and are experiencing what many of us have.

Not just the spiritual exhilaration of conscious awareness, but the social isolation and alienation. These are not easy to brave, as most of us know.

Following that can come periodic belittlement and out-right harassment, sorry to say. We've all experienced it. I'm firmly convinced this is all part of our testing ground. Coming through that strengthens our convictions and helps us realize what is really important to us. At that point we are forced to make decisions – what will I subject myself to and why, how do I deal with it, and where do I go from there?

The most important point to remember is this is a war, a spiritual one. Do not allow yourself to succumb to the negative voices around you. The big lie is on the march and feeling its oats right now.

It will pass. They screw up regularly and can't maintain their barrage. It comes in waves. Let it pass.

Be Strong, and Make Courage Your Mainstay

In reality, this is a time of opportunity like we've never seen before. We're in a fight of epic proportions. When we feel em-battled that's exactly the time to come out fighting. We need these mechanisms we learn from that awaken right impulses which were embedded in our souls in order to remember how to maintain our offensive.

Give it a shot. You'll be amazed at how taking the initiative clears the air, places the enemy on the defensive, and puts everything back into perspective.

See you on the battlefield.

Dissolving the Make-Believe Matrix

These power crazed would-be rulers don't own the earth. They don't own you and me. They don't own all their stupid secret symbols. They don't own the present, they don't own the future. They don't even own themselves.

They're usurpers, in every sense of the word. And absolutely nothing to fear.

That these invading power freaks striving to control the world should try to lay claim to some secret knowledge and power source that is superior to everything else is a fraud. That they think they can bring on world changing events that result in national clampdowns and population reduction is their personal nightmare in the making.

It's only true if we submit to it. Our validation and obeisance affirm their intentions. Without that it would immediately crumble into dust.

Lies have no power unless believed. That's the power of the awakening.

See Through It For What It Is

We need to see it for what it is. A spiritual charade. A flimsy fabrication appearing real that only comes into being when humanity buys into it. Quantum physics confirms this. We get what we focus on and affirm.

While we have to deal with their very real machinations they've unleashed to destroy the earth and most of its inhabitants for whatever sick reasons they conjure, they have no superior super-powers for us to fear. Only those we give them by getting entranced by and believing their lies.

At any point humanity can walk away from it and stop supporting it. Soldiers can lay down their guns, police can join with the populace, employees can walk away from their jobs, consumers can stop consuming what is wrong, and the media can just be ignored.

This external projected nightmare of a world system is theirs, not ours. That knowledge is extremely powerful. We just have to deal with the fallout from their insanity while eliminating its source – our agreement to it. And we can do so consciously and with great peace of mind and heart in spite of all of their efforts to induce fear.

The fact is, there is no secret but that which is willfully withheld or deliberately ignored. And to the conscious, nothing is hidden that cannot be revealed and turned for the empowerment of our fellow human beings and planet.

Their Puny Pride Is on the Run

So much of the big lie that we're witnessing on the world stage is simply projected pride – the big, fat, stinking manufactured pride of pathological egomaniacs reinforcing a fabricated world of their ugly, demented imaginations. Along with their demonic spiritual baggage. Whether world conquest piggy-backing on natural and manufactured catastrophes, or attempting to mutate humanity and terraform our environment to meet their specifications for world control, it's all fundamentally defensive.

Yes, defensive. They're scared. They cannot let things take their natural course. That would mean their demise. They have to forcibly control every aspect they possibly can to prevent humanity from waking up to its full potential. Once we do we just shrug and flick them off like the parasites that they are.

It is they who are running and hiding from something so incredibly powerful they have to erect giant sand castles to hide in with massive security forces while they attempt to exterminate all those who carry this amazing potential to realize truth. Just witness the defensive fortress attitude of the elites and their housing and militarily protected behavior for starters. Look at the massive security details surrounding so-called powerful figures. It boggles the mind. What are they afraid of?

Now you see who really has this innate fear in their veins?

And their underlying problem? Us. An awakened and empowered us is what they're absolutely frightened of. And like the cowardly bullies in the playground, they know their time is just about up.

We're talking together, connecting dots, gathering our wits and growing by the minute in courage and resolve.

Our warfare is a spiritual one. Whether we encase this understanding in one of the more classic socio-political frameworks or see it completely metaphysically, the play we're witnessing is nothing to fear no matter what it appears to be blown up into. The feverish power struggles and social engineering taking place on such a massive scale are all based in fear.

What we need to realize is this fear is first of all theirs which they project on to us. They know they're usurpers and self-serving maggots feeding off of the body politic. They know they're heartless bastards out for what they have deemed is important. And it is contrary to everything natural and nourishing. They know this.

And ultimately this fear is a fear of you, and a fear of me. Because we represent the potential connection to truth that they are consciously denying. That awareness of truth signals their inevitable downfall.

They Cannot Create – They Can Only Hijack and Pervert

While we know this supplanting of authority is true about their false hierarchy and self-imposed "ownership" of lands, natural, and even human resources, they've also cleverly tried to co-opt the inherent powers of the so-called mystery schools, the language of which is fundamentally numbers and symbols.

What people forget is almost all of these symbols occur naturally with wonderful positive, regenerative properties. What these lying entities have done is simply attach negative and destructive and abusive connotations to anything they can.

There are many examples of how these usurpers cannot create but only imitate and pervert. Sacred geometry, occult symbolism–even empowering behaviors they turn into occult satanic rituals. They pervert naturally occurring patterns and energies because they cannot allow natural courses to take place. It nullifies their existence. This is clearly evidenced in the usurpation we see in today's logos from so-called secret symbols of the ancient mystery schools.

This is another shadowy charade of images that only gets power from what one takes on through ignorance. These crafty techniques then cause the unsuspecting to derive the energies these parasitic forces project into this secret language as in the case of satanism, saturnalia, the churches of Babylon, Freemasonry and the like. This permeates society in occult symbolism, whether it be the layout of cities like D.C and the Vatican, film, musical and art references, or corporate logos, all laden with messages.

It's kind of a universal copyright infringement in the alterverse of the fear porn industry. The authority is not theirs, it's attempting to mimic or imitate natural laws and energies. When you wake up and see this it's absolutely pathetic what worms these entities are. Their only power is in our fixation on and attention to their shenanigans. It really is that simple.

This is all to expose how once you're wrapped up in their world of interpretation with an abusive, violent world around you to back it up, you begin to think the lie is true.

Therein lies their only power. Your "belief" and entertaining of their notions, empowered to appear real only by your participation.

Turn it off. Turn off their sources–mainstream media, staged events, manipulated music, shallow publicity, even phony personal responses and relationships.

It's time to get real.

Remember, their whole plan is designed to replace reality with a false matrix of power that's fed by fear. Don't dwell on it, and see it for what it is. And reverse the flow. Their flaky construct will crumble.

Each one of us changes the direction of Spaceship Earth.

Conclusion – Uncork the X-Factor

By our very clarity of understanding, our conscious awareness of the truth and our not submitting to their web of deceit, we throw off the illusory shackles of the would-be controllers. Just one person's total lack of fear, not giving any obeisance to their societal, political, economic or physical oppression network, is a flame in their flimsy cobweb. And those burn up quickly.

Be that flame.

They're lying usurpers – but it only works with our agreement. Our conscious awareness, as vague as that may seem to some, is the ultimate weapon. And it starts with waking the hell up and then keeping on waking up…and rattling as many other cages as we can in the process. It's not always a smooth process, but it requires honesty and guts.

And cutting the bullshit.

As our collective consciousness grows more awake and aware it gains power and tremendous momentum. The x-factor is Spirit which manifests in many ways, including in the profound form of synchronicity. And then when each of us responds to Universal consciousness things change dramatically. Life's signs become increasingly apparent and start challenging and leading our lives more and more, activating us in ways we never knew could have been realized or could have had such powerful influence.

With each and every wake up the war is won.

It was won in the beginning. Stand on that. We need to stop believing the illusions around us and learn to act on our true conscience.

At that point it becomes now. Really now.

That's our event horizon. Be there.

Personal Notes:

The Sad Sad Truth

First of all, it hits you hard. Right in the heart. Your family is at stake, humanity is at stake. We're being relentlessly attacked by some unidentified force and we're reeling, with not a lot to stand on.

Our planet's resources are being polluted faster than we can identify. Everything we just years ago held dear and tried to naturally defend has been so drastically altered it's beyond identification or comprehension.

And we scream as if in a nightmare with no one listening.

The Gulf of Mexico and virtually the entire Pacific ocean have just been killed. Murdered. The skies are being poisoned to incredible degrees, killing our plants, animals and fellow humans.

I like to believe in life's regenerative processes, but we're talking long term. Long after your kids and grandkids have then had to endure the horrors of a mutated world, if they live that long.

These psychopaths are playing for keeps. And people better wake the hell up to that fact.

These earth changes, geopolitical maneuvers and so-called scientific and social changes that are obviously engineered clearly indicate that they have an agenda.

What Agenda Might This Be?

WHY would the elites dig a super underground vault to store seeds from all over the planet while introducing genetically modified seeds growing food they themselves won't touch?

WHY have they built secret underground bases?–that aren't so secret if you poke around a bit.

WHY is the world not told a single fact about the Fukushima radiation readings, and the EPA monitors get shut off and standards recalibrated?…while the media blackout continues?

WHY is questioning water fluoridation considered cult science while multiple millions drink the toxic industrial by-product yet European countries throw the process off?

WHY are they pushing vaccines so hard when they've been proven to maim children and adults?

WHY is cellphone and other EMF technology deliberately set at the range of our brain frequency when it could have been outside that?

WHY is the banking system getting off scot-free when everyone knows they engineered this economic mess?

WHY is war on terror so accepted when it was based on a staged false premise–a clearly government induced false flag millions identify?

WHY is the education system spewing out dumber and dumber kids while more money is poured in to this fruitless endeavor?

WHY is everyone so freakishly fat they can't see their feet anymore and are suffering accelerated off the charts health challenges?

WHY has questioning anything become a terrorist threat?

WHY is our atmosphere so purposely filled with aluminum and other toxic substances our respiratory illnesses have skyrocketed, never mind other complications like increased seizures, memory loss, and even Alzheimers?

WHY is going through the airport now a radioactive exam and terrorizing experience for even children and the elderly?

WHY is the government now allowed to arrest, imprison and even kill you without trial?..as well as spy on you at will?

WHY is the media swill the same on every channel with literally no independent reporting or investigative journalism?

WHY is our DNA being tracked, our irises scanned, blood tested and our movements monitored?   etc. etc. etc.

Getting the picture? We have to wake the hell up, is all I can say. If you don't get it yet, I pity you.

We're under attack.

There's a lot to be angry about. And if you're not angry, you're not alive. Then turn your anger into activity. Do something. Wake others up.

The Zen Spot

Yes, there's always that place of refuge. Of course there's a wonderful "other" transcendent side to all of this, but it doesn't matter if we don't take responsibility for what's going on in front of our noses and do something about it. Observing the essence of a drowning child is bullshit.

Respond.

Inaction while observing these truths of our current condition is mental masturbation and an exercise in futility.

I found out and my life changed. Drastically.

I hope yours will too.

Is It Ever Too Late
to Wake Up?

It's remarkable how little they have to do anymore to get their desired results. It seems it takes just one ripple in the collective mind and the mesmerized masses jump however high they're told.

All of these obvious false flag staged terrorist attacks attest to this.

And what pre-designed Machiavellian step does it lead to this time? "Let's see, we've been doing guns for a while, let's go for…internet censorship." Or whatever. Wow, are you kidding? That's a leap. They're getting pretty ballsy but always have.

The problem is that a major hunk of society swallows all this bullshit and thinks it's real. If enough people would just point the finger at these phony stunts they're putting on and call 'em out on it and refuse to respond or cooperate with any of their machinations, these psychopaths would shrivel up and die for want of an audience.

The Illusory Veil Will Be Rent

It's so far down the tubes now with with lies, deceit and cover ups while they jam their fascist program down everyone's throats that people couldn't bear to start to realize how far they've been taken. The shock would be too much.

Or so they think in their current mind set and paradigm.

When the shift hits the fan big time and the masses are forced to wake up, whatever happens in their collapsing lives to trigger it, we will be living in a very different world. The spiritual reigns supreme so whether people are spiritually conscious or not, the real state of affairs is running around and through all of us like WiFi. And on many frequencies like a radio or television.

Remember the world of pre-9/11? You almost can't any more, but this so-called security insanity and climate of terrorism fear was almost non-existent. It was there but safely remote – which is why they knew it had to be brought to US soil to get the desired effect, same as Pearl Harbor did to get Americans behind entering into WW2, and which the 9/11 perpetrators openly admit was their model and goal in their literature.

But who's looking, once again.

The political aspect is just one side of this designed shift they're trying to establish as our reality. Just as our atmosphere is decimated and our food and water are contaminated, and the bombardment of nuclear and electric radiation continue unabated in massively manipulated weather systems, the social structure of society and the very mindset of humanity is being altered by the day. As conditions continue to deteriorate and the levels of draconian controls and outrageous lies escalate, the veil of disguise they've foisted over their hijinks is going to peel open to reveal the awful truth of what's happened to all of us.

That's going to trigger the mass psychosis underlying the mass belief system and it ain't gonna be pretty. And I suspect they know this.

But to them it won't matter as societies turn into war zones for survival. They've deliberately planned this outcome as well as planned for this eventuality with their own safe havens to flee to.

They Know We Know

When people get detained or their loved ones get questioned or mugged by the militarized police state goons it starts to hit home. When they break into your home and take your guns or shoot your dog for barking you start to wake up. When the airport security assholes pull another old lady in a wheelchair aside and have her strip down -and it's your grandmother – you start to wake up. When your internet connection is monitored and your website attacked by lettered agency hackers you start to wake up.

The dark rulers know we know what's going on. They know it big and tall. That's why the disinformation is increasing, trying to weave through the community with controlled opposition while trolls are showing up more and more with obvious intent. They've having a tough time though, we're bound by a fabric "they know not of". They never will.

Love, compassion, and truth and not part of their vocabulary, MO or lifestyle.

They're simply parasites. Unfeeling, blindly grubbing diseased parasites.

But know for a fact they know a great and growing swathe of us are on to them and their dark, demonic chicanery. That's a fact. They just figure they have enough of the mind-mushed masses under their spell that there's nothing to worry about. They think "those gnomes" will never believe what we say with all the programming they've slipped into them, and they'll get to us soon enough in their "clean-up" campaigns.

It reminds me of Einstein's famous quote, "No problem can be solved from the same level of consciousness that created it."

Hey guys, that goes for you. You really don't get it, us, or anything. Just a short time left to exercise your greed and cravings for energy and control. You will shrivel up and die in the light of truth.

Bet on it.

So When Is It Too Late?

Unfortunately this rude awakening will be too late for most in many ways, although at least finally waking up is in a sense never too late.

It's just that their lives here may likely be horrifically affected and possibly terminated soon after this realization for want of waking up sooner.

We're talking serious suffering that could have been avoided, at least in part.

Obviously there are many levels to all of this, as well as many levels of awakening. Each has its place, and every individual has his or her own story. Fundamentally we're accountable to the True eternal Voice in our hearts.

In order for someone to shut down there has to be a decision or series of decisions involved, at some level, somewhere, to do so. The true conscious Voice and reaction may, and most likely has been, suppressed by outside forces and for that we have to give allowance.

We live in a very dirty dimension of systemic abuse at many levels and we must keep love, kindness and understanding as our guiding force while staying true to truth. On the other hand, deliberate shutdowns are another story.

When it comes to trying to help people wake up, some say you can't mess with people's karma, but I don't know about that. True, we can't force anything on people in good conscience when the point of this life here is to learn to respond individually and consciously to a conscious Universe.

But when the baby is reaching for the electric heater you don't just watch. If friends or family or anyone for that matter is hypnotically marching in a row of people that you know goes straight over a cliff, you don't stand idly by and say I hope they wake up soon.

How can you? That's clearly not conscious. That's sleepwalking. With serious consequences.

Don't Let Environment Dictate Your Actions – You Decide

Oddly enough we're living in an engineered, numbed-down world now that is just so conditioned to not respond to the obvious. How many times do you hear about people watching a robbery or beating in the streets and doing nothing. Or Stockholm syndrome submissive behavior in the face of horrific, abusive circumstances.

Life has become a spectator sport people are not fully engaged in.

How soon will the main act in the coliseum be the captured awakened vs the militarized police lions to entertain the rulers and their zombified masses?

You won't find me there. If I'm going down it's gonna be taking the real fight, for truth, straight to them.

The point to all this is our awareness needs to be full, truthful, and pragmatic. Helping someone realize what's really happening here, and preparing for the inevitable break down that's about to happen, are very conscious actions. They aren't radical or weird.

You're alive in a virtual petrified forest. It's matter of fact. If it was any clearer to us we'd disappear into the next dimension. And that serves a purpose.

It gives strength. It encourages faith – which is knowing, not believing.

We know what's going on. We must tell others. We must be examples of such to the very best of our abilities and speak and demonstrate it forcefully.

We must detach, we must be true to the truth.

Personal Notes

A Time for Letting Go

I think one of the keys to understanding everything going on is letting go. The very process of our minds to which we subject the reality around us is limiting.

We habitually use this linear reasoning process trying to sort everything out by previous understanding and knowledge, consciously and subconsciously classifying and sorting information into little bins and folders in an attempt to accumulate enough evidence towards some level of knowledge and understanding.

We ideally should be experientially based and transcend our limited minds, going by heart intuition and raw contact with a greater reality.

But the world we live in doesn't work that way. Call it the matrix, the grid, the collective ego, the illusory maya, an accumulated social construct or a manipulated hologram.

Whichever, how we process information here is extremely important, especially in this day and age.

Why Things Stick

The goo that collects on our spiritual windshield is not the problem. It's the windshield. We shouldn't need one, we shouldn't have one, and what is projecting and producing this protective windshield is the source problem. Call it ego or some kind of artificial sense of self, it's a lie, a mistake, an aberration from true reality brought on by the nature of this limited dimension we're inhabiting.

It thinks it has something to protect. All a false, created construct.

There has been a lot of intellectual wrangling about whether the ego is beneficial and essential or not. Without it, it's argued, we couldn't survive. Of course they'd say that. What do you expect someone who's attached to ego to say? That's like asking a Zionist if we even need Israel. We'd all be better off without it, it's not necessary, in fact it's hazardous to everyone's health and well-being and has been nothing but a parasitic cancer on the earth. But what will the Zionist say? He'd go batshit and sic the authorities on you, if not kill you himself.

Ah, the lovely, protective ego.

Of course we all come equipped with this muscle called the egoic self. Some spend their lives strengthening, polishing and exerting these things over others like blind race car drivers plowing down the highways of life destroying everything in their paths.

Even those who think they have the game down and play it just right for "success" to either gain power and self aggrandizement, or those fighting for personal fear-based security, this false projection of who we think we are is a fabricated lie.

A blinding virus nourished and protected by its carrier.

Sure, it's real unto itself, just as anyone can create words and make a sentence, or make their body do this or that, or build a life of stuff or accumulated knowledge and experience. But what is it in comparison with real truth beyond this illusory self-reinforcing veil?

Who's Your Helmsman?

Who or what is steering this thing called our life? Is it all ultimately reflexive and reactive, either to our current surroundings and input or that of previous knowledge and experience, or some combination thereof? Or is there something else at play, a higher consciousness that gets buried under the rubble of ego and all it has created to assert and protect itself?

When we find that out we're home free. The real us is our eternal spirit connected to everything. It is not separate from anything, which is what the illusion of this world is all about. Separation, competition, survival. But even in spite of the self-serving survival instinct that comes with our corporal experience called our bodies and minds, there is love.

Spirit emerges via the human heart, expressed in deeds of kindness and unselfish caring for others.

It's totally contrary to ego. Of course certain forms of love also stoke and strengthen the ego game. But in spite of the separation ego reinforces, real love comes through. It's learning to detach from the limiting egoic world and letting its mechanisms dissolve that releases more and more of that underlying, all permeating Love.

The Importance of Letting Go

The times we're living in are extreme. Every age throughout history has its own challenges, but the current information explosion we're experiencing and the draconian control mechanism attempting to crush an awakening humanity is a lot to take on board. So it must be handled wisely.

The wisest thing anyone can do with all this is to let it go. And to do that we have to relax the egoic mindset and turn off its reactive nature and our attachments to any beliefs or coveted non-conscious perspectives we've accumulated.

We have to learn to let things pass and not try to understand everything so hard. To handle what's coming down the pike we'll need to learn to relax and observe. As Heraclitus said, no man can step in the same river twice. It's not the same river, and you're not the same man. You and the water have moved on.

Let things move on. Trying to grasp the full nature of what we're experiencing in this world today is like trying to set up camp in a hurricane.

Just let it blow and step back and enjoy the ride. As far as understanding everything? We have no idea what's really going on compared to the true reality of things. There are going to be a lot of surprises, big ones, so the less attached we are to our current understanding the better. Just as we can see the issues the unawakened are having and going to have as things unravel, we need to similarly see ourselves in our own new paradigms and realize we can't get set in our ways either in an accelerated state of rising consciousness while dwelling in a society that is unraveling

Besides, until we're in that point of conscious awareness, any understanding or action based on that previous limited understanding is only going to reinforce the old system, no matter how reformed, it will just be another unconscious mind construct.

We Become What We Think

I'm not saying here to not think or analyze. I'm saying to not get attached to not just the information, but our hard set conclusions or even ways of thinking. Nothing is as it appears and in these rapidly morphing times illusions can compound quickly, or even come dressed as truth, and we need to remain aware of that. We need to process information, but without getting attached to it and thereby dragged down by it to lower levels of consciousness.

We also have to draw practical conclusions. Life is a series of decisions. The purpose of life is to find and release the inner Source of our being including true information, and express it through personal realization – ideas, words and resultant deeds.

But it takes time to arrive at conscious conclusions which is why the internet is such a valuable tool to help precipitate this current awakening.

The power of these realizations is that they become our guideposts. What we think will become our reality as we make decisions and judgements. So the more conscious, awake and aware one becomes the more their life will be a manifestation of the conscious, loving world we're bringing into existence. We're literally channeling a conscious existence and lifestyle and changing the course of humanity in each of our personal realms and that of those we influence, directly and indirectly. To operate from any lesser level of understanding will have negligible benefits and cause way more problems.

Paradoxically all this new information leads to more detachment from what we're finding out is going on around us, as we realize our essential nature and let go of our old ways and detach from this world system. And responding to conscious awareness by taking responsible action provides a great wrecking crew for the ego. We can't be the old, dead self when we're busy being conscious. Awareness breeds activism and your world changes completely as a result.

Learn we must, but in the words of Lao Tzu, "To attain knowledge, add things every day; to attain wisdom, subtract things every day."

Epilogue

This outside information we're processing can be empowering or toxic. Our perspective and how we process information makes the difference. Learning to let things pass, or if we hold them for awhile to then let them go, is imperative.

The world of the matrix is in the midst of manufacturing and disseminating a mega shitstorm, trying to confuse, intimidate and distract humanity with anything it can. Rather than trying to catch and analyze every bit of crap they're throwing at us, step aside. The crap they fling doesn't have to stick to anyone. Just don't be in the way of it. Our minds are like virtual window screens – if they're tense and cluttered with stuff that's chattering amongst itself then the less conscious we are and the more stuff sticks to it. That's when confusion and darkness set in and humanity becomes prone to manipulation.

To the contrary, when we're not cluttered or clinging to whatever we're attached to, the more the light gets through.

The less there is of us in this equation, including a cluttered mind or muscular ego, the better.

Light shines through openings, not closures.

Wanna be a good pupil of life?

Then dilate.

Let's get out of the way so the light can shine through.

Personal Notes:

Changing in the Face of Accelerating Change

Things change more than we think. Way more and in more ways. Even when we're aware of the underlying reality of constant change, we reference new changes by our memory and perception of old changes. Those are based on previous reference points. And they're all in transition.

We're judging change by points of attachment. That cannot be very accurate. Nor fully conscious.

I'm continually shocked to realize how attached I am to my various "points of view" while thinking I'm not. But that's how the mind is wired and what we're up against.

The Subtle Reflex

Simply put, everything's shifting. And in shifting ways. In a shifting perception of change. What I realized I was comparing to was an emotional imprint. I was looking back to different periods of time in my life in comparison to what I'm going through now. Consciously conjuring up old impressions in contrast to a current experience.

It's all relative.

And for whatever reason. Understanding, nostalgia, encouragement, comparison. There's so much that flows through our minds as we seek meaning and definition.

I realized how I frequently use old imprints to gauge comparative changes. Not necessarily bad in itself as there's no doubt something to learn, but I shouldn't compare to times in my life when I was relatively unconscious. That's the catch.

On top of that, these current vibrational changes are completely new, as am I. Recalling old imprints only reinforces my attachment to them. They're good reminders of my unconscious past with perhaps a few lessons, but nothing more.

Conscious Climbing

Another analogy might be a rock climber who won't fully let go of his gear attached to the lower rungs he made in his ascent. He'll only get so far. As you go higher your perspective shifts phenomenally, but he won't get to those really inspiring views if he won't let go of those lower footholds that got him started.

And physically these memory reference points are embedded in emotions and memory clusters. Very similar to the crystalline knots a massage therapist works out of muscle tissue that then have to be flushed from the system.

Memory can be an anchor. Beware.

But never stop climbing.

Letting Go in a Shifting Reality..or Not

It's all good…if we let go into this shifting reality. A lot of people are fighting it. I'm seeing it in people I'm close to, and hearing this happening to folks from many sources. We knew the shift was hitting, but as we get further into it and our noses are closer to the details it starts getting very personal.

I should hope so. But when it hits it can be a stinker.

It's again like the mountain analogy where it's easy to see the full mountain range from afar but up close to the big climb and vast range of mountains you lose that view as you get all caught up in the foothills and the real climbing work begins as you bear down on the climb ahead.

A total change of head.

It's really a lifestyle shift. Or it should be. That's what grabs the stubborn souls by the throat. Practicality. If someone doesn't budge and they keep refusing to acknowledge the evident truths around them and then yield to those truths by consciously making the needed changes in their lives, it can be pretty tough.

These include disengaging from the system more, letting go of unfruitful and hindering relationships, adopting a healthier lifestyle both physically and mentally, and preparing spiritually and practically for the upcoming economic and social storm.

Those who refuse to see this will not be peaceful people or happy campers. You can spot them by their stress levels, and a fundamentally angry, confrontational attitude. They also vigorously put down anyone pointing out these evident truths being made manifest.

You know who they are. Hopefully this will help spot them easier and faster, as we don't need to be subjected to their demeaning behavior or tainted information.

Defying the Control System

There's really no reason not to disengage from the matrix, at least in stages. Those imaginary handcuffs of the mind are weaker than cooked spaghetti. It's the habitual fear programming that keeps people from doing the obvious.

That's the design, to paralyze humanity.

One of the real toughies has to do with relationships. There are many couples who have diametrically opposed attitudes and perspectives, leaving very lonely and isolated individuals feeling lost in spiritually unfulfilling situations that wear on them pretty heavily. People do wake up all the time, but that type of situation I find particularly saddening and I know it's taxing on the individual as well as collective consciousness.

There's no blanket solution, everyone has to go according to how they're led. But if you're in one of those relationships, always do everything you can to keep strengthening your spiritual convictions and conscious awakening. Some local meet up groups can be very encouraging.

The internet of course is the meeting place for most of us. I'm very blessed with an amazing mate who has gone through much of the same stages of awakening as myself and we now share every nuance together and can easily talk about anything and everything.

I've also developed many wonderful relationships via the internet that's become an expanding, amazing community of awake, aware and loving souls that I'm so very privileged to know. I know that's the case with many other people.

Our little email communities are the seed and fruit of the awakening.

Keep on and keep growing.

A Time of Change and a Time to Choose

But overall, it's a challenge, especially for those caught in compromised situations. Reach out to those in need. Don't necessarily meddle, but be there for their encouragement and a listening ear. Just letting someone know you understand and care is so very powerful. As things take shape in people's lives, more choices present themselves and as consciousness raises we'll all know what to do, or not to do.

The awakening cannot be thwarted.

More often than not ours is to simply defy the system programming...disobey, disconnect, disengage, from anything they throw at us.

The rest will follow.

"No man ever steps in the same river twice. For it is not the same river, and it is not the same person. - Heraclitus

How To Handle the Awakening

I received the following comment on an article on my website. It sparked several thoughts as to what happens when we wake up and have to deal with the ensuing repercussions, both spiritually as well as in our personal interaction with our immediate circumstances.

Zen,

I am continually refreshed by the content of this site, thank you for providing the "soul-food" I need. I have a question for you or the group. I feel like I am trapped in my "lower level" of self. I recognize the actions, and some of the triggers, but despite this, I plow ahead like a stubborn bull repeating the same behaviors. How do I break the cycle?

I realize it is different for all individuals, but any direction would be appreciated and most helpful. I have a strong inclination that I am an agent of change, but I also know I must conquer the base first. Much love.

My response:

Hi J. Here's something encouraging for you. The fact that you are observing yourself shows you are profoundly awake. This separation between the programmed old self and the conscious true self happens over a period of time as you learn to identify, and operate from, the conscious self, which then permeates your behavior one conscious decision at a time.

This is the struggle people go through who have this awakening, and there are a lot of implications to it that sometimes bring on conflicts with the conditions we've gathered around us from our previous unconscious life. The beauty is that they peel off as we continue our heart felt pursuit of truth and activate according to what we're newly learning. That's why I talk about this so much – it's a dynamic that simply awaits activating. We just have to be willing to pay the price of letting go.

I know it sounds simplistic, but it really is that simple. The repercussions are usually pretty dramatic, which shouldn't surprise us as we've virtually found out we're operating between conflicting worlds, basically illusion vs reality. Nothing we were prepared for by any means.

Stand strong and watch things change around you. That's what happens. Stay the observer, and operate from that viewpoint and perspective. You'll find your way one conscious step at a time. Much love and keep on.. – Zen

Finding Our Way Back Home

It's not complicated, as life regularly teaches us by its simple illustrations. It's we who have been separated from these fundamental, simple truths, by ourselves as well as the ignorant and often manipulative influences of others. Now we need to find our way back home.

This takes trusting newly aroused sensations and instincts that were laying dormant within us.

What each of us experiences is awakening in its most fundamental sense. Information begins to take on new dimensions with a clear interpretation and which continues to rock our world, but rock our world it must to get things back into a conscious perspective.

When we finally begin to taste that place of true freedom of thought and personal autonomy it is a wondrous experience. Disconcerting, to say the least, but liberating and oh so exhilarating. We just know it's right. But to look around for confirmations of our new found convictions of this clear personal experience is a mistake – it's bound to disappoint, save finding others like yourself with whom we can relate, which may be few and far between at first.

That's OK, as this is part of our development. We lacked courage in our previous existence, and this teaches us how to hold fast to and develop the courage of our convictions, without which we'll wither and die on the vine like so many others given this precious opportunity. Think of the butterfly coming out of its chrysalis and how the struggle is essential to driving the circulatory system to enable it's newly manifesting wings to fly.

It's the perfect metaphor.

Oh the True Friends You'll Find

One of the most marvelous results of fighting through this transformation, besides the personal discovery and empowerment, is those you soon meet on the same path and wavelength. The dearest friends of my life, whom I now count brothers and sisters to me, soon emerged as I continued my ecstatic journey.

I became active, communicated wildly, and searched the information field like an awestricken new born cub in a brand new world, and sure enough, there were many others just like myself going through the very same experience.

Not only that, the words and teachings of the sages of the ages came alive. I'd been a student searching for these truths all of my life but suddenly there was newborn life in their words.

Everything erupted.

It may not be this dramatic for everyone but it was for me. After a life long search for truth and meaning and purpose in life I'd finally found the key. I don't know what brought it on exactly as it was a culmination of a life long quest, but it happened. Learning what to do with it was next.

But finding others on the same divine mission? Priceless.

Conclusion

The awakening is obviously a very personal experience. There's no formula for it, just the sincere hunger for truth, real truth. That we can share experiences and insights as to our personal experiences in such depth at lighting speed in a world on a collision course to who knows what is a very special gift, and I would add essential tool we need to utilize to the max.

That's what drives me. For me it's a personal calling. But we each have one, and it's ours to find it and fulfill it with everything in us. That is truly awakening.

To be shown truth is one thing; to respond to it is another.

It's all in the response. If you want my two cents, therein is the key to the real awakening in all its glory.

Keep on keeping on, no matter what…

Personal Notes:

So You've Woken Up - Now What?

Many people ask about this or something similar so here's some thoughts on the subject. I don't mean to tell anyone what to do, as that's completely contrary to consciousness and conscious development, but I will share my understandings at this point and my passion for truth and you can do what you like with it.

Question:

"What do you say to people who have woken up but can't leave the system because of family and friends?"

This and those like it pose a very broad question since we're all different and need to be led of our own convictions. However, the answer is fundamentally similar in every case. Do what consciousness tells you.

There's really no time for fiddling around once you've found what you know to be the truth, which is always something clearly outside the realm of what you've been indoctrinated with. It's always life altering. And if it isn't, you didn't hear correctly or it fell on deaf or distorted ears in some fashion.

I don't want to be counted amongst the deaf or unresponsive. Do you?

Especially when you found out that that's exactly what perpetrates the big lie you found out about–a compliant, non-awake populace.

System Dependence is the Name of the Game

That's the trouble with the "system"; it teaches dependency, hierarchy, and canned knowledge, where your choices are carefully narrowed down to "acceptable" alternatives within carefully confined parameters.

That's why people feel like fish out of water when they wake up. They never learned how to truly think freely, nor did they have the knowledge tools. Instead, most everything was reversed, scrambled, confused and filed away in seeming useless obscurity while their particular "Truman Show" marched on.

The result is not just a marginalization of empowering truths into the catch-all dustbins of "conspiracy theory" or wing nut stuff, but worse yet, the system does not cultivate original thought or true personal freedom or responsibility.

That wake up in itself is enough to send anyone on a quest for truth.

The real truth is not an option in such a controlled environment. Oh, you get smatterings of truths, but drawing awake and aware conclusions is not an option to humanity's would be Controllers.

And do know, they work hard at blocking any such understandings never mind conclusions.

The Wake Up Starts with a Bang – But You Have to Keep It Going

When someone awakens to the true nature of the manipulated world we live in, as well as the vast resources for truth at our immediate conscious fingertips, it takes some doing to fully realize what that information means, as well as the vast implications on your personal life.

It can hit hard and may need some time to be digested. It can also be quite disturbing at first, but that will pass.

How it affects each of us individually is really a question of simply putting what we've learned into action and trusting the Universe for the consequences. I don't think there's time for much else. In fact, there never has been.

If you know the truth, what are you waiting for?

While many are hoping for some kind of soft-pedaling of any kind of action call, it's not a set formula. You just find out, and you react..consciously. And just that takes some doing, breaking off the rust of your True Self to animate and start to call the shots that were previously hindered by life long programming.

Stages of Development

For me the wake up took on many stages of development, but the full blown realization of the vast extent of the manipulated lie and its fleshed out intricacies was a head splitting explosion that blew me past the pull of convention's gravity so fast I'm still grinning from ear to ear as I zip through the universe.

The point there being, the wake up takes on many forms and evolves. What gives the wake up traction is commitment, putting feet to your realizations and keeping on in spite of opposition.

You think TV's bad? Turn it off. Banks are a rip off? Get out except for perhaps necessary operating funds if need be. Trapped by the ownership of housing, "might needs", and all kinds of dumb stuff?

Dump everything you can, if that's your understanding.

Knowing "stuff owns you" is fundamental to consciousness. We all get there, but it depends on our enthusiasm...or "spirit in us".

How many respond to just that?

Do What You Know or Face Confusion

Until people put into action what they already know, there isn't going to be much more to follow for them. Just a lot of flailing about in frustration because they don't do what they already know they should do and are looking for excuses or compromised solutions to assuage their guilty conscience and hopefully preserve their personal status quo.

Sad, but true.

That also includes getting right with people, making relationships honest, and disengaging from situations of compromise. It takes courage.

Know You Are Nobody–Yet Everybody

All of this is a whole lot easier when you realize you are nobody. There's nothing to defend.

Your old senses of self were the very strings the lying matrix played upon. Get conscious and the sirens of the system don't affect you except peripherally.

Conscious awareness is number one realizing and seeing through the higher level of awareness that is detached from this life's experiences, and thus free us to discern and identify without attachment what our life experience is.

Seeing through those eyes will bring tremendous peace and understanding.

Get Along But Don't Compromise

Don't fret the next steps. If the universe is so vast and full of infinite possibilities there's going to be something for everybody. Our job is to find it and when we find it, act on it. No, it's not the "safe" way, or the "accepted" way.

At all. We do what we have to do and thus break free.

In reality the parasitic system has been sucking you dry and lying to you and everyone you love. You now no longer owe it any allegiance and can and should disengage any and every way you can. No guilt trip necessary. You are doing what is right.

And that is not contingent on relationships, financial security, self image concerns, or what have you.

So get any and all attachments possible out of play. Happily. You are freeing yourself from the spider's tentacles.

There's Real Peace in Commitment

When you've resolved to go ahead and "make the break" with convention and stand up for what you know is right, it leads to a new lifestyle. How do you think these wonderful websites were formed of like-minded people who found each other and decided to make an impact with videos, interviews, articles, participation in events, etc?

How were Gandhi, Martin Luther King or other world truth bearers including the present day alternative luminaries birthed from their previous lives?

Something gelled, made total sense, resonated, and they just committed. These truth enthusiasts on the internet also somehow found each other and it clicked. It's all about responding to the need and call and openly networking...true response-ability.

The Truth Glasses

I read this fantastic metaphor and it's never escaped me.

Finding out the whole truth is like putting on these amazing truth glasses, much like the movie "They Live".

Here's how they work:

#1. You gotta want to put them on.

#2. You can't force someone else to put them on.

#3. Once they're on, you can't take them off.

If you've found and put on the glasses, that will make total sense. If you haven't, keep searching.

Let your heart lead you.

In the words of Lao Tsu:

"At the center of your being you have the answer; you know who you are and you know what you want."

Personal Notes:

Part 2 -
Navigating Our
Changing World

Personal Notes:

Living in the Climax
of Awakening Ages

Much is being said about the transition we're now undergoing. Is it a cosmic occurrence, a societal awakening, or perhaps a spiraling convergence of timeless influences destined to bring humanity to its true conscious awareness?

It's never healthy to over-spiritualize any occurrence or phenomenon but these have become very real, howbeit esoteric, questions.

It's clear the current paradigm of deceit is crumbling before our eyes and that a major transformation in human consciousness is taking place. We cannot deny that, despite the furious socio-geopolitical activities unfolding before us and the naysaying of skeptical observers.

What tends to be seriously minimized is our empowered place in all of this. What can we do in the face of such an onslaught? Is there a role for us to play? Why the feeling of helplessness as we watch our skies, food and water close in with toxins and our societies constrict as if destined to bring our demise?

Standing Up to the Storm

Knowing we are called for such a time as this is essential. There's sound footing to be had despite the mayhem we witness day by day. It's no accident we are here, never mind awakened at this time. That we see clearly what is transpiring all around us is perhaps the biggest clue there is that the solution is within us, and its manifestation closely at hand.

But it needs our participation. That's the key.

Activating in conscious response is our unified call, in whatever form we are called. Individually and collectively we are the force they fear and hence are dealing with in such a draconian fashion, which in itself is testament to the power we possess. This cannot be emphasized enough.

This Has Happened Before

Not many are aware of the fact that Buddha, Lao Tzu, Confucius, Zoroaster and the early spiritual Greek philosophers were all alive within the same short time period approximately 2600 years ago. It, too, was a time of great awakening, without the aid of today's communication abilities afforded by the internet. Something was afoot during that golden age of opportunity, the truth of which has rung throughout history.

This makes our awakening exponentially more profound as well as powerful in the grand scheme of our planetary history.

We have been given the tools to respond. In love, in truth, and in full knowledge and understanding. This again is why our generation is so fiercely feared as well as opposed. To realize this is a source of great encouragement to anyone wavering in their new found discoveries and convictions. We truly are a tide of empowered truth that is sweeping the world, despite all of the outside appearances to the contrary.

Ages and Sages – The Time is Now

The convergence we are experiencing is everything to be excited about. Do not doubt your inner voice. We stand in full conviction and need not be moved by the barkings of technofascism or police state tactics. We must operate in calm, trusting knowing that what has been established in our hearts is the true nature of humanity and our planet and that these machinations from some sort of imaginary hell are simply that – false, fabricated weapons of fear-based intimidation designed to destabilize our heartfelt footing in the true reality of the world as it should, could, will be, and already is.

It's all about the individual. We stand alone, yet together. We move with honor and dignity. We speak truth, and in love. Our force, even if it be just one alone, is more than the lie can handle. In that conviction the heart wins. No matter the seeming outcome in any surface skirmish, we win. Because truth always wins out. Always.

Know that. Your actions will follow, one at a time. Trust your heart.

But do know the hour is late. Delaying your true role is no longer an option.

Stand and deliver. The rest will follow.

Standing with you, with love and respect.

Sailing the Uncharted Cosmic Sea

Learning to handle these exciting new vibrations and cosmic changes is very much like learning to sail in uncharted waters.

We really need to learn how to navigate these unknown waves and currents and be ready at the helm for the many fluctuations pounding our ships of life.

I'm also feeling for the people who have no clue as to what's going on.

To think there are so many who don't even know there is a cosmic sea, never mind that there are huge energetic wave changes reaching our planetary system that are now rocking their proverbial boats, is sad.

I guess it's like Plato's cave analogy, only here it's blind people in a boat who think all the world is the small structure and items they feel around them, while the real cosmic reality is expanding around them well outside their "boat" reality.

Stay on High Alert

There's a lot of very interesting information available on this transition we're going through with many interpretations, and some great advice on how to manage these vibrational changes. My personal take is to stay very alert and aware on every front, most of all with my thoughts and feelings, remaining the observer monitoring what's going on within and without me.

Don't ever forget, your very thoughts and feelings at times may not be your own but some morphed projection from unseen realms or these hyper-technological insane driven would-be controllers to steer humanity as well. This is especially so when our guards are down.

For me staying on alert also means keeping abreast of the news, the real news. It's watching for trends, not just in the NWO rollout or political news, but following earth and space changes is very important. How our planet and solar system are behaving is intrinsic to getting a deeper sense of the energetic changes we're undergoing. And sensing the spiritual changes around you is also imperative, much of which is intuitive. Once you get a rounded picture of the current situation the dots connect.

But we have to keep at it, especially now.

Real information is everything. It's our spiritual food. Either we're getting the adulterated stuff or we're getting real nourishment. It makes a world of difference in how we feel and think and affects the very course of our lives and hence the rest of humanity since we each affect it so profoundly. I avoid raw

TV as much as possible. It's toxic and completely destructive. If there's something worth watching you'll find it on the net where you can be in control of it. If you have to watch anything, limit it carefully and always mute the advertisements.

Conscious, Observant Living Is A Must – Beware the Unconscious Crazies

Learning to listen to our hearts, our real consciousness that taps into the central Source, and observe from that point is the key. As things start to pick up more speed as they are now this will be more and more important when mental processes get more and more affected.

The mind is much like the computer that is susceptible to an EMP blast, a large electromagnetic pulse, the same kind that can stop your computer controlled car and shut down the grid. The heart, however, your conscious spirit, only revels in the additional energetic bursts and will never let you down.

Now that's empowerment. But we have to be careful.

Now I drive slower than I used to. We all should. We need to watch out for erratic behavior on the roads when we're out, people are going to start unraveling before our eyes. Many will have psychotic type reactions to these vibrational changes and we need to be wary wherever we are.

Make Friends and Help Each Other

This has changed my life. I spend almost my full waking time on the internet, writing, doing interviews and discussing with associates and loved ones about what's going on. There is so much to learn and there are so many amazing wonderful people who have been researching and compiling empowering information I just don't have time for anything else.

I get my walk and take breaks but it's my full time passion because it to me is the essence of what's happening and where I can help and be the most effective in a world in dire straits.

Contributing to this massive wake up is all that matters to me.

I'm a communicator. And I'm not afraid to ask questions, or to thank those who have contributed so much to this truth revolution.

This has led to the best friendships of my life. I wrote how many of us seem to be alone when in reality we're most likely where we're supposed to be, yet we're united in spirit.

I received many touching comments to that post as it apparently resonated with quite a few people. Many also said they don't mind the isolation. That's the world they work and learn best in, and I relate to that.

Most of the people I correspond with are the same. We savor conscious awareness and spreading it. It's an act of love that gives tremendous satisfaction that at least we're doing what we can.

And we do the same in our daily interactions.

These friendships that have come with meeting fellow activists are the best. They're almost like broadening your antenna array to where you can pick up clearer signals and bounce your "readings" off those you love and trust.

So often a little inkling or sensation or an email and link from a friend can lead to new realms of understanding and even new researchers and whole areas you weren't aware of and a fresh re-synthesizing of what you've come to learn.

It's just fabulous. But we have to reach out.

Conclusion – Activate or Else

These energetic changes are not the answer. We are the answer. Those they affect who in turn willingly transform and pass it on, helping others understand and utilize what's going on, are the answer.

You and me.

With or without these new energies our mission is the same. But what a great time to be alive as it clearly appears we're getting a boost...good for conscious humanity, but bad for the matrix whose minions are scared to death of what's happening.

This is why the frantic implementation of the control system. Poor puny bastards. It's like a bucket of water on a raging forest fire. Sorry guys, you already lost. You really think you can fight the truth?

But we do need to keep exposing them so others can see through their false projection and find empowering truth and reality for themselves.

Sail On

We're sailing the cosmic sea, the wind is picking up, and it's all hands on deck.

We're here to act out our mission, however we're each called. We can follow, we can lead. We can sit by the wayside.

I don't personally condone non-action in the least. We need to be conscious responders. Not inexcusable idiots. That's thoroughly pathetic. I think we've all been through enough of that..and so have the enslaved.

Raise your voice.

Radiate the change any way you can.

When Worlds Divide

This question of a coming divergent world, a just one that separates in some way from the wicked one we're currently embroiled in, has been with us for some time. We are watching parallel phenomena of violent, threatening darkness pounding at our doorstep while a simultaneous absolutely awe-inspiring and empowering awakening is taking place around the globe. These are being contrasted before our hearts and minds as we each deal with these incoming realities at many levels.

As we know, they cannot contain our awakening no matter what draconian measures they try.

The dark Powers that have cleverly slipped into place can kill, maim and destroy to their wicked hearts' content but it cannot stop the truth nor extinguish one soul. That glorious fact is a reality that has been carefully kept "behind the veil" of mass human awareness for eons, even though every living soul senses otherwise.

Awake and aware consciousness and those daring to live there have known this all along.

What we call bravery in the face of their onslaughts is this very simple understanding. It's a knowledge and conviction that we are eternal and indestructible and have a firm grip on the reality that the truth for which we live is unshakeable. Living by that simple steadfast knowledge and proactively helping to manifest it in others is called being alive.

That's the definition of true freedom.

Growing Into Realizations – Screw Escapism

I'm not a fatalist in the sense that everything is predetermined. That is purely a programmed shut down mechanism to the degree anyone adopts that mental paralysis.

Complicated, arrogant, philosophical gobbledygook such as that has been the stifling academic controlling answer for all of the not-already-religiously-programmed subjects.

Same old mechanism. Get 'em from both sides.

We are very much alive, gloriously free willed entities in this wonderful cosmic fabric and are intrinsically connected together with the infinite creative Source. It couldn't be more wonderful, profound or simple. Just like your heart has told you all along.

I find myself chewing on this question of where humanity is going quite a bit, not even consciously, but it's always there as I attempt to "grok" the events in the world around me and the vast body of knowledge and esoterica at our fingertips. It's totally cool. I wouldn't have it any other way.

There is no greater purpose in life as far as I am concerned than to keep growing in understanding and empowering awareness and helping others to do the same.

From a new, enlightened perspective is the only way we can achieve the loving intentions we share for this planet...and beyond.

The Wheat and the Tares

This parable always struck me and it is apparently full on appropriate for today. We may not know who came here scattering their evils seeds but one thing for sure, over time we will see "who is who" when the plants grow to maturity. Which is clearly happening now.

"The kingdom of heaven is like a man who sowed good seed in his field. But while everyone was sleeping, his enemy came and sowed weeds among the wheat, and went away. When the wheat sprouted and formed heads, then the weeds also appeared.

"The owner's servants came to him and said, 'Sir, didn't you sow good seed in your field? Where then did the weeds come from?'

"'An enemy did this,' he replied.

"The servants asked him, 'Do you want us to go and pull them up?'

"'No,' he answered, 'because while you are pulling the weeds, you may uproot the wheat with them. Let both grow together until the harvest. At that time I will tell the harvesters: First collect the weeds and tie them in bundles to be burned; then gather the wheat and bring it into my barn.'"

The powerful statement of this parable is how the plants have to grow up together to find this out. Is this what we are experiencing now in a very profound cycle of distended time?

Clearly the mimicking parasitic weeds are sucking the good nutrients out of the soil that nourishes the good plants. No doubt they're good talkers, persuading their neighbors how needed they are in the community – in fact, "we should rule over you and help take care of things".

Ever notice how fast and tall weeds grow, and in the most unlikely places? And how much they can mimic the plants they're killing? And they DO kill off young sprouts if you don't catch them. Crowding them out, sucking up the water and minerals.

Sound familiar?

The usurpers at work. They were hidden, but are now being exposed to a growing swathe of humanity. All part of the division.

Light vs Dark – A Cycle of Change

However you conceive of or phrase the paradigm we're living in, what we are engaged in here is a struggle and it is a form of warfare. While it has become obvious even in this age of exploitation, as you become more spiritual you find this to be true and ever present in life changing ways. As said many times, religion and phony spirituality buries this reality in dogma, ritual, fearful obeisance and hierarchy. They know, therefore they conceal.

It doesn't matter to what extent we realize the depths of their perfidy, once we realize we have a very real enemy of bodies and souls it's time to take action. By each of us manifesting the light that is within us via acts of love and truth we increase the conscious energy field. When we affect others to do the same, and wake others out of slumber and they in turn pass it on, it grows exponentially.

This has been a battle throughout history, but my contention is that this time around something different and much more dramatic is taking place.

It has everything to do with communication. Knowing there are so many others who know, who are connecting, who are compelled to share this experience, who have as a result changed the course of their lives to do so more effectively, is absolutely empowering. And motivating.

We want to care for each other, we are compelled, our compassion continues to grow until it's uncontainable. That's all good.

The internet, designed by military agencies of all things, has been the key. Talk about backfiring.

The Cycles Tell the Tale

There's hardly a religion, metaphysical school or spiritual science that doesn't allude to cycles in some form or another.

The question is, where in cosmic "history" and the cycles of time and creation are we? And do we need to know?

I know we do. Because we're clearly being told. Our hearts are receiving and broadcasting this reality at massively increasing rates.

Why did the ancients track the stars so precisely? Why are the "gods" of ancient civilizations all cradled in astrotheology? Why is modern Luciferianism and even accepted religion steeped in astral symbology?

The cycles tell the tale.

We're apparently at a point of division. For each of us individually this is ever present. As a society and a species, it seems we're at a precipice. What we are witnessing in a spiritual sense is remarkable, and we need to be able to interpret it in its most positive sense, without losing the knowledge of the gravity of the geopolitical and spiritual realities.

They do all go together. And everything is empowering when taken in true conscious perspective.

May this give you something empowering to chew on.

It's with sincere love, and heartfelt appreciation to all those who soldier on for love and truth.

Ultimately, there's no doing anything against the truth. Only for the truth.

Truth By Consensus - How to Control Our Thinking

Funny how this works. People actually think they can arrive at the truth by averaging out what they hear.

Seriously.

That's how most people are taught to think. I get this argument all the time.

It totally explains the power of the mass media. Just think about this dynamic. How do people arrive at conclusions? What information or lack thereof are they deriving them from? Pretty stark reality if you're willing to look it in the eyes. People are incredibly similar in their outlook and understandings. And hence behaviors.

Incredibly so. Like we're following a script.

Look at yourself. How you dress, the expressions you use, what you're into, no matter what segment of society you're living in. I remember when I decided to grow out my facial hair and looking in the mirror thinking, "Am I following some meme being broadcast by these bastards?"

Paranoid? Totally. It's the only way on this planet. Completely healthy. If you're not, you're not awake yet.

Truth is Never Popular

While a defined consensus gets established and reaffirms the status quo, "contrary" eddies of thought and realization make their way through the public psyche. These are carefully ferreted out by the watchdog media cabal and portrayed as "fringe" ideas and "conspiracy theories" of course.

Carefully and dutifully packaged and sublimated into a negative subconscious arena for the mainstream unawakened. Anything contrary is now anathema and resented; spuriously thrown overboard as wing nut conspiracy talk.

Typical. And more importantly…very effective and very efficient. In their world.

Getting To the Point

I'll take truth over BS fairy tales any day of eternity. No matter the pain and seeming loss of emotional or otherwise investments, bring on the truth.

9/11 is always the standard reminder of how duped the world can be. Plain as the nose on your face those towers were brought down by some sort of exotic and carefully planned out demolition technique, but what the hell.

No one cares. Or very few. At least that's the portrayal we get and it seems to hold way too much water. People are even afraid to discuss the subject. That's when you know society has been seriously hemmed in and is headed for dismemberment.

As obvious as it is, the truth can just be right there without people being able to see it. It's the condition of our "race"… we want to believe what we want and will cloak it in "positive thinking" or "idealism" or imposed bottom line security needs whenever we can for peace and comfort.

Very, very sad from the truth perspective, but oh so understandable.

Blindness until awakened. What a tale.

But behold the awakening in spite of all this.

Enter Psycho-Sexual Addiction

This psychological pandering we're witnessing is simply a ploy to keep the masses asleep. The populace has been duped, hypnotized, seduced. It no longer can contain, maintain or control itself. It must have the savories and goodies of the system or it will go berserk.

This addiction is firmly established.

Football, advertising, game shows, reality dramas, zombie and vampire horror and sci-fi movies while sucking down addictive, poisonous foods………"Please bring it on. We want more. We want another reality, not our own."

Scantily dressed young girls, sculpted feminized men, cross sexual weirdness of every type and genre....

...bring it on. Chaos is our new middle name–in fact, their manipulated shifting world is apparently our New Normal.

"Chaos is the new normal" is as cognitively dissonant as the "war on terrorism". Orwell, you must be howling.

Summary

Know what you "believe" about not only their false structure, but our true reality, to the point it's not a belief. Please know each of those as facts...not an emotional extension of some hope or sense of idealism. Be sure you're deciding for yourself and not following anything unconsciously.

We're not used to that kind of truly independent thought, having been taught all our lives to just follow, obey and repeat, so it's a lot of work and a new set of muscles that have to be developed. You'll see what I mean as it goes along.

Affirming our conscious awakening in spirit, word and deed is our primary purpose and most potent weapon. Not only against the usurpers and the ignorance and darkness that seems to rule our current paradigm, but for the development and realization of the true conscious reality that is there to be expressed into this dimension.

Get busy being and doing what you know is right and the rest will follow, I guarantee. Because that's how it works.

And do it in love.

If we can wake up, anybody can.

"If you're not free to follow life's signs and live in synchronicity, you're not free."

– Zen

Personal Notes:

The Land of Don't

"The more corrupt the state, the more numerous the laws."
– Cornelius Tacitus (55 – 117 A.D.)

Everything on our planet is regulated – as in ruled by law. Whether they be outright laws, local ordinances or any type of restrictions, in not just physical activity but also social rules over interactions. Under the guise of so-called democratic societies giving the impression that we agreed to all of this or even thought it up for ourselves, we now live seriously restricted lives, with the penalty of fines or incarceration looming over our heads if we don't obey.

It's all about control.

Carefully manipulated control.

To regulate means: "to control or direct by a rule, principle, method, etc." When you identify just how un-free we are to live, think and operate as we are naturally intended to, it can be quite a wake up call. Most people can see this to some extent, but the full on reality of this imposed prison on humanity needs to dawn on a heck of a lot more souls. The matrix concept is no joke – it's an insidious yoke upon the human soul, trapping and sapping our very energy while spellbinding humanity with its giant jumbotron of deliberate misinformation.

The Mounting World of Regulations

Just look at any set of regulatory rules. They're beyond natural description. The US IRS code alone would fill up over 80,000 legal pages of rules and regulations for the falsely entrapped American, binding them to conditions and stipulations that boggle the mind. Or just try to build a house, or buy property, or start a business and the paper work is beyond surreal between the legal contracts, banking conditions, zoning issues and on and on.

Try to enjoy a public park or any such facility, and the rules will be full frontal. Don't do this, don't do that, "punishable by….."

The conditioning is intense, and has been carefully sculpted to encroach on humanity for millennia, but now much more than ever. The inquisition was mild compared to the control power of this massive programmed legal and social grid thrown over humankind. We need to be aware of the extent of it and not blinded by the sugar coated glitz and glamor and flashy ads and products. Just walk through a supermarket or down a city street – it makes "They Live" look tame once you see through it.

Recent Regulatory Insanity

The following was just shoved down Americans' throats with much more to come. Not only are they absurd mandates but they will cost billions of dollars to comply to, another effort to break the backs of an already overburdened and suppressed populace. Even more disturbing are the Agenda 21 programs being incrementally woven into public policy, such as the so-called "Clean Water Act" that greatly expands the EPA's power to regulate even small bodies of water on private property.

From the Daily Caller:

"White House Quietly Releases Plans For 3,415 Regulations Ahead Of Thanksgiving Holiday

"The federal Unified Agenda is the Obama administration's regulatory road map, and it lays out thousands of regulations being finalized in the coming months. Under President Barack Obama, there has been a tradition of releasing the agenda late on Friday — and right before a major holiday…

"A more pressing EPA rule set to be finalized is the so-called coal ash rule for coal-fired power plants. A final rule will be issued by Dec. 19, and could be bad news for the power sector, which will bear the brunt of $20.3 billion in compliance costs.

"But probably the most fought-over rules to be finalized by the EPA next year will be its redefining of the "Waters of the United States" under the Clean Water Act.

The EPA will issue its redefinition next year, according to the agenda. Federal lawmakers from both parties, along with companies from virtually every sector of the economy, have opposed the rule, saying it greatly expands the EPA's power to regulate even small bodies of water on private property.

"The 'waters of the U.S.' rule may be one of the most significant private property grabs in U.S. history," said Louisiana Republican Sen. David Vitter, adding "they want to take another step toward outright permitting authority over virtually any wet area in the country, while at the same time providing a new tool for environmental groups to sue private property owners."

Always a Can't, Never a Can

Their message is never empowering, but always disempowering. It's not what you can do, it's what you can't do. Restrict, bind, inhibit, control.

That's their agenda and it's on us full frontal. The behavior of those around us is testament to this. Once you wake up to it it's shocking.

Look around you – read your labels and advisories on anything in print, on line or in public – it's never empowering, always qualifying their intention to protect themselves and "the public" while putting the onus on you, the consumer or participant, to stay within the "guidelines" and not step over the boundaries.

The real problem now is people are accustomed to it. After decades of mental infringement, the general mind set is to yield and obey and acquiesce in the face of these limitations imposed by "authorities". A very sad "state" indeed. The sheepleization seems to have been a success to a large degree.

But not for me. Or you.

Pavlovian Entrainment Takes A Toll

Stimulus-response mechanisms when repeated over and over entrain the mind and hence behavior. It may appear obvious at the time or even in retrospect, but understanding the depth of the programming can be disconcerting. From school buzzers and bells between classes, fire alarms, honking horns, warning signs, flashing emergency lights, everything interrupted by ads and commercials, signs with "don't" instructions, threats of violent police reprisals and the like, it takes a toll.

Then add to the mix pop culture and its many mind steering attitudes and perverse inclinations.

The key concept of the social engineers is conditioning. Repeat repeat repeat. Be they lies, misrepresentations, omissions, violent images or scare tactics, just keep the barrage going is their MO.

As long as the herd mentality stays pinned to the matrix wall they're happy. That's why shirking the whole thing is so important. It can't be a partial separation from this evilly intentioned insanity. It needs to be a clean break. Every one of those tendrils sapping our life force and direction, attention as well as intention, is lethal.

Just as their insane worldwide plan of decimation is designed to literally kill off humanity and transform humans into a different, more easily subservient entity on a deliberately eviscerated planet, so this social and so-called legal slavery enhancement and reinforcement is eroding humanity by our continued exposure to it.

Incremental Encroachment

They're very clever, and very patient. Bathing humanity in their concoction of social and physical engineering has been playing out a long, long time. We're at the apex of their attempt to put the clamps on the planet so anything goes now with these psychopaths. They assume humanity has been so dumbed down by their social, spiritual and physical programs that they have free reign to do as they please with absolute impunity…as if that hasn't been the case all along, but now it's full frontal and for all to see in our interconnected world.

The programmed mass media mush is full on evidence of this at any level you care to perceive it.

The United States of Amerika is the primary target for decimation, but it's really an idea they're killing. The UK, Canada and Australia as well as many other countries are parallel targets having this "freedom disease" and are going under as we speak as they bow to the globalist agenda. There are way too many alive and motivated individuals in those countries that may cause trouble. Besides, in their plan the "American dream" has been a beacon of freedom and empowerment for far too long and needs to be taken down and erased as a distant memory in the body politic. Revisionist and blocked out history have served them well, but individual rights and freedoms must now be stamped out.

They're not for the world they've designed.

That's how they see it. Sick psychopaths on a very sick warpath. It really comes down to wake up—or pay the price.

Their True Agenda

We're seeing this aspect put squarely in our faces via predictive, esoteric and even occult programming. If you haven't seen the movie Branded yet it's worth the watch. It's quite the confessional, along the lines of They Live about the deeper realities behind this surface programming and mental conditioning. As the public imbibes and accepts these realities they are unwittingly accepting, endorsing and empowering way more than they bargained for.

That's the deeper aspect of spiritual contracts which we'll get into more in the near future.

Will We Wake Up?

That's the ultimate question. We're being sickened, abnormalized and driven to distorted mind sets and eventual capitulation one day at a time. That people can't see it is the most disconcerting reality for any even partially awakened individual.

It can appear pretty bleak once you catch on but just keep pursuing. There's an underlying way greater reality waiting to be revealed to you.

The fact is, people are awakening at an incremental and even exponential rate, grasping the simplest of tactics being waged against their way of life. It may appear political at first, but it evolves as they pursue the deeper ramifications of what's going on and why.

That's cool. And we need to encourage it.

The point is empowerment, taking control of our immediate situation and personal direction is what it's all about. And one changed life and voice against tyranny and dystopian control represents and encourages so very many others. Most of all, the fact that the solution on each of our parts is to unsubscribe. Detach, let go of your legal and moral obligations to any such usurping entities be they by birth, financial, social or spiritual contract. Break them, and be free.

They're fraudulent. Just step away.

Conclusion – Break Your Contracts and Bust Out!

Forget the restrictions and shirk the programming at every level – grow your own food, collect your own water, speak your own words, live your own dreams, share your own truth. The collapsing system of control is in a downward spiral and furiously attempting to exact every possible restriction on human life and expression.

Why isn't this more evident to the masses? Because they've been cowed into submission while their hunger and desires are being channeled into televised events and day to day drudgery as they slave to make a living in this very system they think they cannot afford to challenge.

A closed loop of control. Until we wake up to it.

Once we get it, the shackles come off. That's what people are nervous about stepping into. Freedom for most is very frightening, and not necessarily something to be desired, unless virtually experienced at a football game as they salute the flag and get all weird, patriotic and high on displaced emotions.

Take heart from the growing sovereignty movements where people are getting free and standing tall in the reality of already having overcome. It might seem a bit foreign and simplistic at first, but dig deeper. That's a real space to operate from. When we truly wake up we realize we're not subject to all these fraudulent laws, licenses, and "certificates of registration" unless we allow them to govern us. They really only apply to the false legal entity they attached to us at birth which is not even us. The whole system is basically a convoluted con job and only works because people subject themselves to it.

Such is the matrix. But we are overcoming just by our conscious awareness and spreading of enlightened information and then acting on what we learn. There's a lot more to be done to effect the changes we need at the grass roots level, but awakening to the reality of our situation and what powers lay at our fingertips to arise in our true form is all important. From there we find perspective and true freedom and derive strength and resolve to reach others in whatever manner we can.

But we must get there first and operate from there. That's the key.

Cut your contracts of all sorts and steer clear of the programming – live for what you know is true, honest, loving and needed.

And keep on keeping on! If you think you haven't found it yet, you haven't. Keep on, and you will....and you'll know!

Personal Notes:

Dancing in the
Vortex of Change

We currently appear to be in a kind of vortex, or a roiling series of etheric vortexes and scattered eddies of changing, swirling currents, carrying newly manifesting energetics as well as debris of all types, sizes and dimensions.

It's wonderful exciting energy but it can be disconcerting at the same time.

We need to be careful to dodge the spiraling flak while maneuvering into and even reveling in the energetic vortex. It's nothing to fear as long as we're aware of what's going on around us and stay on our toes. The changes are changing and the winds are picking up.

A great time for letting go – but it will not be a pleasant ride for those who refuse to loosen their grip.

While this may seem "spacey" and weird to those not picking up on these new vibrations, this may explain the strange feelings many of you are having. But I'm convinced this is what is going on right now.

The Changes We're Sensing

I'm certainly experiencing it and from what I'm hearing, it's happening to a lot of people. People are wondering, "Why did I lose my job", or "How come things just aren't working out as I thought or hoped they would?" "Why this terrible issue with my dying relative?" Easy.

The Universe is giving opportunities for change by nudging us towards entirely new paradigms in our lives. It always is but it seems to be stepping up. And the only way to experience what Universe has for us is letting go into it and letting go of all the trappings. Old hangups, outdated understandings, wrong attachments, etc. Love is all inclusive, as well as all dissolving.

The fog in the heart must go.

And that takes commitment. Changing friends, locations, means of provision, trusting your new awake outlook, and... telling the truth. It means not going along anymore with the lie and letting go of old habits and frames of reference. It's imperative if we want to move on to the good stuff. Things are coming at us fast and furious and from strange directions so it's get with the awakened program or get knocked out of the game.

Once you get into it it's like dodge ball in dance class with your fellow psychedelic mariners. A laughing, riotous mishmash of fun and creativity.

Dreams, Visitations and Climate Screws

There's a sense of movement and disorientation but there's a stillness at the same time. Many are also having profound psychic or spiritual experiences; floods of dreams, waves of spiritual intuitions, rapidly changing emotions or sensations for no reason….and perhaps spiritual revealings and even visitations of varying sorts.

Those getting the heavier doses of these experiences know what I'm talking about. It's nothing to fear. Draw close to Source most of all but also loved ones, share what you're going through with those you love and trust.

And let go.

And get to where you can dance to it. We can interact very consciously and poetically to anything and everything. The challenge is the changing tides of change coming at us right now. There's not very much regularity, rhyme or reason, yet we feel called into the vortex despite the seeming chaos.

Actually, there is no choice as far as entering into the vortex. It's here, like a massive, morphing yet loving spiritual hurricane. To handle it consciously and grow with it is the key.

The weather often parallels these changes for me. This inspiration came while weird gusting winds were blowing around our home and area, which they've done for days. In fact, in general the weather just feels different to me, like that expression "something's in the air" – and it's not just chemtrails and radiation, obvious assaults on human connectivity to consciousness.

155

Something wonderful this way cometh. But it ain't anything we've seen before. And that's a good thing.

So why not dive in and make an interactive dance out of it? Spiritual yoga, tai chi or a host of other rhythmic conscious disciplines are a perfect solution for releasing your ki and tuning into the true essence of it all as the changes whirl about you.

How beautiful to behold.

Know Your Way Around

I'm just trying to lay out these etheric sensations that appear to parallel the increasingly nonsensical changes we're witnessing. Hopefully it helps others grasp the nature of this experience, but more importantly to help people know they're not alone in all of this. We're all together here, and we have others involved in this apparent transcendence working and manifesting at many levels.

Be aware, awake, and awash in love and the innate knowledge that all is ultimately well and under control. We are unstoppable infinite consciousness. Bottom line. Stand with conviction, spiritual warriors.

But we have to do our part. More than ever. Never negate or minimize our role. There's a type of cosmic directive that pivots on the state of conscious awakening and our response to it.

That might sound a little strange, but responding consciously is our daily commitment and lesson in life. Just floating down river with all the flotsam and jetsam is not living consciously. Think of the receding tsunami in Japan and all it carried and that's what the world is currently experiencing – a massive backwash of debris that's heading out to sea.

To the conscious mariners who have prepared it's game on. And we'll be busy trying to awaken and rescue anyone we can.

This is Not a Drill – Conscious Warriors Arise

What's exciting is the spontaneity of our shared experience. We are encountering a time in our evolution that has perhaps never been experienced before. While the world may currently seem strictly suicidal in nature in the context of our current Machiavellian rulers' agenda and their reign of terror, there is something wonderful happening at the same time that is much more profound.

There are many lessons to be gleaned during our stay here that are invaluable for eternity.

Number one: Our true state of being and who we are. The realization of our potential is the ultimate answer.

I realize finding our way is not a process that can easily be explained. We don't clearly know where we are or where we came from other than by intuitive understanding and some pieces of difficult to find research. But one thing massive that we do know: we are conscious awareness discovering itself. That in itself is enough for the conscious voyager to keep going and experiencing.

Following that is truly manifesting...with great and profound assurance that we are the living and loving answer. Just as we are. We're each becoming the world to be, as it already is in its own right which we know in our hearts, and we should continue do so with complete confidence and authority.

Conclusion: Behold the Beauty of Change

What beauty we have the privilege to live and participate in, no matter what the circumstances. Our lives during these temporal events are filled with wonder, excitement and change – expected in some cases, and unexpected in most. If we fearfully resist what's swirling around us and drawing us into new realms of realization and experience we'll only meet serious disappointment, followed by sadness, angst and frustration.

That's exactly why our state of mind and heart and living in a higher vibrational state has become imperative. When we release our old ways in order to embrace the unknown with an attitude of trust and wonder it becomes the ride of a lifetime.

Dance with it. Let go consciously with spiritual awareness and enter in. Look around, find your way, make wise decisions, detach from attachments, and don't be afraid, even if it seems to get a bit "freaky".

We're in this together. They try to make us feel alone but we are all connected. We always have been and we always will be – because we always are.

I'm having my own wild and wonderful experiences I'm currently tapping into – although it can be a bit daunting when these new spiritual sensations arise and manifest I'm having a blast. But hey – would you really refuse a ticket out of here that's clearly a path to a wonderful new world of experience that can be shared with any and all?

Take all this on as you feel led. But most of all....turn it into a powerful, consciously aware dance.

We are all entering into new horizons of living consciousness, and should utilize and enjoy it.

Much love and empowerment to you all.

Keep on "wondering" and dancing to the tunes of the Universe.

Personal Notes:

Let Go of the Baggage or Go Down with the Ship

It's a very freaky time right now. I'm really removed in every way possible away from mainstream anything. The only news I follow is alternative sites, and much of that is esoterica or practical ideas for the real world we should be living in now and how to go about it.

Being so removed has also brought on some very profound new sensations.

We're well into our second month of detoxing again from life in the US and it's a very strange experience at this time. Almost immediately, besides the exhilaration of a beautiful and humble new land to learn about and explore, it's as if the static is gone and I can feel the real spiritual atmosphere the planet is experiencing.

And despite the local peace, it's not a good overall vibe.

I thought it was the location I was in but I don't think so anymore. It feels like there's this creeping crescendo of oppressive darkness that's getting exerted on the planet, like a gravitational or magnetic pull downward. It's the same feeling you get when you watch an ominous storm gathering on the horizon, only it's all around and pulling downwards.

It's very much the old gloom and doom scenario, only in this subtle, almost visible inky heaviness seeping out of the earth and trying to draw everything down.

Maybe, Maybe Not

It's hard to quantify intuitive feelings like this. I've also had a series of incredibly clear dreams that have gone along with this sensation, so it could signify things I'm going through personally, which no doubt is to some extent true. Someone was commenting on Is "It Ever Too Late To Wake Up" about a similar experience they're having and that's what triggered this article. And I quote:

"I have this feeling that peaks and then subsides a bit. I have quit watching any news (just to see what is being fed to the masses) and stopped swinging by MSM websites to see the latest "story". Yet, it is as though I can feel the waves of BS rolling in. There is a storm off the shore for sure. The waves are more powerful and coming in faster and faster. I scream louder, but others cannot hear me over the crashing sounds. I am hoping the salt water gets in their eyes to distract the hypnotized eyes and allow them to see for a moment before the storm rolls on shore. I want to slap people, but I know it won't really matter.

So, I throw out a statement here and there to get a mind that has even began to peek out to find the food it needs. We all have to keep trying. I agree with Martine – anything is better than nothing. It all adds to the collective that we want to raise vibrations and hurts the collective that is bringing us down. Tilt the scale, one little ol' pea at a time." – Little Mama

Well put. What I'm sensing and trying to describe here sure fits this climate we're witnessing in the world today. The forces of darkness are exerting more and more draconian control mechanisms to where there's no way things can be reversed without some sort of conflagration. Too much has been set in motion, which is why I keep repeating to prepare accordingly, as it will give you great peace of mind.

Letting Go – Or Else

That's why letting go of this world is so important right now. This gravitational inertia is pulling on a lower dimensional level. Only those who operate in that vibrational field will be seriously affected by it. When someone awakens to conscious truth and awareness the matrix crap starts to fall away.

But there are a lot of conscious choices to make in the process.

How much stuff should I have? Are my finances out of the reach of the banksters? Where should I live and with whom? What will I give my daily energy and attention to? How can I help further the awakening and lend a helping hand to this wonderful spiritual revolution? Is my ego still in charge rather than my consciousness? Am I as fully a part of the solution as I can be, and not still part of the problem?

When thinking about this whole subject I was reminded of those that grabbed their valuables and jumped off the Titanic, only to sink all the faster. If this increasing gravity has anything to hold on to it's going to take down whomever won't let it go.

That's a Huge Lesson for Us All

Disengage, disassociate, disconnect. That's all I can say. The parasitic beast is consuming everything in its path that exhibits inertia.

We need to let go of the net of shallow understanding lest it catch the evil birds of control and draw them in. We need to relax our egoic contractions to these affronts by the controllers' snares and sidestep their idiocy in conscious awareness.

We are intrinsically free.

Free, seriously, free.

Just do it. Don't delay.

Freely.

Drop the Rope

It's interesting how we get entangled in compromising situations and interactions, often unwittingly. We all face this challenge continually. So often the very encounter itself is predestined to failure without our even knowing it and results in a sense of energy sapping futility.

If you find yourself in such a tug of war, it's time to rethink your entire stance. In fact, it might be time to drop the connection all together. So called winning ain't what it's cracked up to be, nor to your benefit in most cases in these circumstances.

This happens because we get snared into lower level thinking on a preset playing field designed to do just that. Ensnare and entrap. This societal mechanism is designed to set the parameters and disguise the real solution which is way outside this constructed paradigm. When we join into the "contest" we subject ourselves to the win-lose dialectic, the pitting of one versus another trap that has beset humanity for eons.

That's not to say there isn't a time to attempt to illuminate ignorance or expose manipulative mechanisms, we just can't expect to "win" in an arena built for pointless conflict that distracts from seeing the essential and empowering reality that blows their entire construct to bits.

If we're too busy fighting amongst ourselves, physically or intellectually, we'll never see that bigger picture where the true problem truly lies.

The Conflict Dialectic

Society has been manipulated to such a degree that the easiest way to control us is through simple distraction. Bread and circus competitive sports and similar mind-stinting entertainment, right-left paradigm political charades and society dividing issues such as race, immigration and social, economic and class status are furiously alive trigger points of distraction running rampant in this seriously dysfunctional world mind.

We help define and reinforce these memes ourselves by our participation. Without rising above this imposed playing field and understanding the world we're already living in we certainly cannot find the way to change it, never mind the way out without their constrictions.

Simply said, if you don't want to play their insidious, pointless, draining and distracting games of tug of war, simply drop the rope and move on. Let them fall in their own devices.

Dropping the Rope

When dealing with this seeming "conflict resolution" we appear to be confronting on many levels, "dropping the rope" is a very interesting way to break this sycophantic relationship with our oppressors. What invariably surfaces in our left brain human response in these sorts of circumstances is a sort of contest between people or situations. One side opposes the other in some form, and one or the other or both sides express umbrage at what the other is saying.

It's a programmed and mass entranced conflict, the "strategy of tension" as they call it, utilized by the media and military with very successful abandon.

When we find ourselves in these situations it can be quite stressful. Reflexive thinking usually kicks in and we take sides, concentrating on the "issues" at hand while ignoring the overall. Even in a personal heated exchange, subtle or obvious, no one wins. They can't. The overarching truth is being missed in this morass of "logical" confined thought subscribed to by the perspective of the participants within a fogged emotional state.

Overall social psychosis perhaps, or the left brained reptilian mind going to work, who knows. It's just futile in that type of paradigm. These types of conflicts are an exercise in futility.

Oh, we may bring some light of truth to the conversation or situation but the problem is that we're buying into their boxing ring. Someone has to come out the "victor" and the game goes on, without addressing the underlying reality outside the ring, or imposed and deliberately created stadium of conflict.

This realization is a blow to the egoic mind set and, while essentially counter intuitive, it's only destined to be repeated. And the pointless game goes on. Don't fall for it. You're well above all this.

Spiritual Scoliosis and Letting Go of the Unchange-able

The application of this realization can get quite personal. Those we're closest to can often display usage of this dialectic and it's not easy to discern up close and personal, nor know how to respond to it.

There's often an embedded agenda to what is being said or proposed, as exemplified by news outlets, or as we usually see it by people around us, that is much more profound than the surface argument. You'll often hear sweeping language with generalities that appear to be true in such contests of mind but these can have a much more insidious nature.

People, as well as social engineers, often use this technique.

It's usually very cleverly embedded, be it by an individual or ideology. But on an individual basis it can get pretty dicey.

The Personal Touch

It's naive to think we could correct spiritual scoliosis or perform some kind of exorcism or somehow overwhelm this mechanism to get it into its proper place and perspective when dealing with an infected individual with such a mindset. Those are the things and persons that conscious people sidestep until the subject really wants help and starts to see the light of day and fully lets go of their petty shibboleths.

These are issues that really aren't so petty when you get down to the spiritual nature of it and difficult to discern as well as confront.

But when you're awake to these traits you don't argue with them or plea with them to let go. They either do when confronted with conscious awareness or they don't. Otherwise you leave them alone until there's a change, and move on to those open to real dialogue. This kind of conscious awareness is sadly thin in today's world but people are catching on.

No players, no game is a great default setting.

Their approach has a lot to do with posturing, as if they're authoritative on some subject. Unthinking people often submit to that. When someone comes on pretending to be an authority on anything and speaks in that tone and posture it's time to sit up and take notice – carefully. Not sit back in acquiescence. Real truth sharers propose and entreat. Remember, words, which carry spirit, can eventually overpower you if you keep listening to where you sense either it's empowering and rooted in truth and love, or it isn't healthy.

It'll be clear. Just listen.

Be Like Water

Avoiding these kinds of obstacles is a bit of an an acquired art, but it can be learned. This has to do with the nature of ongoing change. Water just goes around the rock, or over it, or both. Sometimes rocks move with the water a little but never fully. Like those set in their ways.

They're rocks. That's the attached baggage people won't let go of in their hearts and it clogs up the works and infects anything it embeds in. They're fine, or should I say less dangerous, on their own and they have their place despite their issues. But they're not water; and if you expect them to come along like water it's going to be a long and arduous journey that pretty much is playing the rock's game.

Water moves on to where its welcomed. Go with the flow. Let the rocks be, i.e; let go of the rope.

Conclusion

It's important to not get caught up in futile and ultimately destructive contests of any sort, be they relationships or unconscious dialogue as they can have very deceitful and disempowering consequences.

That's how the system works. Getting everyone caught up in lower vibrational interactions that muffle the call to conscious awareness and activism in avenues that have real meaning. It's something to which they are clearly diametrically opposed. They're more than happy to entangle you in anything petty to keep you from realizing that.

You can't win on their level. Don't even go there. But if you do and find yourself in a tug of war with ignorance, egos or manipulating entities…..just drop the rope. It's that simple. Let 'em fall on their asses and you go merrily on your way.

And go take a nice walk in our majestic freedom and glory in your independent magnificence. Then turn and do and say what's right – in every situation you come up against.

Screw the programming. We're free.

That's how truth wins out.

Crossing the Threshold

Time is once again behaving strangely. Little slippages here and there, abrupt realizations that it's not the time or date you thought it was. Are you noticing? Weird sort of head spinning feelings when trying to track your thoughts, memory lapses, strange sense of fatigue, or ringing in the ears with a touch of vertigo? It's freaky. A lot of influences at work right now. Some good, some bad.

Personally, I think we may have hit the edge of the wormhole.

Exotic thought perhaps. But that's what appears to be happening in many ways. The awakening was easier to see from afar just a year ago. Now the picture is getting muddled and appears like a hodgepodge of swirling influences and resultant reactions. Things mix together like paints on a happy child's finger painting palette.

It's apparently because we have entered some kind of vortex perhaps, where time and space subduct like esoteric tectonic plates.

Going through a wormhole can't be an easy experience, unless of course you've been distilled to spirit. Which we all will be.

Behold the Plan

As if. Who knows the plan? But we can track and watch and learn and experience. And knowing it's all just a ride will save your spiritual hiney and keep your engine cooled during all this insanity.

I'm so enraptured with the awakening that's happening.

It's clear, yet it's hard to put your finger on in many ways with the crap we're being told. What we're being shown by the big media projector is the exact opposite of what's really going on. Thankfully dot connecting makes things very plain, and when you learn to speak that language, damn it's clear.

Your Personal Choice

So, you've walked up to the wormhole of truth and transformation. What do you do? Run in fear and hide from what could be a path to a greater reality and cling to the old world addictions to whateverthehell keeps you entrapped and ensnared?

Or venture on.

It was an easy choice for me, thankfully. Adventure towards freedom vs trudging towards slavery? Are you kidding?

Resist, and affirm, by being.

The Tipping Point At the Crossroads of Time

It appears we're hitting that infamous tipping point in many arenas of late. So much is getting revealed and reaching the collective consciousness as the truth manifests. Remember, to finally tip a scale it just needs that last grain of sand to completely reverse perceived reality in the mass mind.

Just look at not just the grains, but the flood tide of truth being released into the public mental, spiritual, economic and political domains, never mind the profound vibrational morphic field shifts with so many souls awakening in a whole range of areas. It's astounding.

There's still a lot to be done but the landscape is changing fast.

No doubt the external world situation grows more dire by the day, but it's important for people to be able to identify these powerful shifts now taking place for their own encouragement and inspiration. While the forces of abuse and control seem to be making monstrous strides toward their end game, their machinations are becoming more obvious and clearly malicious. As people are able to step back and identify the fact that their world is a completely manipulated one, they shed their fear of it and soon find their true spiritual and consciously aware footing.

This is the very definition of empowerment and drastically weakens the power structure's control over people's minds. As a result the flame of true freedom grows brighter continually, further propelling humanity's awakening and continued empowerment.

The Alternative Mosquito Swarm

Every email, every blog, every website, every post, every conversation, every independent media outlet broadcasting the truth is a massively powerful influence towards turning the tide in the perception of our world and hence its actual operation. It happens one seemingly small act at a time, but it's spreading like wildfire, in spite of the doubts of naysayers and and even alternative cynics.

Doubt is akin to fear, and its end result is apathy; i.e. disempowerment and inaction. It's similar to one of the biggest lies ever perpetrated in the heart of mankind. "After all, what can little me do to make any kind of difference that matters? I'm just one little person."

The absolute opposite of the truth. As the oft used expression goes;

"If you think you're too small to make a difference, try sleeping in a closed room with a mosquito."

Now picture multiple swarms of truth-bearing mosquitoes, replicating as they go. Can't you just see the wicked minions in assumptive power fleeing their pretentious little bastions of lies and pompous superficial sandcastles as a result of such an onslaught? Absolutely glorious.

The Power of the Awakening Factor

Few realize the power of change, whether it be conscious awareness or fundamental knowledge tools. What we have been handed is a very limited viewpoint that needs continual challenging, especially once we become aware of their vast array of social engineering programs.

Researchers have discovered a very powerful dynamic in our social milieu, something we know in our hearts to be true but sometimes it's good to have it affirmed by so-called scientific evidence.

"Scientists at Rensselaer Polytechnic Institute have found that when just 10 percent of the population holds an unshakable belief, their belief will always be adopted by the majority of the society. The scientists, who are members of the Social Cognitive Networks Academic Research Center (SCNARC) at Rensselaer, used computational and analytical methods to discover the tipping point where a minority belief becomes the majority opinion. The finding has implications for the study and influence of societal interactions ranging from the spread of innovations to the movement of political ideals.

"When the number of committed opinion holders is below 10 percent, there is no visible progress in the spread of ideas. It would literally take the amount of time comparable to the age of the universe for this size group to reach the majority," said SCNARC Director Boleslaw Szymanski, the Claire and Roland Schmitt Distinguished Professor at Rensselaer. "Once that number grows above 10 percent, the idea spreads like flame."

Pretty damn powerful, and personally empowering.

Turning Tides

Just look how the ISIS "terror" operation cover has been blown open for what it truly is, a ploy masterminded and funded by cooperative surreptitious interests out to destabilize and control the Middle East and beyond. This recent attack on Yemen by Saudi Arabia, of all despotic nation states, is another massive blip on the radar, as if that fascist state is interested in representative rule, all with the full on backing of Israel, the US and NATO.

And into another spectrum, how about the moon mission being thoroughly debunked as NASA admits they can't pass the Van Allen radiation belt? This fact has been known for a long time but is now evident to all. Not only the whole space program, but all of the information coming from NASA all these years comes into question.

A new 9/11 novel titled Methodical Illusion by a former airline stewardess is chock-a-block with real information regarding what really transpired that day that's going viral in the mainstream media, with pilots buying the book by the box to pass out to friends.

The truth is being revealed by the minute in all kinds of arenas.

Clearly multitudes are seeing the world's economy is manipulated by central banksters, and that the unending war on this scripted illusory concept of terror that they keep propping up with new false flags and boogeymen has become a worn out old saw for anyone even half awake to see. Now rapacious Israel has openly declared its intentions to eviscerate Palestine and other foes while its vice like grip on America is laid bare before the world.

And more examples are surfacing by the day. The obvious nature of this world game is now naked in the eyes of millions of people worldwide, despite Amerika's comatose state – and these realizations are rapidly growing as lives change in the light of this awareness.

Yet you won't hear a peep about any of this in the scripted media. After all, big money and controlling elites rule all in this metastasized Orwellian spin off to which we're subjected. Another aspect is the vast discrepancy between fat cat incomes and the rest of humanity that continues to distend as these psychopaths think no one is noticing, all while subjugated citizens' income and food supplies run thin as the elite's bankrolls blossom and our food supply is systemically attacked.

The outrage is boiling and reaching the tipping point, in multiple ways. The tide will certainly shift, and already is via massive undercurrents. But now is the time to put our shoulders to the wheel of change while we can still operate freely in order to stave off as much of this draconian insanity as possible.

It's time to rise.

Express these realizations loud and clear in whatever way you can to make the message heard while encouraging others that are sensing this same reality. The doors of opportunity are closing fast. If and when the temporally induced night comes, we need as many hearts ablaze as possible to light up the darkness while our work continues.

When Humanity Awakens and Arises

We're about to see some fantastic cataclysmic changes on our planet, but way more importantly within human consciousness. This is not so much "their" doing even in lieu of the obvious socio-geopolitical arena, but is of cosmic proportions in ways they will never see coming. This awakening is what they inherently fear, as global takeover progenitor Zbigniew Brzezinski articulated, and the very thing the would-be controllers are preparing for in their attempts to kill off, drug, cripple, transhumanize and militarily control humanity.

The tide is turning, the scales are tipping. This is not wishful thinking. It's fact. The question does remain however: what will we do with this empowering dynamic? Observe, or participate?

Change, awareness and activation don't just happen on their own. They work through you, they work through me. If we respond to them the changes happen. If we just observe, pass the buck and let it all just continue, it doesn't happen or meet up to its full potential.

It's a choice. It's yours, it's mine. To not enter in at this point is stupefied insanity.

Will you go all the way? Because that's the type of commitment it will take at this stage of the game. All it is is simply responding to the need at hand. It's not all that difficult. When push comes to shove most everything people are now preoccupied with will vanish as if it were a dream. That's when the remorse sets in for all those who refused to take action.

Something to think seriously about. We are now at the crossroads. What world are we helping to manifest? Or will we irresponsibly let things slide along as they are? The answer is up to you.

It's ours in which to participate. Passionately and with dogged determination. Because everything is at stake. Here and now.

Fulfill your calling.

Personal Notes:

When Your Back's Against the Wall, Don't Be There

That's simply it – just don't be there. If at all possible you shouldn't be in a place like that. If you can avoid getting pinned against anything, that's your smartest move. That's why I like to keep changing and moving. But you can't be carrying a lot of baggage if you want to do that, physically or spiritually.

Now's a good time to free yourself from attachments and be ready for anything. Each according to his own, but you don't want to get caught flatfooted if you can avoid it.

In my basketball days we had a defensive drill where you'd take your stance and the coach would come and try to push you over. If you were on your heels you'd fall back quick and easy. But if you're in a ready stance, knees bent, arched back, on your toes with your hands extended for balance, you not only couldn't be pushed over, you could easily move side to side, front to back, block passes and shots, and even steal the ball.

Being in a ready stance to take the initiative is the key to freedom. In a world where we're so bombarded with influences and imposed conditions we need to be able to sense converging conditions and not allow ourselves to be corralled into any kind of corner, whether in social exchanges or immediate living conditions.

Preparedness

I honestly believe preparedness is more spiritual than anything, although the physical is also imperative.

We're going to see more and more weird stuff in the coming months and years and our antennas need to be up and our listening on full alert. I'm sure you've heard the stories, but many a time people get premonitions – intuitive forewarnings – that often turn out to be life savers for whole families.

We need to learn to operate in that realm.

That type of conscious awareness cannot be hacked, spied upon or blocked. The only thing that jams it is fear and distraction. When those conditions seem to close in it's time to heighten your sensitivity in order to determine what is really going on around you, in the microcosm as well as macrocosm of life, in order to make conscious judgements and decisions.

The Power of Distraction

If you've ever had your pocket picked you've probably experienced how deftly distraction can be used. One of their techniques is to put pressure on one part of your body–usually your shoulder or upper back - while they lift your wallet out.

Your body sensors are concentrating on the main pressure and don't register the other. They'll also do a complete hit as if they were accidentally bumping into you so something gets spilled and everyone is distracted looking at the effects. Apologies are exchanged and you don't realize until afterwards that you've just been robbed.

Another interesting technique is they'll work in a group, which is usually the case, and one will say "watch out, there's pickpockets on the train (or bus or street)" as they walk past. You'll instinctively reach down and pat the pocket or wherever you're carrying your wallet or valuables to see if they're OK. Guess who was watching just behind you?

Scam on. And the whole matrix is just such a scam, never forget that.

Stay on the Offensive

They say the best defense is a good offense. I'm not totally sure about that as it's a a bit two dimensional but the point is a good one. Try to stay on the offensive and not let yourself get put on the defensive. You learn this in conversation or if you've ever had to deal with the media. Really aware and prepared people will take a derogatory or leading question from some talking head and say, "I'm glad you asked that question.." and then go on to say whatever they want, ignoring the trap-laden question altogether.

We just have to be smart, especially in troublesome times, and now with this militarized gestapo and snitch society mind-set moving in on us it's even more important to stay vigilant.

Fear is the killer, but mobility, taking the initiative instead of just reacting, and keeping a listening heart, will keep you and your family safe more than anything and keep you free to be a force for good.

But What If You Get Pinned?

That's entirely up to you and your situation. I just don't think it's healthy to have a stand-off mindset as it invites trouble and plays into their hands. But don't over spiritualize a situation that warrants force to protect yourself and your loved ones.

My point is it's better to simply not allow yourself to be funneled into those types of situations, especially if you're already aware that some confiscation program or search for so-called dissidents is afoot.

Be well. Stay alert at all times. Driving consciously is a good illustration, noticing every little thing around you and listening for warnings. You can be the best driver in the world but if you didn't slow down, stop or turn when consciousness tells you to, the consequences may not be the optimum outcome you're looking for.

So-called accidents can usually be avoided and don't have to happen. Don't resign or relinquish yourself to anything by unconsciously going along with what is awash around you no matter how "normal" it appears to everyone else. You may never see that accident or traffic stop or mob break out that you avoided by making a pre-emptive conscious choice to take another route, or even move out of dangerous areas.

Stay tuned in and turned on. It actually makes all this insanity a fun ride. We're in a very energetically empowered time but it requires wise choices and a very real degree of commitment to learn to operate by spiritual radar instead of living inside their "reactor" climate.

Surf's up! The power is infinite and for the taking. Practice operating in this mode and you'll see synchronicity and confirmations abound, and a whole lot of empowerment!

Personal Notes:

Co-opting Consciousness at Awakening's Door

The concept of deliberately controlled opposition eludes public awareness to an amazing degree. It's similar to the brazen reality of false flag operations, the epitome of carefully planned societal manipulation by unseen forces who have no regard for the human condition other than to control it – those who are more than willing to attack their own to provoke a desired response.

This is so very similar to the slogan of the nefarious Mossad: "By way of deception, thou shalt do war." The Jesuits are no better and on the same page. Nor is the CIA and a plethora of other deliberately obscured agencies.

Agencies, as in clusters of agents, are all subhuman tools in the war for the subjugation, exploitation and control of humanity.

Controlling the opposition is a practice of misdirection and deception disguised as genuine questioning and resistance to the party line in order to accomplish certain goals. It's a game of ruthless deception that is endemic to the fabric of the entire matrix of control.

It's not anything really startling in the grand scheme of things once you've woken up to the big picture, but for those still under the spell of the official narrative it's an extremely powerful weapon of mass manipulation that they are very cleverly subdued by.

And it has many forms.

"The best way to control the opposition is to lead it ourselves."
-Vladimir Lenin

Useful Idiots and the Puppeteers

The obvious NATO/US backed insurgencies such as the bogus clearly outside-funded and supplied ISIS charade leading up to these military supplied pogroms on Syria, and the entire middle eastern region for that matter, are perfect examples of controlled opposition on the geopolitical stage.

As awful as that reality is, the problem is way deeper than that.

We've all been useful idiots at one time or another. No one's been fully conscious or completely independent of these influences all of their lives. We all have had to compromise in some manner just to survive in the matrix. In that state we unwittingly contribute to the official narrative by our silence and willful ignorance which is handily garnered as humanity's imprimatur of acceptance and even approval.

This social landscape is an engineered one, and we help build and maintain it at varying degrees of conscious unawareness until we fully wake up and disengage. Some aspects become more obvious than others to different people. The clearly manipulated banking system for example has been getting roundly exposed by the awakening. The full extent of its control is known by very few, but people are getting the idea to a massive degree. And it leads to more questions, as well as fundamental doubts about the world around them.

That's how it works. It only takes one vector into the heart of true reality to wake people up. The issues of health and food freedom, geoengineering, clearly destructive fracking and GMO and vaccine issues, all eventually lead to the heart of this deceptive matrix of attempted full spectrum control.

Arriving At Awakening's Door

Many people come to the awakening via the health crisis we're facing, with contaminated and mutated foods and vaccines being forced into the marketplace without the slightest compunction from our ever-so-caring crypto-fascist central State. Just going to natural food or natural or alternative medicine sites is another way to get into the wardrobe and enter a land of the Narnia of Truth they had no idea existed.

For those looking to help others awaken, this is a great way to approach someone still under the spell to get them started looking around. GMO awareness and the invasive fracking issue have also jerked people up and are great entry points.

Just like the bankster revolving door with government, the similarly favored and government promoted Monsanto/Big

Pharma, big oil, and other infesting so-called "interest" agencies will make their heads spin if they're willing to see it.

Geoengineering and Fukushima are other possible portals to the awakening. The surreal potential extinction level event (ELE) nature of these assaults is seriously disrupting many entrained minds to where the dots are beginning to connect.

They'd better. These are extremely serious times.

Finding out the extent of our own involvement is a trip in itself, and will lead to many wonderful, sometimes disturbing discoveries. Even more so is realizing the source of information we were trusting was tainted, twisted, distorted, re-written and infiltrated with specific purposes beginning in the socially engineered education system and reinforced by corporate media. And in almost every case completely infiltrated with fabricated lies, propped up by the energy of those that believed them.

This effectively makes humanity unwitting battery pods powering the controlled collective.

What Really Matters

Religion, politics, education and the economic meme are of course the most predominant factors in the mainstream mind. But important things like where we came from, why we're even here and where we're going are barely addressed. If they are, it's all scientific or pseudo-philosophical gobbledygook designed to confuse and stifle the human spirit, or worse yet freeze it into a debilitating religious paradigm where we wait for the cavalry to save us and are told "the powers that be are ordained by God".

This is the true controlled opposition, although we'll get to the modern oracles of this insidious ploy soon enough.

We have to see this for what it is. Anything short is not going to cut it. Just about every aspect of the opposing paradigms we've been handed as the absolute truth are designed. And even outside seemingly opposing elements who seem to know what's going on are often generated by, or soon channeled by, these same overlords.

Therein lies the power of controlled opposition on the world stage. A very powerful tool in the hands of psychopathic liars. It's essential people catch on to this reality, as they play skillfully on the heartstrings of sincere citizens and in their newly awakened state they are quite vulnerable to a seemingly "sympathetic" vibe. The staged and oligarch-financed "color revolutions" are a perfect example.

Dastardly clever.

How They Cultivate Credibility

This is where and how the manipulation kicks in. Just like the controlled State media propaganda, there have to be enough apparent facts to cultivate credibility. Just enough. They won't overdo it unless it's some innocuous subject. Many of those "facts" will be wrapped in fear and violence, designed to cauterize your sensitivity while heightening your anxiety. That or smug mockery.

Religions have effectively done this for eons. Tapping into our inner knowledge of the spiritual and mixing in a few truths, they have no problem steering us straight into a numbed state of docile subservience to some strange hierarchy of spiritual and physical abuse. In the name of God of course.

Name dropping, anyone? Oh, and in the name of that Guy they can send you and your kids off to fight their wars, build and support oppressive exploitative corporations, hate an unseen enemy due to their religion, or be a professional sports gladiator and gain fame and fortune pounding other contestants into the ground to the roar of the frenzied, flag waving mob.

Nice paradigm. Competition, parasitic capitalism and war all built into the fabric

It's Rarely Black and White – Deliberately

Layered into the imposed matrix are many overlapping memes and projected illusions, rendering fundamental empowering truths either hidden altogether, and/or disguised and distorted. In a loving, uncontrolled conscious world there would be no need to hide anything. Instead, this mutant matrix system is built on deceit and compartmentalization in order to spiritually disconnect and disempower those subjects they wish to exploit.

Think of the mega volumes of information and in-place technology being withheld from public knowledge under the guise of "national security". How about "classified" or "closed door meetings" or "need to know basis" or the vast labyrinth of secret ops operating in their occult network built on compartmentalization in the name of science or military confidentiality.

Now slide over to the Vatican sitting on brutally gained secret historical and scientific accounts for centuries. Take another step into the City of London and its secrets.

Does this make any sense to you?

Why do they keep all of this withheld or only release partially available information in separate categories? Because if we connect them they form a picture, a very clear one. Our entire manipulated society is completely staged, controlled and with vastly sinister intent.

They don't want you or me to wake up.

Who's Controlling Whom? Examine the Opposition

I try to be very careful about what I read and certainly what I "take on board" in my mind and heart. I'll look at just about anything, even mainstream drivel occasionally, to keep an eye on stuff and get the pulse of what's going on.

But I'm very careful. I know I get misled sometimes like anyone, but I'm not afraid to admit when I'm wrong. In fact it's a joy every time that happens. "Hey, I got another damn velcro hook off my spiritual body."

Media outlets and information sources are something to look at very closely and carefully. And keep watching. It's never, or should I say rarely, totally clear cut as to who is who. Someone can be piping out a high percentage of true information, but then throw in some massive monkey wrench that few see coming.

Sometimes it's the tone. I'm skeptical of crass self-promoters who are caught up in their image. If there's that much ego there's that much less conscious awareness, and the love starts running thin. If people can't forget themselves and see past all the evil in this world to the wondrous beauty of the Universe and the amazing unlimited potential of the human spirit, I wonder about their information, or at least how it's used.

But no one's perfect, so we need to see and process the good and the truth, and chuck the husks in the trash. It can take time and things clearly morph, so it's all part of the process.

Snowden, Wikileaks and Other Corruptible Things

Keep a close eye out on these supposed whistleblowers. While we need real ones to come forward desperately, those that attain public acclamation by way of major media attention are always suspect. This is because the corporate media is completely controlled so when they give someone headlines there's a reason. They may let out some truth, but it's always to inoculate us against the full truth. There is no more responsible mainstream media today.

Only 6 mega corporations control the media and they are a corporo-fascist cabal.

I've written much about Snowden and my suspicions, as have many others. When the Wikileaks phenomenon appeared, I and many others were again very skeptical. It was playing right into the globalists' plan, not the least of which is to smokescreen real events and give reason to muzzle the internet while conducting a cleverly controlled release valve of information for tracking and other purposes.

Why do you think these supposed whistleblowers withhold the explosive information they supposedly have and let it out in carefully planned stages? Would you do that if you were sitting on a gold mine of exposing information in such a crucial time in history? You can conjecture all you want as to the "why" but ultimately it tells the same old tale.

Humanity is being played from both sides.

Like most disinfo outlets, it conveniently sidestepped, minimized or dodged many of the really important issues. Assange was groomed deep in the oligarchs' machine for years. While that doesn't mean he can't wake up out of it as Snowden says he did, when Assange came out and said 9/11 was not an inside job that cemented the deal for me.

Just like NPR – at least no balls or conviction, and with that come self preservation and ultimately massive compromise of some sort. Some of the information appears to be bonafide, but just watch where it leads you. Don't get corralled into a certain limited or infected mindset.

Channeling people into political expression is just another ploy, as is rage and violence. All very controllable expressions they can condemn and contain which is why they push those buttons.

It's very similar to how these "partial" whistleblowers never mention Israel nor the Zionist influence and their massive programs of outright genocide. Notice the black out on the Ukraine and Yemen genocides as well. Always a very serious warning signal. Co-opted right out of the gate.

Control the opposition and you control the populace on every side. Always give this and any stuff that comes at you the sniff test. And trust your heart. It's an elaborate game they play so it's completely healthy to be extremely skeptical and judge things from a fully conscious perspective.

The influence of these embedded social engineers is vast. We have no idea how many inroads have been made and how the military industrial government complex has infiltrated and controlled all we see and hear at this point, even within our alternative community.

It's staggering, but it doesn't frighten me. It's expected once you begin to understand how they work and how elaborate their scheming is.

Follow your heart. You'll know. And it becomes laughable.

So Will the Wake Up Be In Time?

Clearly we're up against massively orchestrated activities, outlets and manufactured disinformation, and there's much controversy on this subject. It's a huge part of their agenda. Don't let it bother you too much but be aware of it. It's just the matrix at work. Rise above it.

But will humanity "get it" in time?

It's always in time...individually and collectively. Once you've popped into Now awareness and even begin to grasp the fact that all this is a sham and a fabricated facade, you're virtually home free. Your participation in propping up this fake social landscape will fall off like over-sized pants and your new role as a node of empowering information and healing vibration are instantaneous.

It just happens.

Enjoy it, but be responsive to where it takes you. We've all got to do our parts in making a difference which we naturally do as we truly awaken. That's where the real revolution of conscious awareness and activation lies.

Respond. Consciously. And in love. Take it to new levels. You are a unique expression that needs to be released to its full potential.

Personal Notes:

Burning Dross and Distilling to Consciousness

I frequently correspond with a close friend with whom I shared a large part of my "middle life". We were recently talking about how it can be dismaying realizing how many stupid things we fell for in our previous limited understanding yet we can't have any regrets, as whatever it took to get us to an awakened state was all good.

Whatever it took to get here, so be it.

I was musing on this thought and the intense pressures we all endure going through life and all of its challenges and wild changes. So often things seemed insurmountable with no end in sight to those particular situations we find ourselves seemingly trapped in.

When thinking on this and how I literally exploded into this wonderful new awakened conscious awareness, I had an interesting analogy come to mind that made me smile inside. During all of that compacting pressure and often feeling like I was seething in a cauldron of trials and tests I was actually getting distilled down to "truth concentrate". When the alive crystal clear waters of true liberating and enlightening truth finally got into my then ready container....wham! And I've been exploding ever since.

I was getting distilled down to the elements that would be essential for my eventual role in life. As the old analogy goes, gold is purified by intense fire whereby the dross is burned off to give us the refined end product – in this case: consciousness concentrate with a heck of a lot of learning along the way.

It's Not Easy – The Scylla and Charybdis

It's a lot easier to look back on all of those trying life situations and experiences than it is actually going through them. But we do get through them. If, that is, we keep up the pursuit of truth. I'm by no means minimizing the seriousness of life's trials, they literally are life and death, both physically and spiritually.

Getting through those dire straights, real or imaginary, is no picnic.

I loved Homer's The Iliad and the Odyssey as a teen and learning about Greek mythology. The imagery and stories were fascinating. I just knew there was truth in so many of those so-called "myths" and ancient legends.

They resonated with me very deeply and surfaced in my consciousness repeatedly all during my journey.

One particular story comes to mind that is the archetypical backdrop for idioms like "dire straights", "between the devil and the deep blue sea", or being "between a rock and a hard place."

What's interesting about this metaphor for life's challenges is the extreme nature of the obstacles, painting them as aggressive energetic forms out to "sink" the life traveler.

All fear based, again sometimes appearing very real, but after all is said done fear is our biggest obstacle. Once we learn to overcome that we're well on our way.

But life's circumstances can sure appear this way:

"Scylla and Charybdis, in Greek mythology, two immortal and irresistible monsters who beset the narrow waters traversed by the hero Odysseus in his wanderings described in Homer's Odyssey, Book XII. Scylla was a supernatural creature, with 12 feet and 6 heads on long, snaky necks, each head having a triple row of sharklike teeth, while her loins were girt with the heads of baying dogs. From her lair in a cave she devoured whatever ventured within reach, including six of Odysseus' companions.

"Charybdis, who lurked under a fig tree a bowshot away on the opposite shore, drank down and belched forth the waters thrice a day and was fatal to shipping. Her character was most likely the personification of a whirlpool. The shipwrecked Odysseus barely escaped her clutches by clinging to a tree until the improvised raft that she swallowed floated to the surface again after many hours. To be "between Scylla and Charybdis" means to be caught between two equally unpleasant alternatives." (Wiki)

Pretty apt as to how life's challenges often appear.

Putting Truth In Action and the Duality Game

It's a whole lot harder to know truth and not respond to it than it is to find it out and take action. I pity people who are coming across so much empowering and enlightening information now yet refuse to budge.

There's something called accountability that I think people minimize to try to keep their conscience at bay. Once we know something is true the next obvious step is to do something about it.

If we don't, there are spiritually derived consequences at many levels.

It's not always clear what the next step is, but as I often say the boat has to be in motion for the rudder to take effect. Too many are afraid to venture out into what appears to be unknown territory, but that's only based on our previous understanding of what is known and unknown, what is a so-called safe and secure course of action versus a life of thrilling fulfillment and a greater sense of real security, what awaits anyone willing to push off from that seemingly safe shore.

That fundamentally "forbidden territory" is now my number one destination.

But when you finally step out you immediately realize all of those fears were unfounded, and in most cases you'll find are deliberate social engineering memes rerun over centuries to keep humanity frozen in place. Ultimately they are just fabricated dragons and demons as in the above metaphor, only given power by our entertainment of the illusion.

This is where duality comes into focus, setting humanity at variance with besetting ogres and fabricated concepts and enemies to keep us apart from realizing we are all one in a completely connected universe.

In other words, transcending the board game called life and seeing things for how they really are is the most empowering and thrilling experience you'll ever have. The rest simply comes into focus as an opportunity to learn and grow and help others to do the same.

The cauldron used to get you here wasn't so bad after all now, eh?

Living With Yourself

This is the crux of the matter. Our personal universe is ourselves. That's our battlefield. When we get sorted out we can help sort out others, not before. Once we've found greater truth which we know needs to be manifested and shared, our lives drastically change, whether we handle it responsibly or not.

For those who respond constructively life gets brighter, happier and more meaningful. Certainly new challenges present themselves but tremendous empowerment kicks in, even if we feel absolutely alone during the first phases of this transformation, an aspect of the birthing process I like to address to help those during this seemingly estranged period.

The most wonderful realizations come when we see this entire movie set we're on is a fabricated one, and that we each have complete control over our personal reality.

But all this can be addressed in a very simple way. You have to live with yourself. All day every day. For the non-enactor, when you know better than to do or be what you are living or participating in, life is very conflicted and unpleasant. Such is the power of truth. It will not go away. It's here to stay and always has been here and will eat at you. That's a good thing.

You just discovered it, or a good piece of it. Now it's your turn to respond. If you don't, there's a price to pay. Your conscience has been more fully awakened and will not be satisfied until you respond to it. You too have been changed for life.

This is obviously why the "whirled" is the way it is, to keep everyone comatose so they don't feel, never mind respond to, these callings of conscience. For those unwilling or too lethargic or selfish to answer the call, these distractions become a source of solace, an enabling mechanism for their apathy. They're also addictive, all the better for the unwilling to hide behind. Such is the state of much of society today.

But the price is high. Personally and socially.

Dispelling the Hologram

It's a time to awaken from slumber. Realizing everything that has transpired in our lives only makes us stronger is wonderfully empowering. We hear that at many levels, but when the break through happens it really comes into focus.

Know your life is a process, a wonderful one. What each of us has to endure in this magical journey really is part of a wonderful design, but the most important aspect is to see it as such from an awakened perspective. I spent decades "trying" to forgive my father for how he serious damaged me as a young man, having horrendous consequences throughout much of my life. I knew forgiveness was intrinsic to moving on but I just couldn't muster it.

When I woke up forgiving him was a piece of cake, and I've been happily "corresponding" with him on the other side ever since. A dramatic shift in consciousness was necessary.

If things are troubling you and don't make sense, it's time to rise above this entire paradigm. Whatever it takes, get there. There's no secret remedy except a sincere heart and a driving passion. Once you transcend the old understanding model everything will make perfect sense, and the gratitude pours in like sunlight into a darkened room.

See you there. Love truly does rule the Universe.

We just need to get above the fray and see things for how they truly are.

Personal Notes:

Don't Worry - Everything's Not Under Control

What a farce. Telling everyone "everything is under control" is perhaps the most dulling and disempowering phrase ever uttered.

My fascination with language just keeps expanding. I love looking at expressions, words, colloquialisms, so-called "sayings" and the like with fresh awakened eyes. I can't help it. The supposed, accepted and unconscious meanings of these imposed "expressions" are what direct our minds and turn our attention.

So much of what we've been handed down is contorted, manipulated and eventually nestled in the collective mindset to twist our hearts away from simple truth.

How many times has this expression been used to bring seeming comfort to someone; "Don't worry, everything's under control." Really? What control? Who's controlling what? And why?

So often this is used to imply some powerful force is behind everything directing what's going on. Remind you of anything? Yes – religion, hierarchy, and social, political and economic so-called "controllers". How debilitating can you get when it comes right down to it, playing on people's insecurity and lack of conscious awareness?

"It's under control" is comforting to people? It's the picture of ignorance and personal disempowerment.

External Control? Or Creative Freedom

Sure, there is a wonderful creative Source we are all intrinsically part of, but it's not "controlling" anything in a living, expanding Universe with beings of all sorts with free will and self determination in an alive multidimensional environment. If anything, this Creative impetus is tearing down control systems that attempt to foist themselves on its process, put there either by conscious intent or the manifestation of hardening mindsets in the social fabric.

Earth processes attest to this, as well as our spectacular expanding and ever changing Universe. Nature itself is alive with new sprouts of life in the animal, plant and mineral worlds, never mind other realms of existence.

Look at earthquakes and volcanoes, or the sun and astral influences. As much as some try to analyze or predict major events that affect earth that still brings no control, only a measure of preparedness on rare occasion. And that type of insecurity is good for us. It's humbling and keeps us in check.

This process is what the awakening is all about.

While some earth changes may be exacerbated by human activity, the big stuff is way out of our control. Thankfully. That's what makes life life, and also why the insane would-be captivators of humanity and its planet work so feverishly in their mad pursuits to try to control natural processes. Control is their yardstick and without it they have no temporal security or power, which to them equates with some weird form of normalcy or equilibrium.

How upside down can you get.

Be it geoengineering our climate, genetically modifying the natural progression of life forms, or attempting to install artificial intelligence to run their soulless programs, these maniacs are desperate for control in every shape and form. Why? They cannot meld or harmonize with what's natural since their psychopathic, demonic intentions have nothing to gain, all while the rest of us thrive on being part of the fantastic empowering natural processes of Creation Itself.

Therein lies the rub. Quite apparently we're in a world of conflicts of interest. That's our current playing field, if you will. Or won't. It's just the way it is.

Let Go Into Conscious Anarchy

I like the anarchy approach. Anarchy is an example of another twisted word. It's doesn't mean putting a society into deliberate chaotic destruction, it means living without hierarchical control mechanisms. Something most groomed humans are scared spitless of thanks to generations of social programming.

You mean to tell me if we didn't have so-called "government" that everything would fall apart? Baloney. People are resourceful and essentially responsible, at least their inner nature is that hasn't been perverted by all of this programming to the contrary. That very dependence on external control systems is what the hierarchy is literally banking on which is why the repeated memes of fear of scarcity or blown up worries about personal security.

There's plenty for everybody. All we need to do is work together locally and share with other communities in a range of sizes and distances. Real commerce in loving cooperation, not the regulated systems that have been foisted upon us.

We've been weaned from personal responsibility into a system of statist dependence, like someone who's stopped using their muscles and is dependent on some mass produced contraption for their mobility when there's nothing wrong with them at all.

They just need to exercise their innate capabilities.

Just because people have become spiritually atrophied in large numbers doesn't mean that's the way it's supposed to be. Exactly like waking up, it's time to arise and use the magnificent body of capabilities we've all been given, and let go of these false crutches and systems of hierarchy and walk into life and live.

Epilogue

That false assurance that everything's under control by external forces, as if we individually have virtually none, has got to go. Being comforted in times of stress and turmoil is one thing, but propping people up with some external dependence reinforcement is fundamentally wrong.

It's time to be conscious – in our words, our thoughts and our actions.

It's really not that difficult. The main thing you'll confront is ignorant, unenlightened opposition from those who've grown deeply accustomed to this dependency programming, as if it's some form of respect for the "great ones" who rule them.

It's very deep and will take time to overcome for most. But remaining in that conscious space, no matter what ridicule or obstacles assail you, lies the very solution we each are longing for.

It begins with each of us. Standing our ground and then moving forward in conscious, loving action.

Do it. Bravely. The time for humanity to arise is now.

Personal Notes:

The Matrix Program
is Crashing

It is. It's outdated programming and the engineers of deceit can't keep up. The vibrational changes are exceeding their capabilities. You know how your phone or computer's software goes out of date, and new programs can't operate? It's the same thing. The imitators of creation can't maintain a current operating system any longer in the face of this Universal shift.

And it's driving them nuts.

Just look at the desperation we're witnessing. Crude military and police state maneuvers are only one aspect. The biggest clue is seeing the previously incremental and now hyperbolic use of monstrous lies that are becoming so transparent and unbelievable to just about anyone.

Agreed, there are the entranced apathetics who swallow anything, but we're witnessing a meltdown before our eyes.

If you can't see it, look again.

You Want Proof?

First of all, you're in the wrong mindset if you're looking only for data or left brained evidence, although it's out there for those who can see.

When we come to understand the vibrational workings of our holographic reality everything takes on new dimensions and opens us up to understanding these more esoteric notions.

Those with hearts that can see feel this. I say hearts because much of what we need to grasp or at least track is intuitive.

Taking all of the information and dot connecting and personal spiritual experience together paints very clear pictures, we just need to trust what we're seeing and learning. When we explore these realities we're sensing we start to notice how they're manifesting.

Forbidding free speech, shooting civilians with no cause, obvious blather and disinformation in the news, wars with no possible end, deliberate poisoning, starvation and dumbing down of populations? It's beyond surreal once all this becomes clear.

It's kind of a conscious or spiritual symbiosis we're experiencing. They all work together. But ignoring the spiritual and metaphysical as "evidence" in conjunction with such obvious manifestations is why this world has devolved to its current state. Previous enlightened civilizations and earth connected tribes took this to heart. Our current imposed paradigm does nothing of the sort.

The Computer Analogy

It's just like expired or outdated software. Their programs can't keep up with the changes the cosmos is bringing to our planet and race. That's exactly it.

While they've literally gotten away with murder for millennia and are working furiously to enforce their "programs" on so many levels, the time's up. Sorry Charlie, but you've been superceded, or should I say "super seeded", with an exponentially exploding worldwide awakening. The new upgraded paradigm is taking over fellas. It's just a matter of time before your whole wicked system crashes.

The shift is moving through their lower level grip and on into massive empowerment and transcension way beyond the net they've laid for humanity.

It's got to be frustrating the hell out of these creeps. Imagine, the very thing you're trying to encase in every way possible keeps morphing before your eyes. They can throw up matrix program after program but their perceived petri dish subjects just keep finding ways to survive and grow.

What irony the Universe has.

Hence the Transhumanist Agenda – Things They Think They Can Control

Humanity is getting out of hand, in their eyes. All the while we're being empowered – by our own awakening and resultant commitment to truth, but also by a fundamental vibrational shift we're undergoing. No savior, no galactic battlestars. It's us, and an organic consciousness evolution at the deepest level with a living, expanding and all-enveloping multi-dimensional Cosmos.

Awakening with Creation Itself.

Anyone who's woken up to almost any degree understands everything is interconnected. Even "modern" physics is arriving at this reality, all while mainstream thinking ignores the profound ramifications. That we're all interconnected not just as a race, but with the earth and the cosmos in such a fundamental way is a game changer. While this has been known for eons, our current control model cannot even begin to acknowledge this fact. To these oligarchs and self-appointed maniacal masterminds, no matter what powers they're summoning, that truth is something apparently well beyond their debased comprehension.

It's out of their league.

Sure, they have their satanic rituals and tap into other dimensional entities, but it's child's play compared to the True picture of our all Powerful Creative Universe. That they live in rebellion against this Force is a known reality for millennia, and even alluded to by spiritual traditions and native shamanic teachings alike for ages. Bringing this understanding "down to earth" is another story.

This is why the transhumanist agenda is so important to them. This merging of man with machine has been in the works for a long time. Clipping the link with our humanity by short circuiting the human creation is an obvious next step for these would-be controllers. Agreed, they've made it a fad and carefully groomed acceptance of such a trend, but it's going to fritz and die in the junkyard of temporal existence. It can't stand, never mind last, in such a creative force field.

Time will bear this out, as has happened to previous off-course civilizations.

Is This For Real?

It's up to us. We have everything going for us. But our will and actions need to be aligned with this transition. We can ignore it or respond. The sanctity of our free will cannot be violated. Either we get paddling and ride the wave or it crashes on us and perhaps dissipates on the shores of time for lack of recognition or response. And the whole cycle may need to be repeated. Not a nice destiny if that's what we choose.

I don't know.

I know I'm not coming back. I'm done with this insanity and am doing my damnedest to change things this time around. If we all did it won't get repeated, but time will tell. Not many seem to be willing to respond, even though their lives and their children and grandchildren's lives are at stake. Talk about self imposed defeat and debilitation.

Either way, the matrix will collapse. But the true civilization of love, peace, harmony and abundance awaits manifesting.

Is it time?

I think so. It is for me.

How about you?

Stormy Weather on High Cosmic Seas

I don't even need to ask who's feeling this. We're all experiencing turbulent vibrational times right now. It's a very real challenge.

Whatever the source, we're going through a kind of vortex of change and disturbance that needs to be acknowledged and addressed.

I don't know the so-called "reason" for it, but it's there. This is confirmed by good friends and a variety of sources, but with even a cursory look at the world around us we're passing through some serious stuff. And it can be quite disconcerting.

I've said many times in previous articles that this was coming, but as always, when it hits it's another story. We can observe something inside the "washing machine" from a safe distance between the event and ourselves, but when we're actually in it personally – man o' man.

Symptoms and Possible Contributors

The affects in times like this include scrambled sleep cycles, a sense of tension and difficulty in concentrating, low energy and health challenges, emotional turmoil, and even degrees of confusion in our thinking processes. It really helps to look outside for influences so that we don't lose perspective on the event we're part of or get lost in futile introspection.

Astrologically speaking, we're in a very powerful vortex. The mercury retrograde that just passed was having its usually somewhat disempowering effect. It's said to always be a good time to back away from major decisions in our lives when this is happening.

More substantially is a major influence called the Pluto-Uranus square, an infrequent alignment that has drastic implications on social and personal situations. This was brought to my attention by a dear friend who has been deeply immersed in astrology for much of his life and follows these trends passionately. Apparently it was the aligning of Pluto and Uranus that happened in the '60's that contributed to the rise of the cultural and spiritual revolution at the time, and a similar effect will begin again again once this direct squaring passes.

Which happily is soon, and it portends an uprising of convergence of social activism and increased awareness which will give tremendously greater impetus for spreading this awakening amongst a much larger swathe of humanity and help dismantle the ruling oligarchy.

Happy thought? I thought so too.

Surreal Signs and Screwing with Humanity

I don't know about you, but just observing the daily news and events is enough to make your head spin. The obvious lies, reversals, omissions and outright blather, negativity and fear we're being bombarded with is surreal. That so few can stand back and take notice of this charade is another mind-blowing factor.

It's increasingly hard to even peruse the headlines as it's so shockingly bad. But remember, that's the intention – "shock and awe" at their sorcery and draconian power plays as a form of mental conditioning.

For many of us, that anyone can even begin to fall for the mainstain portrayal and explanation of anything is hard to believe. But to so many this is their way of life, as incredible as that may seem. How they'll snap out of the hypnotic trance is a question we all ask ourselves.

Again, remember that detachment is the key to keeping a well balanced and conscious outlook.

What's Going on in the Etheric Realm?

Good question. There are a lot of explanations being posited. Spiritual and inter-dimensional attacks, electromagnetic influences, chemical, radioactive and genetic degradation, mind control programs and on and on.

Personally I take them all seriously and put them into the mix. It's out there to be investigated.

The point being, a very serious affront, or bombardment if you will, is now accosting our planet and spiritual sphere. That's what we're feeling and is twisting and turning so many and causing this sense of disassociation. We can't lose our conscious footing due to "circumstances" and outside influences.

This may seem like ethereal cereal to some but those who are experiencing what I'm talking about will understand.

Know you're not alone, first and foremost. This is hitting all of us. But it can be weathered with full empowerment. Those on the cutting edge of understanding and consciousness already know this, as it's not a new routine. We've faced these onslaughts many times over, and much of it continually.

My intention here is to bring clarity and a general sense of common awareness. In unity we are strong, and as we share these common influences in open communication we're able to better understand and ward off these affronts.

Much love, and power to the True People.

Personal Notes:

Personal Notes:

Part 3

Language, Beliefs and Other Hazards

Personal Notes:

Can the Awakening Be Hijacked?

Once we understand that everything is an illusion we're home free. Knowing we're eternal consciousness having this in-body experience is the greatest gift anyone can possibly have.

It's wonderful, it's free and it's forever…and it's for everyone. People just need to wake up to it.

That would seem to be fairly simple, especially once it has happened to you. The fullness of life you expand into, the realization of infinite possibility, is so exhilarating, liberating and profoundly simple that you can't help but wonder why everyone doesn't see it.

This is especially so once the grand conspiracy being foisted on humanity comes into focus. Things really kick into high gear upon realizing fully what's going on and why we're here at this crucial time.

The notion that this wonderful realization should be apparent to all soon tempers though, when we remember being in that entranced unconscious state ourselves and how we thought we understood pretty well what life was all about. A healthy spiritual check for our attitudes.

How Did It Happen?

Almost all of us were once encased in something that kept us apart from this simple experiential realization. That encasement was both natural and engineered. Natural in the sense that we are spirit born into a physical body, so there is a dimensional challenge right there.

The real problems arise with the cultural and societal constructs we are raised in. As helpless infants for an extensive period of time after birth, we are at the complete mercy of whomever is caring for us. Although we are inherently spiritual beings, if this is not corroborated by the spirit and behavior of those around us a type of callous begins to grow to obfuscate that knowledge. Much like waking from a dream and not being able to remember it as a whole different "reality" takes over our senses.

It just happens. If people have dumbed down parents they will most likely be dumbed down as well. At least on the surface. In later years they perhaps can wake up out of that environment as many of us have done.

The War On Consciousness

Children are very often extremely spiritual, often remembering their previous state in detail. Children are born pure. If this inherent spirituality is encouraged and the reality of our true nature reinforced, this would be a very different world.

However it rarely is. Those indigenous peoples who were not raised in engineered societies but only within simple cultural guidelines are very spiritual and natural. There is no "waking up", they just never went to sleep. This is why these spiritually rich, conscious native cultures and their shamans have been systematically decimated by the ugly Controllers. They do not want an awakened populace, nor for these simple empowering truths to be propagated. Period. And these spiritually free, unharnessed indigenous peoples carried this awareness and connectivity that the Controllers so despise.

So in the overlords' view the children of the world must be made to conform to a system as limiting and spiritually confining as possible. This will include drugging, mind control, restrictive false education in militaristic institutions, treadmill like jobs, mindless diversions and constant propaganda.

In other words, the imposed world system we see around us.

If you're wondering why the global crack down is so fierce and Orwellian and is accelerating at breakneck speed, this is why. The awakening is spreading like wildfire. And they know it. This is why predators like Zbigniew Brzezinski see the awakening as a threat and say things like "It is infinitely easier to kill a million people than it is to control them."

This is the type of monsters we're up against.

Original Sin – The Seed of the Matrix

The most clever and effective tools to control mankind are religion and belief systems. Instead of fully denying our spirituality, they acknowledge it, then channel and control it. Win the masses over by appealing to this innate drive in each of us to realize our spiritual potential and take them to another nicely decorated cell they think is freedom.

They use this tactic proficiently. Just look at the infrastructure of the Catholic Church for probably the most blatant and elaborate example.

The other religions and denominations aren't far behind, nor the socio-political structure. Anything to "protect" us from reality and personal responsibility.

Original sin is one of the most colossal reversals of truth of all time. That and the fear of death. From start to finish these parasitic overlords lie, steal, destroy, manipulate and kill. They're never satisfied. But that's how they do it, reverse and confuse everything until your true orientation is almost impossible to find.

Or so they'd like to think.

That we were born in "sin" and need someone else to pay a fee to get our innocence back couldn't be more binding, never mind exclusive of everyone who doesn't see why they have to pay this toll for just arriving here. It's like having to buy land and water on our own planet. Who the hell thinks they own this place?

This is why we're "tagged" at birth with "certificates" that connect us to this false, imposed legal matrix. It's a contract, and one that needs to be broken. Consciously. An essential part of awakening.

In reality we were born pure until they put their filthy matrix trip on us. Even then they will never conquer our indomitable conscious spirit, but untangling and disengaging is ours to fully pursue.

If You Can't Beat 'em, Lead 'em

Who can you trust in this day and age, even with the internet communication and information revolution? It's obvious the powers that shouldn't be will try to subvert or nullify the truth movement, or whatever you want to call it. They must think we're naive dolts like the majority of asleeple and just awaiting their fascist harvesting combine. Quite the arrogant disconnect there, when their machinations are so obvious to the rest of us.

But that ignorant assumption on their part makes sense, when they live in a lower density mind trap and can't even conceive of our state of consciousness.

Overall there's a lot to be wary of. And that's a healthy attitude. Am I paranoid? Damn straight I am if that's the definition. They are after us. Reminds me of Arthur Conan Doyle's The Most Dangerous Game where the ultimate hunt for the psychopathic gamesman is a human being. That's their mindset in a nutshell. Just look at the war and genocide programming and soft kill depopulation agenda.

I Don't Believe in Believing

When it comes down to it, don't believe anyone. Belief is a form of spiritual weakness. Faith (not religious), or knowledge, is a whole different animal. It's actually knowing on a personal level despite the baggage that comes with the term, but belief will get you in trouble. Pursue until you are fully convinced. Sometimes it takes some doing – many times you just know something in your heart to be true.

That's not a belief, that's knowing. That is where we derive our power, our happiness and our effectiveness.

Belief will have you living in vain, vain repetitive prayers or rituals, vain longings for what you desire as you await the graces of some deity or all powerful ruler or government; and vain hopes for things that could be realized through knowing affirmation. Even the quantum physicists know better. What we intend and focus our attention on becomes manifest.

Our knowing creates our world.

I tell people all the time not to believe me or take my word for it. People need to find out for themselves. Hopefully I can help point the way but it's up to each individual to find out for themselves.

That's what's wrong with the world today. Everyone just blindly follows the dictates of others, especially the vast matrix of deceit. What choices they do make are within a carefully contained compartment, giving the illusion of freedom.

I'm just sharing my take and if it resonates or helps people on their way, great. People need to get their own knowledge and perspective. I just want to help turn over a few stones as I'm learning myself and stir people up a bit and maybe inspire and spur them to action to free themselves and others.

If someone thinks I'm full of it that's fine with me. They go their way and I go mine. But let's at least acknowledge the sanctity of having the freedom to each pursue and learn for ourselves.

I like it when people challenge anything, as long as it's constructive and in a spirit of wanting to learn and find the truth of the matter. When someone shoves their program too hard or it's for self justification or aggrandizement watch out. We all get out of it sometimes but when there's a regular pattern that's off kilter we have a problem. But even then, take the good stuff and leave the rest. You'll usually find yourself looking at other sources of information naturally, and leaving the questionables behind.

Truth Psyops

The truth community or alternative research community is already infiltrated, you just know it is by simple logic. The controllers' motto is to lead the opposition, that's how to control it. So you know they are amongst the places we all visit for information, trying to mislead and misinform, whatever the source, be it spiritual or clearly misdirected or agendized information.

Some are obvious like the politicized bullshit or religiously oriented propaganda. Some aren't that easy to spot, much like these new computer viruses that appear and disappear. They're shape shifters of every sort.

With real conscious awareness comes discernment. We need to listen with our ears and minds, yes, but most of all with our hearts.

I can't say I know for sure who's who myself but you can usually sniff them out. For example, there are some who've captured the so-called "patriots'" attention with mountains of exposes and angry rhetoric and most don't have a clue where they're being led and what a diversion it potentially is. Even some of the alternative health sites have some very questionable viewpoints and allegiances. The information in these compromised outlets is mostly bang on, otherwise it wouldn't work. But there are usually major gaps missing from the full truth, or it's caged in a structured paradigm that by definition is limiting and will only land us in new versions of the same problems.

Eternal vigilance, as has been said, is the price of freedom.

Maybe it's all karmic and what has to happen with people getting waylaid by partial truths, I don't know. I do know what my path is and it's not based on a destination or outcome. The path is what I'm doing and living every day, and I'm an extremely grateful and happy person. I did have to go through several major traumatic life changes to find the full "Now" way of life as is the case of many. But this awakening is something I feel I'm still just learning about and at childhood stage which I'm very comfortable with. In fact I feel I know less all the time and it feels good. The wonderful mystery of it all just gets more fantastic and I'm learning to just let go and enjoy it instead of trying to figure everything out.

Funny thing is, the more you do that the more wonderful things just come at you.

Like many of you reading this, I couldn't help keeping on until everything became clear. It's very humbling to wake up, everything is just so so wonderfully evident, like "where have I been?". But it's a massive responsibility at the same time. If we don't manifest and utilize this awareness, it will not only fade and many others we could have helped will suffer.

Therein lies the catch.

Belief System Diversions and Hijacking the Awakening

The NWO is a spiritual model most of all. They want control and ultimately the spiritual is supreme and they know that. While they don't have the conscious awareness and wonderful empathy we have, they do operate on a spiritual level, just a different frequency. The New World Order includes a new world religion, and they're warming up to it.

There's a plethora of disinfo tools laced into the alternative information and spirituality arena. Most are obvious. If it disempowers, it's wrong. If it directs your allegiance, it's wrong. If it robs you of your sovereignty, it's wrong. If it's dogmatic and hierarchical, it's wrong. If it leaves you angry and tense and upset with no course of action or peace, it's wrong. Most lies and lying systems have all of those traits, while other aspects are more subtle. There are other attributes but to me the ones above are the most prominent.

The so called New Age Movement is rife with phony baloney trips, false messiahs and deliverance doctrines. Many will be tempted to rest their weary minds and park their energy in any one of these false peace spaces and expect someone to cover for them.

Walk on your own two feet. There's nothing more empowering and liberating.

We have to understand there are plenty of way-stations, indefinite stopovers, sidetracks and diversions on our path to conscious fulfillment. For these psychopathic control freaks to try to hijack this awakening in every way possible is clearly a priority for them towards our continued subjugation.

Be savvy.

The point is to get past them, and not fall for their mind candy and rhetoric, no matter how appealing. We are divine in our entirety and do not need some kind of system or group identity other than love and truth. Sure, groups will form as action or fellowship gatherings, but when those symptoms listed above start appearing it is probably time to split, and enlighten those around you. Until we have a clear, consciously aware picture of what's going on and our real situation, shortsighted actions are just rearranging deck chairs on the Titanic.

So, hijack the awakening? Let them try to put out the light of the sun and stop the other stars from shining while they're at it. What fools.

Meanwhile, keep an eye out for these maniacs. They're getting more desperate by the day. These psychotic parasites are on the loose. We need to be smart and on our toes. And most of all keep the light on. Those in the approaching darkness will be needing it.

Game on. They don't know what or who they're dealing with. Let it fly.

Fruit Loops and Perilous Pitfalls

There is plenty of valid information to keep us satisfied and busy with productive insights and empowering ideas to go around.

What we don't need are time and attention wasting wild forays into areas that are pure conjecture based on fanciful mind tingling speculation.

It is of course fine and wonderful to explore theories and potentialities, but at this present juncture in our burgeoning awakening process it's important to keep on track with truly productive information and fruitful modalities.

Let's face it. It's fun to explore and I do it continually. That's part of the learning process. It just appears far too many are jumping headlong down energy vamping areas that ultimately have a negative impact on the awakening process and hence its effectiveness.

Explore – But Remain the Observer

Each to their own of course, but the trend I'm seeing of late reeks of deliberate as well as unwittingly planted sidetracks, trip offs and focus-fuzzing diversions.

We're well aware the alternative research community is increasingly infiltrated with plants, shills and distracting psyops, so it's my intention that this forewarning will help forearm those not yet fully aware of these devices.

People should be willing to take a look into just about anything for informational purposes. However, anything adhered to in a dogmatic fashion to where it brings contention, division and wildly derisive accusations is very unhealthy, whatever the latest trends may be.

It can be any field of information that brings about these effects, usually with questionable, unverifiable sources. I'm particularly leery of channeled information, unless I personally know the source, as well as unfounded sensationalist conjecture, revelations from "off planet" civilizations, hard core sensational "cataclysmic event" date predictions, most of all so-called inside information regarding secret deals and events within presupposed warring factions inside the cabal of the banking and globalist structure that have zero factual backup.

I'm not saying real information can't be attained in these and other matters, but is it really worth your time, energy and attention to "buy into" such questionable information to where it throws your spiritual compass into a tailspin and absorbs your very being into an ultimately pointless vortex?

Watch out for anything that generates false hope. That's the carrot on the stick that has led many a soul down the path of confusion and even destruction.

Knowing by Its Fruits

What effect does it have on you? Are you getting your hopes and desires falsely pinned somewhere? Does it lead to a tightness or inordinate longing in your gut to where you're looking for confirmations for whatever newly adopted theory you're becoming attached to? Even defending this new found position in a proud, contentious or self righteous manner?

This happens to those not yet grounded in the fundamentals of standing back and simply observing new information in a detached frame of mind and heart.

We're going to be very surprised when the real picture comes into focus, and much of what we've learned along the way will get jettisoned as old baggage. They were stepping stones toward a greater truth and awareness but we have to remember they were just that. Stepping stones. Even the missteps and booby traps never mind the soon to be obvious diversions we entertained along the way.

It's just a learning process, and something to be enjoyed and definitely not fought over.

The Dark Secret Key of Belief

A big red flag should go up when anything requires leaping the imaginary hurdle of belief in order to enter into some secret realm of so called "knowing". This is how religions have literally gotten away with murder for millennia. You have no footing in this co-imagined realm whatsoever once you enter into this acquiescent zoned-out mode. All you have to guide you then is the word of others who have surreptitiously taken control of the reins of your life by their adamant espousal of some belief system and insistence that they are right and you need to believe as well.

This dark key to nowhere is where many have fallen in their hopes to attain a deeper understanding of the world around them. It's subtle, it's entangling, and extremely persuasive. The loss of personal control is the key indicator. Once someone is enthralled with this new "exclusive" world view, whatever it is, it is very difficult to speak in an open manner, never mind dissuade them. The reasoning is cyclical, with emotive reactions furiously reinforcing this new found belief system.

The matrix is the perfect example, laden with microcosms of such self-reinforcing mind traps that are ever present in the socially deprived milieu we inhabit. Day to day people defend their outlook and mindset in the world around us, yet this is counted as "normal" in some weird fashion.

If the entire ship is awash with sewage for a length of time it becomes normal. Such is the state of the whirled of today. Filth and garbage are good. Clean truth is now anathema, a pain in the ass to the status quo who are swimming in a whirlpool of toxic lies and deceptions.

Don't Take Yourself So Seriously

One of my personal yardsticks in measuring character as well as proposed information is humor and outright personal happiness. Besides people being natural, affectionate and easily approachable, I so appreciate the quality of a good sense of humor and someone who doesn't take themselves so damn seriously. What do any of us know? Who do we think we are?

This in an inherent quality that cannot be faked. And those who are so serious about it all, though it does have its place, can be a real downer when it comes to realizing our inherent freedom here and now.

After all, this is a not a work load or arduous journey to a destination, but a dance with life to be thoroughly enjoyed, no matter in what capacity.

Epilogue

The journey to enlightenment is paved with a lot of stuff. It's hard to enumerate here fully, but learning to point our antennas straight up to real verifiable information is paramount. It's no easy task, especially when the interference of relative ignorance and belief systems come into play.

Take your time. Go slow and methodically and keep your wits about you, despite the amazing new discoveries you're making along the way. Put ideas into a processing coffer that gently grinds the information in a fashion that makes it palatable and you can digest, or reject it, in due time.

There's no hurry. We're all learning, and true learning requires analysis and digestion before we react to it. Hasty decisions that are put into action have a serious price, whether physically, spiritually or intellectually.

Enjoy the ride. Just know what you're up against and watch your step.

And most of all stay happy and free. That's your barometer.

The Manipulated Matrix of Language

Powerful things, words. This subject has always fascinated me. From "In the beginning was the Word" to the metaphysical explanation that creation began with one sound and spread out as some form of electric plasma and that we're all simply vibrational expressions of varying dimensions of a primordial signal.

And how do we communicate? In person–with vibrational words, of all things.

But we also think and write mostly in words to express feelings, concepts and images. Do words therefore have some sort of intrinsic power even when not spoken? One thing for sure – how we formulate and express concepts can be helped or hindered by this pre-designed cleverly coopted medium called language.

Alas, generations of hand-me-down languages, some clearly better than others, some lost to antiquity.

The Language Matrix

Language to me is one of the most intriguing, under-appreciated and carefully veiled 'mediums' in human existence.

Everyone knows describing something can never take the place of an experience. You can write books about what it's like to fully submerge your body in water, but it will never come close to actually doing it. If you've ever had a psychedelic, kundalini or peak experience of any kind, this word limitation and restriction comes front and center to your consciousness.

Life just is and it's amazing far beyond words. You realize everything is essentially inter-connected vibrational energy at all kinds of wondrous levels. And language cannot begin to convey these realities.

In fact, language usually hinders its full expression.

Sadly most of humanity are observers and not full participants in this glorious potentiality of life. Instead they don't just read and think in the terms they've been handed, they literally watch others play life out on a flat screen in their home while living boring, hum-drum existences.

Language can do the same thing. Separate us from and chop up and impose false or limiting definitions of experiential reality.

Enter the Manipulators

From my worldview, while language itself is obviously an essential medium of exchange with fascinating empowerment potential, I think it could also very well be the controllers' most cleverly crafted and effective tool of mental and spiritual containment and limitation to keep most of the world blinded as to humanity's true identity and infinite potential.

I propose that the matrix of the Big Lie thrown over humanity is intrinsically reinforced by our deliberately poor, limiting and manipulated language, its very vocabulary, structure and tools. In addition, what language and crude weapons of expression we do have, and what enlightening vocabulary there may still be, is being deliberately degraded and stripped from our lexicon in their continuing campaign to dumb down, disempower and spiritually blind the world's citizenry.

Words simply have imbued power.

This subject isn't new by any means. I'm sure you've thought about examples of language limitation before. While English has one word for love, Greek and other languages have several to include the many "types" of love you might want to describe. One culture just recently discovered in the jungles of the Amazon don't even have a word for time.

You've also no doubt felt the frustration of trying to come up with the right word to express something. The beauty of writing and communicating is that your language skills come alive and improve. You don't give up until you find the right term. Or if you're a learner you'll look up synonyms till you find and learn a new word or group of words to convey your concept.

That's empowering, but still limited compared to our true potential of expression.

My point is that the tools we've been handed are not only relatively primitive and tend to limit conscious awareness, but societal engineers have been slowly replacing enlightening ideas and concepts with moronic epithets, while taking acute and illuminating words away through oversimplification, repetition of crude concept mantras, and starvation through omission.

We learn to repeatedly use the same forms of expression and descriptions in this form called language. We're inescapably corralled into a society of similarly communicating beings who speak the same way with the same formulated ideas following the same trends. This society inevitably subjects you to information through education and popular media using the same conceptual ideas and methods of communication. This becomes your inherent language tool. And we're seemingly stuck with it. Or so they would have us think.

Where Are We on the Evolutionary Communication Scale?

Early man used simple tools, or so we're told. These tools eventually became more sophisticated and efficient.

Where are we with language as a tool? Are we able to express what we're really trying to communicate, or are we being literally limited in our ability to experience due to the lack of latitude our language allows? Could we be communicating much more wholly, efficiently and dare I say, spiritually, with expanded resonating sounds and intimacy bordering on the intuitive or telepathy? Some already are.

Just think about the language-framed archetypes spoken of by Carl Jung. These are huge concepts that liberate the mind to freely roam consciousness for how the collective chemistry of the Universe works. It's open, inspiring and liberating.

"The archetype is like a black hole in space: You only know it's there by how it draws matter and light to itself". - Carl Jung

But that too is classified as "psychology" and put on a shelf in terms of daily communication potentialities.

That Brings us to Logos

This is a much more powerful language, and guess who speaks it? The elite controllers.

The word logos literally means "word" in Greek. These symbols are the language of the Illuminati and its hierarchy. Whether it be corporations, political parties, military branches, banks, sports teams, clubs or secret societies, there is more power in a logo than there is in a long explanation. The use of symbols throughout history to impose and perpetuate ideas and goals is one of the most fascinating studies there is, and probably one of the most revealing.

As Confucius profoundly stated:

"Signs and symbols rule the world, not words nor laws."

Indigenous Languages

If you listen to earlier indigenous forms of speech you'll notice a more musical sounding quality, with greater use of tones and breath. It conveys not just concepts but spirit and a much deeper awareness.

Native Americans for example use rich sounds and picture words that have an inherent respect and reverence for nature and the Universe built right into their language, using profound analogies and metaphors referring to their shared interaction with the wondrous natural world around them. You hardly have to know what the words mean it's so enriching and fascinating to hear.

Modern languages, however, have deteriorated. Why?

Culling the Language....1984

Here's a profound example by a renegade thinker almost 80 years ago who apparently saw what was coming on mankind. It portends exactly what seems to be coming to pass in today's society, and his references to language are ominous:

Newspeak and George Orwell's 1984

"Newspeak is a fictional language in George Orwell's famous novel Nineteen Eighty-Four. Orwell included an essay about it in the form of an Appendix after the end of the novel, in which the basic principles of the language are explained. Newspeak is closely based on English but has a greatly reduced and simplified vocabulary and grammar.

This suited the totalitarian regime of the Party, whose aim was to make subversive thought ("thoughtcrime") and speech impossible.

"The Newspeak term for the existing English language was Oldspeak. Oldspeak was supposed to have been completely eclipsed by Newspeak by 2050.

"The genesis of Orwell's Newspeak can be seen in his earlier essay, Politics and the English Language, where he laments the quality of the English of his day, citing examples of dying metaphors, pretentious diction or rhetoric, and meaningless words – all of which contribute to fuzzy ideas and a lack of logical thinking. Towards the end of this essay, having argued his case, Orwell muses:

"I said earlier that the decadence of our language is probably curable. Those who deny this would argue, if they produced an argument at all, that language merely reflects existing social conditions, and that we cannot influence its development by any direct tinkering with words or constructions.

"Thus Newspeak is possibly an attempt by Orwell to describe a deliberate intent to exploit this decadence with the aim of oppressing its speakers.

Basic principles of Newspeak

"The basic idea behind Newspeak was to remove all shades of meaning from language, leaving simple dichotomies (pleasure and pain, happiness and sadness, good thoughts and thoughtcrimes) which reinforce the total dominance of the State. A staccato rhythm of short syllables was also a goal, further reducing the need for deep thinking about language.

"In addition, words with opposite meanings were removed as redundant, so "bad" became "ungood." Words with similar meanings were also removed, so "best" became "doubleplusgood." In this manner, as many words as possible were removed from the language. The ultimate aim of Newspeak was to reduce even the dichotomies to a single word that was a "yes" of some sort: an obedient word with which everyone answered affirmatively to what was asked of them."

Pretty bang on, eh?

It reminds me of the expression "my bad", and all the violent words in today's pop lingo. Rap music is a perfect example, although it can be used to convey some great things as well.

Language is predominantly how it's used as well as the medium. My problem is how most of humanity takes today's language for granted and doesn't see how they're being brainwashed and manipulated by this and other types of social engineering. In spite of all this...

Humanity thrives.

The human spirit always comes through. We have infinite consciousness within each of us, what manifests as personality, or spirit. It cannot be quenched or contained, as hard as the social engineers try.

But I believe we MUST be aware of these relentless attempts to dumb down and suppress and limit humanity and realize the parameters we were born into "ain't necessarily so".

It's worth thinking about...

When you realize natural foods and remedies are called "alternative" medicine and have been inherently marginalized by the wording, whereas "modern medicine" is the bastardized alternative, you start to get it.

When you see how "conspiracy" is automatically attached to "theory" and thereby auto-debunked, you start to get it.

When you see how the power of "political correctness" steers masses of peoples' activities and produces paralyzing self-correcting thoughts and sets off fear-inducing alarm bells as in "anti-semite – racist – hate speech – homophobe – or dare I say terrorist" you start to get it.

When the assumptive terms "Sir, Your Majesty, Doctor, Your Highness, Mr. President" become strangely surreal, you're starting to get it.

It's all about words and language.

In the beginning was the Word…and the end, if you're not careful. Use your tools deftly, and always look past the veil.

There's more to life than meets the mind.

Personal Notes:

Not Without Our Consent

Nothing happens without our permission. In one way or another, consciously and/or subconsciously, we give our approval or disapproval by our actions, words and intentions.

Over time our accountability increases.

A mad world swirls around us in this manifestation with our inherent agreement. Without our complicit cooperation in support of this insane system none of this would be happening. No worldwide massacres without soldiers; no economic rape without bankers and merchants; and no social degradation and control without willing teachers, administrators and enforcers.

It takes the cooperation of the people. We cooperate with them, they succeed.

We don't, they don't…

Why?…

Because waking up to the true reality around us is too much work, and way too uncomfortable for most of the entranced masses. If you acknowledge things are as seriously wrong as they are and their true devastating effects on human life, you might have to change and do something about it.

Most people have developed coping devices that have become a way of life. The most effective is outright denial that it's all that bad or even happening at all. You'll see that everywhere if you're an awake and aware soul, and it can be disheartening at times.

It's somewhat simplistic but denial is a pretty good catch all.

The Belief Bamboozle

The subtle yet stronger partner of denial ironically enough is belief. Playing on your dreams and elusive sense of hope, beliefs, as opposed to true spiritual knowledge, effectively co-opt your subconscious aspirations and ability to take fully conscious and effective action. After all, you "believe" the answer is coming, everything will be OK all by itself, or an outside power will save you.

That's how many have chosen to cope. And there's a massive support system for that...not without a whole lot of help from the manipulators who have identified and scientifically used this human weakness to their advantage.

The thing is, belief systems and schools of thought, even drippy new age wishful constructs, they're such a convenient escape for all the accumulated undigested junk stuffed into that over-populated 'state of denial' in the mind of humanity. But heck, why not go there for refuge? It's comfy. "And there are so many others there. Just look at all the churches and religious institutions..must be truth to it." Yada yada..

The overall result? No true conscious rationale for behavior, no clear right and wrong or loving or unloving boundaries, just mindless acceptance of the status quo–with some anesthetized escape system waiting around the corner.

Suspended Animation

Hanging on to false hopes can't be a more inhibiting phenomenon. That's why religions are so effective.

Trapped in little "hives of hope", so called faithful believers of every persuasion are co-enabling each other on massive scales world wide, hoping and praying for deliverance and salvation from a world they themselves help to build and support on a daily basis.

Do you see anything strange there?

After all , Christians justify by "scripture" that the "powers that be are ordained by God". Argue with that if you're in the belief camp.

An off the charts blanket assessment, and yet it's applied in a timeless, unconscious across-the-board fashion that makes your head spin. Same with unquestioned loyalty and support to Royalty or the murderous Zionist state of Israel.

And so few can see it for what it is.

Response is Neutered

What's revealing is when you realize the amazing extent of this false hope escape/denial system. It's massive.

The inaction and lack of response it spawns is the perfect disarmament tool for these dastardly controllers and social engineers.

This is all over not just religions, but intellectual circles, scientific explain-aways, dumbed-down education, the new age movement, media mantras, and on and on.

I don't want to do a blanket diss of anything, I just want people to be cautious and most of all conscious.

As soon as you give away your autonomy to group-think, you're going to have serious energy depletion problems and a loss of conscious truth.

On Guard

Any form of truth is way too easy to co-opt and twist, which they effectively do.

A lot of issues are at work, and basically people should continually be on guard. There are plenty of entangling belief systems ready to suck people in. Some are outright, some are very subtle.

Challenge and question everything.

Stay fully conscious and you'll be fine.

The Spiritual Abuse Sting

The thing about belief systems is the subtle yet powerful spiritual and mental abuse involved. Much of this is because people are basically debilitated from birth in today's world and they don't catch the nuances of deceit in the societal fabric until they wake up…or it's too late.

Just observe when there's a fad or perceived social shift; the masses sway like seaweed in the social tidal flow.

They see no choice. It's apparently right because it seems it is. And the medium, the social swirl about us, not truth, is pressuring them to conform.

It's a serious social disorder, and belief systems are a logical and perpetual byproduct as well as major perpetuator of this fabricated illusion.

And remember, there are plenty of parasitic forces ready to pounce on the naive new "believer" when they reach out for something more. Plenty. Many of them sincerely thinking they're "carrying out the program" so it can be hard to spot.

Beware. Be aware.

Conclusion

This short treatise is in response to many comments and articles I've seen of late that smack of wrong dependency.

It's so endemic in our less than conscious world. It's entrained in us via education at all levels, the media, religious propaganda and any possible avenue. We must recognize these influences and see them for what they are and stay free and above them.

Detach.

It's not hard. Get above it first.

Be the observer you truly are.

It clarifies everything.

Language: Vibrational Key to Conscious Activation

Language fascinates me. It's empowering to realize it's virtually an arbitrary construct when you realize how many languages there are and have been through the course of history. Its development has been partially organic due to our basic efforts to communicate, but mainly it's what's been handed down and manipulated by the would-be Controllers via their social engineers and resultant reinforcing patterns.

Is this being paranoid or just realistic?

Look at how many terms have been either eliminated, restricted or introduced into our lexicon and by whom? The educational system is documented to have deliberately dumbed down the populace. Music and social media terms have turned language to shallow mush.

The mainstain media and our staged, corrupt political structure take our medium of communication to whole new debased depths of mindless manipulation.

If you can't see that, I pity you. The challenge is to reclaim our voice and medium of exchange.

George Carlin Said It Best

Why would a comedian who uses this very same language to convey his exposing message say such a thing as this?

"By and large, language is a tool for concealing the truth."

Because he knows. His life-long efforts were to peel back the false veneer of society and its manipulated phoniness in a manner that was verbally and visibly liberating for his audiences. Laughter is a release of psychological tension, a spiritual reaction expressing liberation and the realization of forbidden conclusions, more than anything.

It's the same basic struggle – they use language to hide stuff and manipulate, we use it to expose and empower. As always it's all about the motive and intention.

Rudyard Kipling appropriately said, "Words are, of course, the most powerful drug used by mankind."

Pretty powerful stuff. It takes consciousness to stand back and look steadfastly at your very method of conceptualization and conveyance of ideas and emotions. Not many are willing to step that far back.

The Vibrational Element

Now it gets interesting.

This recent article about the discovery of Russian scientists and the relationship of language to DNA is so revelatory, and segue's nicely with the above points.

DNA Science and What Russian Researchers Have Surprisingly Discovered...
(UndergroundHealthReporter)

Russian Scientists Reprogram Human DNA Using Words and Frequencies

"DNA science has finally explained previously mysterious phenomena such as clairvoyance ... intuition ... hands-free healing ... "supernatural" light and auras ... and more.

"The discoveries are to the credit of Russian researchers, who ventured into DNA territory Western researchers have failed to consider. Western scientists have limited their studies to the 10% of our DNA responsible for building proteins. That means they have dismissed the other 90% of DNA as "junk."

"In contrast, an innovative Russian team, led by biophysicist and molecular biologist Pjotr Garjajev, refused to accept that such a huge majority of DNA could hold no research value. To probe the mysteries of this uncharted terrain, they paired linguists with geneticists in an unconventional study to test impact of vibration and language on human DNA.

"What they found was completely unexpected — our DNA stores data like a computer's memory system. Not only that, but our genetic code uses grammar rules and syntax in a way that closely mirrors human language.

"They also found that even the structuring of DNA-alkaline pairs follows a regular grammar and has set rules. It appears that all human languages are simply verbalizations of our DNA.

Changing DNA With Spoken Words and Phrases

"Most astounding of all, the team discovered that living human DNA can be changed and rearranged with spoken words and phrases.

"The key to changing DNA with words and phrases is in using the right frequency. Through the application of modulated radio and light frequencies, the Russians were able to influence cellular metabolism and even remedy genetic defects.

"The Russians' work provides scientific proof of why affirmations and hypnosis have such powerful effects on human beings.

Our DNA is inherently programmed to respond to language. Esoteric and spiritual teachers have known this for ages. All forms of affirmations and "thought power" derive in part from this underlying principle.

"Individuals whose consciousness is more highly developed will have less need for any type of device (to apply radio or light frequencies). Scholars of this science believe that with consciousness, people can achieve results using only their own words and thoughts.

"The Russian scientists also found a DNA basis for the phenomenon of intuition — or "hypercommunication." Hypercommunication is the term used to describe situations when someone suddenly accesses information outside his or her personal knowledge base. In our times, this has become increasingly rare."

Amazing?

Not really, if you've been following the power of vibration and it being inherently causal and interwoven into our Universal reality. We're just discovering the real nature of language, a vibrational exchange of the utmost importance – until of course we can communicate telepathically and bypass this manipulable lower-dimensional stage of our development.

Telepathy is real and already available to all. We're tapping into it in our daily lives more and more via "intuition" or whatever you want to call it as the shift continues.

The reason we are so easily tooled around by our controllers, whether psychopathic power freak killers or interdimensional energy vampires, is this very element. Seriously suppressed, low level communication. No activation, no revelation. Nasty to the core.

But conversely this is a great source of empowerment and inspiration.

Have you ever noticed how an enlightened article or conversation elevates your spirit? Or how dampened you feel after a news report or some confusing and downer explanation of something in the mass media? That's exactly what I'm talking about. It can go either way.

Enter The Disgusting Dweebs

Don't worry, no way will the lower level complicit suck-up-a-trons get all of this. They just do it for shares of power, popularity amongst their own, and profit, so don't crack your nut trying to figure all this out and how it's executed.

Someone has to carry out the lower level duties so they hire them. Simple.

Plenty of non-thinking animals out there, unfortunately, groomed to perform these duties and inject whatever needs to be injected; false misleading words into the lexicon, fluoride into the water, heavy metal nano particle into the air, paralyzing vaccines into the innocent.

They'll do it all.

We're Free

Don't let any of this rattle you. To know what they're doing to us is half the battle. Take heart, we see what's going on and what they're up to. And don't worry about the language manipulation. Speak truth in whatever form, but do take advantage of right language which may take some research. Our empowerment does the same thing to them and unravels their machinations.

We are empowered. Nothing can take that away. They can try to deny it, hide it and pretend it isn't there. There's is a losing battle and they know it.

Be free – find your frequency and broadcast.

Matrix Mindscrews and Other Embedded Idiocy

We have to learn to spot the mechanisms buried in our language and the tricks of the media, education and propaganda, mainstream or otherwise. Engrained recitations and parroted phrases are a prime example. Don't assume anything you hear or learn is true, or begin to mindlessly swallow anything you're told from whatever source.

Learn to think critically and give everything serious, conscious consideration. Then listen to your heart.

We have to slow down to do that. Get off the treadmills of pressure, expectancy, and daily emergencies. One of the main tricks to get anyone to do or follow or swallow anything is to put the pressure on and say, "Hurry! Time is short! This is an emergency! It's your last chance! Decide now!"

Just look at an infomercial...no, don't. But that's it in a nutshell, as one dimensional as that may seem. It simply works. It plays on fear and triggers waiting to be pulled. By whom?

Parasitic manipulators. Preying on humanity's innocence and naiveté.

The Programming Falls Off with Conscious Awareness

It takes some doing to change this pressure issue in our lives with all there is going on around us to keep us busy and distracted, but it's integral to leading a conscious life. Don't worry, it comes more naturally as things progress in our wake up.

Conscious awareness is its own solution. Everything superfluous just falls away.

I was a pushy, intense, hyperactive speedy guy most of my life but as I became awake, aware and conscious I learned to live easier. It just came, albeit slowly, with a greater understanding of the big picture. I even began to drive much more slowly, and I didn't allow myself to get under pressure like I used to.

I gradually learned to see so much more around me, with my thoughts flowing more naturally, and life became way more fun and depressurized.

What Programming? Now Repeat After Me...

I've hit on some of these before but it's time to point out the idiotic idioms of the matrix – sayings that are only designed to subdue, dumb down and freeze in fear the human psyche. There are myriad examples but I'll hit on a few that I hope will do some "mind liberating" and elucidation of programming truths.

This seemingly innocent rhyme has been taught to kids for recital before going to sleep for ages. It exemplifies not only the disempowering effect of bludgeoning religious indoctrination, but believe it or not this seemingly innocuous prayer is a perfect example of the embedded trauma based mind control method that's one of the key underlying elements in the imposed matrix of society.

Now I lay me down to sleep,
I pray the Lord my soul to keep,
If I shall die before I wake,
I pray the Lord my soul to take.

Mind control has been around for millennia and here's a perfect example of how it is culturally perpetrated. This little recitation may seem innocent at first, but let's look at it. Conscious trust and knowing instead of fear is clearly a good thing; but rote repetition of half truths and imposed relinquishment of your own authority and personal sovereignty in a spirit of helpless is downright nasty.

Never mind the fear and death mongering.

Holy Crap and Eternal Insecurity

There's an example of a child forcefully declaring their helplessness and vulnerability in the night. "I need protection and I'm going to get it from the great white father in far off heaven who loves me if I'm good and say this prayer every night. And just in case I die tonight (which of course everyone thinks about before bed..not.) please take me to your nice castle. Oh, I hope you will. I'm asking 'cause I'm not sure. Oh God, that makes me feel creepy and afraid but I'm not supposed to because I was taught this and the whole church does it and they make it sound so nice and innocent"…and on and on.

The mind twist and hogwash embedded there is sinister.

Even so called "doctrinally" it makes no sense. Christians are supposedly taught they're unconditionally loved by God— so why do they have to keep asking? Talk about eternal insecurity. If you're so called "saved", why are kids repeating over and over "I pray thee Lord my soul to keep" and then "if I die tonight, lord, please take my soul"?

Anyone see anything wrong here? It's completely disempowering, outright death worship and screwing with their impressionable minds and hearts. But that pretty much summarizes religion overall, doesn't it?

The point is it's not just religion, but manipulative society in general.

How About Rock-a-Bye Baby?

How's this one for calming and reassuring children before bed for the less religiously inclined?

Rock-a-bye baby, in the treetop
When the wind blows, the cradle will rock
When the bough breaks, the cradle will fall
And down will come baby, cradle and all

A great image before sleeping, couched in a soft, rhythmic "lulling" song while scaring the crap out of children with this violent image of a helpless baby falling out of tree.

Getting the depth of the diabolical programming? You might not see it as that severe just yet, but give it time. When the fabric of what we've been handed becomes clear you'll be as livid as I am and want to wake everybody up to it.

Creating Alters for the Altar – The Religion Scam

This psycho-schism engineering of the human mind is everywhere.

—Love your neighbor but bomb the hell out of people of other religions half way around the world.

—Worship the far off "Prince of Peace" on Sunday then go dress like a ghoul and scream your drunken head off at a violent football game.

In mind control that's exactly what they do. By very extreme disconnects from a plausible reality using sadistic trauma of every sort, they force people to compartmentalize to such an extent the subject creates different personalities or "alters" to escape to someone(s) else they've split off into who literally have different lives and viewpoints. The institutionalized mass versions are somewhat less extreme but nonetheless use the same basic psycho-technology.

Cognitive dissonance is one of the mild sounding terms for this type of effect, but there's much more to it than that as I cover in the article, Cognitive Dissonance? Or Mass Disassociative Disorder.

The religious scam is the most infuriating. Talk about alters at the altar. The "conversion", the indoctrination, the memorization, the catechisms and all the levels of condescension, guilt manipulation and heavy handed hierarchy are consciously unbelievable. How we all fall for it to one extent or another is a study in itself, but if you realize the programming began where children in the bedroom are reciting death scenarios you start to get the point.

I mean billions worldwide are hooked on one religion or another. Is it any wonder they're "lulled" to sleep?

Don't be fooled. Your "religion", your supposed faith, your "beliefs" are what you live. Screw the phony ethereal mental crap. Your life is you. What you do, what you stand for, what you live, and what you help propagate. It's where your time, energy, attention and intention go.

Since When Did Curiosity Kill the Cat?

Here's another crippler. Curiosity killed the cat.

Is that right? Are you smacking my hand just for having a question? What the hell is that all about?

I looked it up and yahoo answers has this revealing, dutifully submissive definition:

"It just implies that if you have too much curiosity, especially about things that you should leave alone, you could get into a lot of trouble. You say it when a person wants to know something that he/she should leave alone."

Welcome the world of withheld information. Get used to it, children.

And who decides what's to be left alone, may I ask? The government? Your pastor, parents, friends or some controlling interest group that has plenty to gain as well as to hide?

Another arbitrary cudgel in the hands of any wanna be oppressor, be it prophet, priest, professor or president. No wonder the sanctioned districts like the Vatican can have a secret library, the City of London its secret finances, and Washington its secret government.

Let's Try Some Other Taboos and Conundrums

These will get you going.

–"You can't teach an old dog new tricks." – Nice. Give up on people past a certain arbitrary age. How to justify selfish reluctance. Eugenics and euthanasia sniffing at your heels?

–"Don't talk about politics or religion." – Couldn't be more obvious – Don't debate, don't engage. Might lead to realizations.

–"Quit while you're ahead." – What the f**k does that mean?

–"Children must be seen and not heard." – Muzzles on those pesky, lively children please. They are a nuisance.

–"Do as I say, not as I do." – I know. Nuts, but used like a cudgel on kids.

–"Needless to say" or "honestly now"…what? Are we talking here? Honesty has to be qualified?

–"Look Before You Leap" and "He Who Hesitates is Lost" – put those together. Ha.

–"You think too much." – Another sit down and shut up phrase.

–"Don't look a gift horse in the mouth." Really? Ever heard of a Trojan horse?

The list goes on. Beware the assumptive and confusing programming that's designed to come across as ancient, common wisdom. It's not, which is clear when it's held up to the light of true, empowering words of wisdom. Nothing in this fabricated matrix context is sacred or truthful. In fact, it's outright destructive and debilitating.

Synchronicity is the Name of the Game

I truly am experiencing synchronicities and learning to follow life's signs continually and it's a blast. I'm sure I don't catch them all, but it gives me great peace and joy to know I'm honestly open to them now and in a place I can act on them. It made all the difference when I detached from any entanglements and sold virtually all my stuff and uprooted. That felt great. And acting on and passing on what I was learning was even better.

That's a real key.

But beware of the pressure, as I mentioned above. Think of all the wrong decisions you've made. I'll bet pressure was involved, consciously and/or subconsciously. I know it's true with me. I've made some real doozies based on fear of being too late, missing a presumed opportunity, worrying about what other people thought, etc. It's when we're in that flurried state of mind that these trick precepts and sayings they employ and our years of this kind of programming can be so effectively activated and manipulated.

As well as our own, homegrown stupidity.

Conclusion

It's amazing and liberating to pull things apart and see the truth about the garbage we've been handed. It's all part of getting deprogrammed from the grooves in our minds that the matrix has made over the years. But so very important to do.

Don't worry, lies are powerless and dissipate in the light of truth, wherever they're embedded.

No shrink, no analysis, no fumbling in the dark - just the glorious effect of full on truth.

Radiate in peace.

Personal Notes:

Cognitive Dissonance? Or Mass Disassociative Disorder

This sounds like a false choice, I know, but it's not. Unconscious humanity is in a real pickle. Let's have a little term defining first since these concepts may seem confusing.

Cognitive dissonance, which most people are familiar with, is a psychological phenomenon that takes place in less than conscious human thinking, and is a favorite tool for manipulation by social engineers.

It pits the experiencer between what they're being told and the fact that what they're witnessing is nothing of the sort.

The subject then has to synthesize a middle ground explanation or justification for what's going on in some conscious or subconscious form, essentially ignoring the absolute contradiction before them because they don't know how to reconcile the two phenomena nor realize the motive for the deception.

They then virtually recreate the lying solution being handed them, usually from seeming "authorities" supposedly there to tell us the fabricated lie being posed is truth. It's also known as bullshit.

It has defined most of modern society for some time.

On the other hand, dissociative disorders (DD) are, according to wikipedia, "conditions that involve disruptions or breakdowns of memory, awareness, identity or perception. People with dissociative disorders use dissociation, a defense mechanism, pathologically and involuntarily. Dissociative disorders are thought to primarily be caused by psychological trauma."

In other words, there's an entire psychotic break that takes place. Instead of forming some kind of middle ground fantasy as happens with cognitive dissonance, the subject, similar to what takes place in traumatic mind control techniques, breaks with any sort of reality altogether and has a number of seeming unrelated compartmentalized associations and eventually alternate perception platforms or "personalities" appear.

It appears we're experiencing that now as a mass phenomenon in this media entranced, politically and psychologically manipulated world. And that's how they're getting away with their way over the top, nonsensical doublespeak insanities we're witnessing in the news every day. It doesn't need to make sense.

They can appeal to whatever fractured segment of the mass brain they want and not worry about it making sense.

Concepts and issues just aren't interconnected.

Mind Control –
Way Deeper Than We'd Like to Admit

A lot is coming out of late regarding this dark and most invasive of subjects. From whistleblowers to extensive research, books and articles available online, it's obvious this über manipulative phenomenon is at work in the world around us. And much more than we perceive at the surface level.

I think it must be a kind of sadistic joke for the powers that shouldn't be to watch bent and bewildered singers, actors and politicians repeat inane instructions right on cue.

If you're unfamiliar with this area please do a thorough search on it, and read Cathy O'Brien's The Tranceformation of America and see if that gets you going. The topic is not a fabrication of theorists but a product of despicable scientific elite-backed manipulators.

If you were a power freak, what would you not weaponize? Behold their mindset. And the contrived world around you. It's easy to also understand why the massive production and distribution of psychotropic drugs.

The Switchover – Divide to Conquer

The reason I differentiate in psychoses is the following: It's beyond rational recognition. Look around you and follow the non sequential behavioral attributes of the common human... absolutely psychotic.

Here's the programmed wiki definition of psychosis (I know, they're suspect too, but be that as it may:)

"Psychosis (from the Greek "psyche", for mind/soul for abnormal condition or derangement) refers to an abnormal condition of the mind, and is a generic psychiatric term for a mental state often described as involving a "loss of contact with reality".

People suffering from psychosis are described as psychotic. Psychosis is the term given to the more severe forms of psychiatric disorder, during which hallucinations and/or delusions, violence and impaired insight may occur."

Sound familiar?

America at its finest. And most of the programmed world. Admittedly "reality" is a seriously relative term, but still, this is a serious realization. The break is with some form of reality. Do you think the modern politico/social/media promoted world is a form of reality except unto itself?

Not exactly.

Why? – The Plan

We need to be aware of what is transpiring around us and why. If you can spot what dynamics are attempting to influence yourself, your loved ones and those around you or those whom you are observing, that's pretty helpful, is it not?

To disconnect humanity from its true spiritual nature and co-opt their very consciousness is their basic plan. If humanity woke up to its full potential and realized its purpose of manifesting universal truth within its experience, all would be lost to the manipulators.

We're eternal conscious spirits now having human experiences in a wonderful realm on a loving, conscious globe we call Gaia and all potential is at our fingertips via loving manifestation. To deter us from realizing that innate knowledge and experience takes some doing.

That's what we're up against.

They can't harvest our energy if we're on to their game and we say no. They have no power when we come to the realization of who we really are as it instantly starts manifesting, like crystals continually growing under any circumstance–as they do. So to mask this obvious truth and deter us from finding it for ourselves they will and do use every technique possible.... and with the advance of technology they've gone bonkers.

Sorry, it's too little and too late boys. It's in vain. Contrary to what it appears to be, they're behind the curve, not ahead of it.

When you see that, your head, mind, heart will explode with empowerment.

It's Not Ethereal Cereal – It's Plain and Simple

Don't take my word for it. I'm just sharing my observations and interpretations, but I find it pretty compelling when the dots connect and intuition kicks in.

Don't fall for their crap. It's a shit storm of lies out there; just about everything is either an outright bold faced lie and reversal of truth, or even worse, a tainted half truth or outright omission of essential information.

The answer is to learn to "think" from your heart. Your conscience, aware self, even so called common sense abilities. It's not some form of ethereal cereal, it's all actually quite simple, so don't go running off to a shrink or guru or something, it's time to knuckle down and get conscious and be willing to apply it to your daily life.

Time here is a bit tenuous right now, if you haven't noticed.

Seemingly it's not pleasant, but when you become awake and aware and come to terms with it in the bigger scheme of things, it fits right in. Their desired results don't have to happen, but more importantly we're alive spiritually and doing our best to awaken other souls in whatever way we can and are happily finding our true brotherhood.

And nothing can touch that, no matter what these maniacs do.

Keep on – and enjoy the ride. We're exactly where we're supposed to be – now live the gift accordingly.

Language Leaps and the Information Shuffle

So much can be told by language shifts. Both what's being used more frequently in general as well as substantial new additions, and deletions, to the lexicon. This goes two ways. The controllers keep shifting their language and euphemisms to blanket their intentions, while the awakening community grabs hold of and proliferates empowering and revealing words and concepts that grow in usage at an astounding and truly inspiring rate.

This is a powerful manifestation of the awakening.

Just look how easily and readily words like Zionism, the matrix, the Illuminati, social engineering, transhumanism, freemasonry, psychopathy, cognitive dissonance, geoengineering, false flags and big brother surveillance are being used now. Even the word conspiracy is bleeding into the mainstream lexicon with way less stigmatization. These were considered side line or taboo issues discussed by whack jobs not long ago. Now? They're mainstays of conversation that bleed more and more into the mainstream dialogue.

That speaks volumes as to the effect the onslaught of true information is having. And something to be very encouraged and inspired about.

Droning Psychopaths Tell No Truth

The official narrative of the "powers that shouldn't be" is also a changing landscape. While our heart language is rooted in truth, theirs is a constant smokescreen of disinformation designed to deceive, decoy and disempower.

Examples du jour? We're all too familiar with misleading names like the "Patriot Act" or the always ready handle "national security" and the like, but lately they've taken to covering their tracks even more, no doubt due to the awakening taking place, even in simple language recognition they're no doubt following with all of their invasive computer algorithms.

Mass surveillance has now become "bulk data collection" while torture is conveniently labelled "extraordinary renditions" and "enhanced interrogation techniques." All arrogantly perpetrated as if no one even notices.

But these shifts in contrived perception work on the unwary, which is why the official narrative is laden with such misleading and obfuscating terms and labels couched in complete blather like any one of Obama's wet cardboard speeches.

After all, to them, truth isn't the issue, it's control and getting their program across as seamlessly as possible.

Therein lies the rub, and a very important one to identify.

Look for Real Empathy

What really resonates with you? And what confuses or dis-animates you? These are ways to discern between the lines in the barrage of information coming at us. It's truly an informational war going on in so many ways, but thankfully one that the truth is always destined to win.

It may be ever so incremental, but truth stands its ground no matter what assails it.

There is no resonant sense of love or down to earth practical truth with propaganda. It always falls flat and only appeals to very dry and distant programmed self justification mechanisms. That's the intent. Keep us in our self circumscribed socially engineered limits in a dazed state of some far off distant "belief" guaranteed by some voice from somewhere leading people on with some promised carrot to chase after.

"Hope and change" and "Change you can believe in." There's a BS sandwich if I ever saw one.

However, real, good information feeds. It nourishes. It's clear and empowering in some way. It embraces your soul, encourages your convictions, and leads you to new understandings that positively affect your life.

Know the difference.

You already do, just listen to your heart. And respond accordingly.

Personal Notes:

The Slippery Slimy World of Subliminal Contracts

It happens so often and so subtly. Anytime we bend to the will of a lesser consciousness and address something on a wrong premise, we've agreed to a contract. We've officially agreed to engage at a lower level of understanding and awareness and will now have to operate within that severely limited and crippled framework.

Is it that serious?

Yes it is. How do you think this flimsy, lying matrix gets away with keeping so many handcuffed, bewildered, stupefied and incapable of waking up people in submission? There's a methodology. And a big part of it is the lure into lower, self reinforcing levels of communication and understanding. And there's no intention of getting anyone up and out of there, but instead to reinforce its grip on whomever ventures there.

It's like the sayings about fools. Get down to their level of arguing and they'll pound you into submission. Why? They believe that crappy lying system of thought, they've bought into its manipulative highly self-serving power. And by its very dumb downed lying nature they will deny the existence of anything else and try to beat into submission anything that challenges it.

All the while claiming vociferously that higher levels of understanding and truth don't exist. And you have no leg in that world to stand on. As Mark Twain famously said, "Never argue with stupid people, they will drag you down to their level and then beat you with experience."

Sorry, but you went there willingly. Just don't do it again.

The Presumptive Premise

Look at that word "premise". "Based on a false premise." "According to your premise…" yada yada. Then there's "get off of my premises." Hmm.

This is an important idea that has to do with where you claim to maintain yourself. Or where you stand on something perhaps.

Here's an interesting and somewhat funny example of how a false premise can be easily carried forward:

"An old cowboy goes into a bar and orders a drink. As he sits there sipping his whiskey, a young lady sits down next to him. … She says, 'I'm a lesbian. I spend my whole day thinking about women. …' A little while later, a couple sits down next to the old cowboy and asks him, 'Are you a real cowboy?' He replies, 'I always thought I was, but I just found out I'm a lesbian.'"

Look how easy that was to slip by. We think funny only because it's obviously a male cowboy and a jarring juxtaposition. But the suppositional power of a false premise is much more clever and dastardly than that. Just listen to lawyers and politicians and all the assumptive, contractual phrases they sneak into their language. It's overwhelmingly fraudulent and extremely intrusive and aggressive.

And each time people believe it, take it in and don't identify and deny and resist it, it becomes another contract.

A voluntary agreement to enter and participate within a trapped environment.

> "Don't say Hi, like a spider to a fly
> Jump right ahead and you're dead"

-Mick Jagger / Keith Richards

Friendly Contracts

Same with people. You agree to be a certain person with this person, and they with you. Same with another. The conflict arises when you're with a group of people and you have several different contracts out. Ooops. Finding your footing can be tough if you've been living at that shallow, deceitful level. But it's a question of survival so people make it work.

And work it is keeping so many contracted stories going. Such is life for so many entrapped in the system.

Being real and honest, as unhip as it is in this artificially contaminated world, is so simple. It was actually a big revelation "back in the day" (another give-away expression) to "be real" only 50 years ago. "Do your own thing". Wow, how revelatory. "Do what I'm innately called to do and not what the system is telling me? What a novel idea."

And what were we called for being ourselves? Hippies, misfits, druggies and outcasts.

It all took some time to wear off but wear off it did, after the spiders popularized the psychedelic and sexual features of the movement and slowly beat it into accepted submission. They've got time, and that's the kind of thing they do. We just ride along and comment on the countryside.

Beliefs Are More Bullshit Contracts

I don't use the word believe except to challenge and belittle it. It has nothing to do with truth, consciousness or experience. It is hope made into rigamarole. It is ethereal cereal in a world that needs real experiential food. It is more often than not dreamy feel good nonsense in a massive garbage dump that needs recycling.

Or burning.

And they're contracts. People agree to what they want to project or wish for. It's fantasy. It's not all bad as there are positive affirmations than can help alter immediate situations, but they're still bullshit on a stick.

They're not experiential. They're attached to outcome, phony baloney wishes and desires that have nowhere to go. So we harbor them as a last resort in our fantasy football world of desired outcomes. Play the game of belief if you want, but your idea of spirituality is sitting in the lotus position while a boulder is rolling down the mountain on top of you.

It's either old school religion or new age wannasee and wannabeeism. It's time to get real. Consciousness is knowing. Faith is knowing.

Belief is hope and has no foundation in anything. Get off the drug. You'll see so much more clearly.

Conclusion – Making A Path

When you grow in consciousness you'll recognize these issues quickly and easily. When you're enmeshed in the morass of intentional confusion and control you'll think "conspiracy freak" or something to explain away these pin pricks on your consciousness.

It's nothing to worry about. You'll get it eventually.

That's why we need to wake people up. Any way we can. We each only have our personal realms of influence, but more importantly we each have our ability to align with consciousness and automatically each other. Therein lies the key, our unity. I don't know how it works but I know that's a massive factor in our effectiveness.

When you or I activate, others activate. If we don't, the ones we touch probably won't. That's how it works. We each are part of the path to the safe haven of truth. We are lining up even if we don't think we are or can't feel or see it. Trust your heart and do what's right.

The light will and does show the way…and sometimes the darker it is outside the clearer we can see what's light and what's not.

The Hope and Belief Conspiracy

Here's a good exercise that will help alter your conscious awareness and put punch and clarity where slosh once existed. Don't even use the words "hope" or "believe".

Every time you're tempted to say, write or even think these debilitating, nebulous concepts, replace "I hope" or "I believe" with "I think" or "it appears to me" or something else realistic that clearly indicates what you really mean.

These types of inhibitors are a subtle trick of the programmed language we've been handed.

We don't need full evidence to make conjectures or intuitive surmisings. Just call them what they are. Hope is one of the most misleading and disempowering terms we've ever been handed, as is belief. Drop them entirely.

We tend to know what people seem to mean when using these terms, but they're still just as intellectually and spiritually crippling.

Catch Yourself

When you catch yourself using these terms you'll be surprised at how often they appear and how much this exercise strengthens your perception and awareness.

These misleading terms run around humanity like viruses just waiting to infect the unwary. Just as we wash our hands regularly when going out in public, we need to do the same with our minds and the use of their dirty language.

It's a bit like fear porn and falling for the dark side of viewing the world around us. Sure we need to be aware of the sickness pervading society and the machinations of the would-be Controllers, but these language tricks are all potential traps to sap our energy and powers of true intention and conscious awareness, the very tools we so desperately need to rise above this ongoing fray with the forces around us.

Free Your Mind – Meet the Trivium

The above segues nicely into something I've wanted to bring up for some time. Many are familiar with this rational approach to learning and discovery as it's quite remarkably lucid and helps one stand back and clearly assess the information before us and regain our intellectual and even spiritual sovereignty.

Unfortunately and as expected, this method of learning has been lost or adulterated in today's world as evidenced by the confusion and blind ignorance that are so rampant in society and our deliberately dumbed down educational system.

The ideas of "hope" and "belief" are deeply intertwined in religious thought and hence all of society. They are perfect examples of false, misleading and disempowering concepts that learning techniques such as the Trivium can quickly dispel for upcoming generations. This subject deserves serious study but I'll include some introductory information here to help give the feel of what this is about and hopefully stir your interest in this fascinating and liberating conscious learning technology.

(From GnosticMedia)

"In medieval universities the Trivium combined with the Quadrivium comprised the seven liberal arts. This teaching method is based on a curriculum outlined by Plato. One of the key intentions behind applying the Trivium and the Quadrivium is to distinguish between reality and fiction. By training the mind how to think – instead of what to think – this method provides a teaching of the arts and the science of the mind as well as the art of the science of matter.

Tools of Knowing

The Trivium and the Quadrivium are often presented in a Pythagorean triangle which represents the human way of knowing :

"Any observation enters our mind through the 5 senses. Then we use our mind and apply the Trivium and the Quadrivium in order to process the observation. This process consists of several steps which enable us to understand how the observation relates to what we already know, how we can explain this new piece of information to others and how we can store it in a methodical way.

The Trivium method of thought

"The Trivium is the first half of the 7 Liberal Arts. It consists of 3 elements : General grammar, formal logic and classical rhetoric. Sacred texts often refer to these 3 elements as knowledge, understanding and wisdom. The overarching topic of the Trivium is communication and language.

"Within the process of seeing, conceptualizing and speaking it is important to be aware that the created concept about how we think reality is, does not equate reality as it really is.

"In other words, the map is not the territory.

"Aristotle who is considered to be one of the originators of the ideas behind the Trivium stated that an educated man should be capable of considering and investigating any idea or concept thoroughly without necessarily embracing or dismissing it. If during any discussion it becomes obvious that the other person is emotionally involved regarding a particular subject matter, then it is impossible to have a rational discussion based on the Trivium with them. Any emotional attachment to a particular belief blocks any kind of rational or logical argumentation."

Note the direct reference to those emotionally attached to a belief and how it blocks rational discourse.

Sounds Too Rational?

We're dealing with the rational mind, which works in conjunction with our imaginative/creative mind. These work in concert. Above all is keeping a conscious awareness above both processes, but each has its place, just as we inhabit a physical body that works in conjunction with Spirit.

You can find much more on the Trivium and other terrific information from the TragedyandHope website as well as at GnosticMedia, two great resources.

Don't Hope or Believe – Know or Don't Know

It's not that big of a deal when you think about it. The biggest trick is in the language and how it's been appropriated and used in this ongoing onslaught of group-think. Having a truly conscious frame of reference, if we can call it that, requires us to have a foundation based in detachment first of all.

Learning to let things sit or even pass until reality takes shape is as important as finding seeming factual information.

The reality we're experiencing is fundamentally an illusion. There's nothing wrong with changing viewpoints, perceptions and understandings.

After all, we're continually evolving spiritually within a very confining environment that is engineered to distract and delude our thinking and comprehension of the world around us.

Why the deliberate confusion? For us to draw awake and aware conclusions would mean the inevitable fall of their power structure.

Then so be it. Illusion cannot stand in the face of truth and conscious awareness.

We need to watch our language and what we unconsciously adopt as our medium of exchange. Abolishing the use or application of words and concepts like "hope" and "belief" is a great starting point on the road to recovering our power. There are many such Trojan horse words and expressions.

Beware the conspiracy of language. Use the language, but don't let it use you.

Here's to the joy of getting free and awakening.

Transcending Language and the Leap of Faith

Don't you love dreams, especially the trippy ones where you're sure you were there? I just had another one, and it brought up so many significant concepts and emphasized something I've been thinking a lot about lately.

Manifesting the next level with all that is in us.

The main impact of the dream concerned communication. Not the message being conveyed, but the more than amazing power of our mode of communication. Both in how it can hamper and contain, or gloriously liberate our spirits.

Something that drastically affects the entire state of humanity.

Into the Library of Light

In the experience I was transcended into this other realm by a series of very touching dream events. It was wonderful. I was transported in that spiritual yet physical kind of way "up" into this other realm. There I was introduced to this modern looking library type place with glass walls, and happy people of all kinds and ages. It was hovering over a pristine planet below and filled with awake, beautiful vibrant people, some floating and some walking, with lots of children around this big room with elevated library levels and a hubbub of audibly silent, peaceful activity.

Everyone was effortlessly busy and innately knew what they were supposed to be doing; no pressure, no hurry, and communication was oh so easy and simple.

I was greeted as if I was expected and was immediately accepted and integrated as everyone just kept about their business. I pestered my beautiful "governess" of the outpost guide about contacting my loved ones left behind about what had just happened to me so they wouldn't worry. I was clearly a novice but even that was accepted blithely and in stride and they were checking out ways of contacting them. If there was some "protocol" even that was open for reconsideration.

It was really cool. But so especially so profoundly, and openly communicative.

Conscious Communication is the Key to Conscious Empowerment

The most profound realization and insight of this experience was how everyone communicated. There were many messages and many personal details involved, but the real world of conscious communication is nothing like what we experience here. Somehow everyone who needed to know something knew it.

There was no useless chatter I could "hear", and it wasn't silence in between like something was missing.

It was perfectly orchestrated, but naturally.

What struck me as I thought about this experience is that we are all controlled by our very manner of communication more than the content.

Because in this life we have this huge buffer called our ego or false self, this mind and voice box controller, with which we can formulate what we want the other party to hear. This makes for a huge gap in reality and allows for all these false fabrications of projected truth vs real truth that we witness every day.

Hence our screwed up world of lies, phony nuances and easy deception. And anyone stupid enough to tell the honest truth gets trampled on like a bug on a city street. Here. But not there.

There truth isn't something to strive for, it's a simple and glorious matter of fact way of a loving, vibrant life.

The Medium Is the Message

I'm reminded of the brilliant mind of Marshall McLuhan. He said the medium is the message. And exactly right he was. Just imagine using binoculars looking the wrong way while a bear is attacking you from your blind side. That limited medium kept you from getting the full 360 degree view.

It's much like that.

This limiting medium we share that appears so essential needs serious investigation. Oh sure, now we have the internet and pixels and holograms and such, but it's still all based on this seriously separating premise where there is no assumed unity, when we all know there truly is.

It's this mechanistic "Subject addressing other object…Formulating message accordingly…Sending…Message received… Awaiting input."

McLuhan said some amazingly insightful things. Anyone who says, "I don't necessarily agree with everything that I say."..which he did, is my kinda guy. He's a great study when you get time. Just go to his quotes for starters, they're brilliant.

Whether McLuhan got the "full picture" at the time of his visit here I don't know, as mainstream infojerks used his insights to transform marketing, advertising and mind manipulation into the monster it is today.

Totally controlling, misleading and sinister. As usual.

But McLuhan had a very important message. How we communicate is profoundly more important than what we communicate. Sounds messy to the mind but again, there's a profound element of truth to it. And that it works at such an ultimately wonderful simple level is a glorious discovery to be had.

The Alternative to Lies – Fearless, Loving Honesty

Go to college if you want to get really screwed up, but this subject of real communication is so profound it's barely touched on. Why?

It leads to the culprits.

Those that manipulate how you communicate manipulate you. When we're forced into restricted, crippling language based channels of communication and think that's all there is, we are duped into a lower density reality, just as they want. And we all have been at some point because there apparently has been no choice. At least that's what you'd think from the possibilities we've been given.

Sound paranoid? You bet. And rightfully so. We're under incessant attack, and our most essential life tools are where they strike the hardest. Our health, mental conditioning, and spiritual state.

What we're grappling with is a profound idea of how we interact. If our communications were honest, we'd be in one heck of a different place. When we know what others are thinking the jig is up. The truth is known. While it would wreak havoc if applied in this current world, apparently in this other level it generates a natural homeostasis of peaceful, harmonious honesty.

The Other World

Communication is a life force. It is a life giving interaction. To constrict or limit it is as wicked as turning the lights off in a dark, dangerous crowded room. Yet that's exactly what the extra-dimensional controllers have done and audaciously continue to do.

Here in this new realm I visited, everyone simply knew. What was a concern to you, you knew about. Were you introduced to somebody? "Hi, I'm so and so" etc. but not nearly that clumsy, and it's transmitted with immediate understanding. Something pertinent to your situation? You and whomever needed to be included/involved were in the "conversation" although it's more like a poetic catalytic information process… with a soul.

That simple, that direct, that loving. No froth needed or phony touch ups. Just the loving truth.

Our current paradigm? What comes at you, or you formulate to fit the outside projection, is all you get. There's no "shared" information except what the controlled "media" deems to broadcast or you as an individual volunteer. Or are able to dig up.

Can you say "ripe for corruption and abuse"? Hence the power of the alternative and independent media.

Central Command?

The really freaky thing is the communication is "moderated" naturally. You don't worry about how it happens, it just does. If you're supposed to be in on the conversation, you'll be in on it. Something comes up and it's within your 'jurisdiction", you'll be informed.

It's all natural and normal and cosmically directed in some way, as it should be. You don't look for the big eye in the sky, it's the nature of things.

The akashic records could be another level from what I experienced, or a central storage area. Here was a working station but a home at the same time. I wasn't there very long so these are all from impressions I had there and then analyzing the dynamics as I perceived them.

In such an honest open medium you can imagine that if someone had bad intentions or was doing something out of synch or had a serious need or problem, those around would know. The fabric would be disturbed and the issue would get immediate attention, and the potential problem could be addressed.

A loving fully open society would therefore heal itself should the need arise, by whatever means necessary.

It's Time to Transcend and Trust Our Hearts

This wonderful intuitive power of communication is where our strength lies. If we can develop this "6th sense" and learn to trust it more than the other matrix-driven information channels, we're on to something.

We know we want to bypass the programming but are reluctant to step out and really do it.

There is no other way.

It's time to trust our heart instinct, our intuition, the conscious understanding we sense and learn to act on it. It might seem scary at first like stepping out on thin air, but the payoff is next to supernatural.

Exercising it will bring it into our realm.

Synchronicity and Intuition are Leading the Way

This "telepathic" communication concept is nothing new. What's wonderful is how it resonates and how many have had experiences with it. The inspiring synchronistic events I experience and hear about everyday from friends are extraordinary. And that's good–outside of ordinary. We need more people to see more of these wonderful events and "coincidences" happening around them. And learn to expect and utilize them.

My concern is bringing this into our current paradigm as there are choices to be made. By all of us.

We can do this on a grand scale with intention. We just need to "step out" and get the hang of it. It's already there and we're all practicing it to a large degree in many ways. But we need to see this form of deliverance for what it is. It scrambles their signals, screws up their thinking, freaks out the control boards, and blows up their paradigms ...all while empowering a fledgling truth community that so desperately needs encouragement.

So why hold back?

The dynamics I feebly attempted to describe here are amazing. When this medium is let loose everything else the manipulators are using just reduces into cosmic jello. It's like the ultimate enzyme, or the perfect catalyst. One drop and zappo.

Conclusion

I'm very serious about this. Amongst our enlarged community are many great minds and wonderful hearts. Critical mass has occurred on many levels, but we need to keep the attack up. We cannot sit still or space out into all the wonderfulness when we have brothers and sisters that need our help and a paradigm about to implode on the innocent.

That's how I see it.

It's up to us to do everything we can...in peace, in love and with full conscious intensity as the situation warrants...which this does. Within each of us are so many untapped resources we'll kick ourselves when this is "over" because we didn't use them. Philosophize about this all you want but responding to the call of the Universe is imperative.

That's all nature does.

Go fully conscious, any and every way you can. It's a life worth living. Hesitation and hanging in the fringes is for cowards in twisted denial.

It's time to transcend this outdated, manipulated prison matrix muzzle and communicate in Spirit and in truth.

Time to tap in. And do it with glorious abandon.

Personal Notes:

The Religious Mindset – Gateway to a New Dark Age

There couldn't be a more pertinent backdrop to this article than the socio-religious marriage taking place on the world stage right now. The Jesuit Pope endorsing these global social engineering programs disguised as caring for an ailing planet is a perfect example of mass manipulation using religious mindsets and attachments and a clear demonstration of what is being perpetrated on mind-numbed humanity.

If only people woke up from this and similar programming we would have a different world overnight.

Sadly, most operate from preconceived, purposely placed paradigms and can't see the forest through the trees, to put it lightly. Taking what they're handed at face value is perhaps humanity's biggest weakness, much like hungry, penned in animals heading to the feed trough for whatever is being offered.

There are very powerful dynamics behind religious belief systems. And they're not nice. As is the case with all controlling influences, they're designed to subserviate, subjugate and control, with the appearance of being oh so benign. All with very serious consequences; socially, psychologically and spiritually, cleverly designed to fulfill a hidden agenda.

So let's look at some of these devious disempowering dynamics and where they're taking us.

The New Dark Age – Retreat to an Archaic Revival

Dark ages have repeated themselves throughout history. We're in just such a potential collapse, as disturbing at it may seem, albeit an altogether avoidable one. The Greek dark age is little known but one such example while the Middle Ages are the most recent historical "dark' era, one of rampant torture and persecution and the sequestering of real knowledge.

On a so-called modern geopolitical scale this excerpt from The Raven Foundation website aptly summarizes the current sociopolitical condition:

"Fear, exploited and unchecked, triggers a deep, "rational" insanity. We're driving ourselves into a new Dark Age.

"The driving force is institutional: government, the mainstream media, the military-industrial economy. These entities are converging in a lockstep, armed obsession over various enemies of the status quo in which they hold enormous power; and this obsession is devolving public consciousness into a permanent fight-or-flight mentality.

Instead of dealing with real, complex social issues with compassion and intelligence, our major institutions seem to be fortifying themselves – with ever-increasing futility – against their imagined demons."

On a parallel plane of understanding, there is this perspective as stated by Terrence McKenna who often spoke about an archaic revival of a coming dark age:

"These things are all part of the New Age, but I have abandoned that term in favor of what I call the Archaic Revival—which places it all in a better historical perspective. When a culture loses its bearing, the traditional response is to go back in history to find the previous "anchoring model." An example of this would be the breakup of the medieval world at the time of the Renaissance. They had lost their compass, so they went back to Greek and Roman models and created classicism—Roman law, Greek aesthetics, and so on."

The Willing Subjects of the Penitent Mass Mind

So let's look at some of these devious disempowering dynamics that are attempting to take us to a new darkened age of directed, reduced enlightenment.

When the religious aspect is interjected or amplified upon the human mindscape as it has been, we see very powerful dynamics at play. These very tools are used to manipulate humanity into the willing accomplice in such a retreat to this "archaic revival". These are some of the mechanisms at play.

"I am not worthy" cries the subservient religious practitioner, no matter what carefully contrived religion it is. The abdication of self, sovereignty and rationale, all for a pittance of acceptance and justification for even living at all is the basis for all abusive religions.

How humanity has been decimated by looking outside for help via forms of external authority. A very "captivating" concept and great way to excuse oneself from responsibility in the bargain.

"Please accept me, oh great Being from beyond" cries the abdicating pawn. I know, I've been there, as have so many in one form or another if they're honest. Religious affinity befalls sadly abused, programmed and misdirected souls who are longing for meaning and acceptance. It's the most susceptible of emotions, being very cleverly locked into the natural human hunger for spiritual expression, but so very cleverly manipulated by "smarter" entities of all sorts.

This is an amazing topic as religion and belief systems are the most powerful of all control devices. Even the Gnostic teachings say that of all the Archontic devices leveled against humanity, religion is by far the most powerful. I heartily concur from all I've learned up to this point.

The Guilt Trap – Just Another Form of Fear Subservience

The guilt aspect is surreal, but basically the religiously blind-folded human wants to earn their way to forgiveness since that's the playing field they've been presented with. It's a "pull your self up by the bootstraps" kind of completely mindless, unsolvable conundrum that ensnares more than any other control device. And all according to whom? And what?

Just think about the idea that we were "born into sin". What greater defenseless, innate bondage can you have?

This is very easy to use on less conscious humans. If you know anything about historical trends and the background of religion this is clearly obvious. Sadly we put this type of dynamic and its many ramifications bringing dis-enlightenment into a carefully distanced "historical context". As a result, epochs like the dark ages are "way back when", safely tucked away in the musty annals of times gone by, with people not realizing they themselves are indeed now in the midst of another clever "darkening of the truth" while what they're being directed into is made to appear toward the light of a brighter day.

We've been entering quickly into a new dark age for decades, and all by design. Despite any kind of information explosion or not, people just don't see it for what it is in the socially engineered world closing in around them.

Judging what you're really going through by what's going on around you is akin to abject lunacy.

It's the mindset of dependency that's killing the inhabitants of this planet. Looking to others, "powers that be", "authorities", "saviors", "great forces from beyond", "celebrity icons", "politicians" and profoundly including "technology", or better said "technocracy", one of the very real driving forces of the new age of darkness and the loss of our innate humanity.

But even more so is the overarching religious aspect of the would be new order of world control, much as in ages past. We just lack the true historical perspective, which again has been blacked out by design. It seems unthinkable that another inquisition could ever happen on planet earth, yet we are in the throes of just such a draconian mind, soul and spirit crackdown and on a scale never before seen.

The Sad State of Affairs

People tend to succumb to the latest trend du jour. Whatever it may be, historically as well as in the current social context, we can see that the majority of humanity is going along with whatever is thrown at them. Why? Because it's sold to them without apparent recourse. It's done very cleverly but with distinct determination, waging this campaign to accomplish a desired result. This is not difficult in such a massively media controlled whirled, yet it's cleverly masked from the unawakened.

This is why true information and being well informed and independently questioning and researching anything and everything is so, so important.

Our current situation is uniquely unique. We're at a very profound crossroads in history yet the majority of our world's populace isn't fully understanding it and are clearly on the defensive. That's not a good place to be for anyone. My point here is that the underlieing influence is largely religious, as well as occult spiritual programming, and something to be astutely aware of and broken free from.

The Globalist Mindset – Subdue At Any Cost

We're being maneuvered into a new religious paradigm. Ever so slowly, and ever so slyly. The spiritual aspirations of mankind must be harnessed and channeled to support their intended agenda. This is why the rope-a-dope Pope is integral to all of this. Without spiritual endorsement they cannot nearly have the sway they intend to have. And there will be other such spiritual "voices", guaranteed.

It's all by design, and anyone could have seen this coming even without binoculars.

We're being taken back to another dark age, one of massive totalitarian control with subservient masses, but they know they have to sell it as well as enforce it to get to that stage. We're seeing the obvious dumbing down of humanity and its weakening and subjugation, but the final stage is so draconian it needs a massive marketing ploy, such as this hyperactive Jesuit Pope and all the media hype and concurrent entertainment and UN propaganda support, while they press ever harder on the unwitting masses' minds and hearts.

While espousing Luciferian "light" they bring darkness. While proclaiming unity and prosperity they bring draconian control and subjugation. It's about time people woke up to their agenda.

How It's Done

In a chilling document from GnosticMedia.com about the social engineering of the 60's and the long term agenda to bring humanity into a stupefied state of darkness there is this ominous excerpt:

"The purpose [of the psychedelic movement] was to establish a neo-feudalism by the debasing of the intellectual abilities of young people to make them as easy to control as the serfs of the Dark Ages. One accurate term used for the individuals who were victims of this debasing was "Deadhead," which is an equivocation for a "dead mind" or "a drugged, thoughtless person".

"Aldous Huxley predicted that drugs would one day become a humane alternative to "flogging" for rulers wishing to control "recalcitrant subjects." He wrote in a letter to his former student George Orwell in 1949:

"But now psycho-analysis is being combined with hypnosis; and hypnosis has been made easy and indefinitely extensible through the use of barbiturates, which induce a hypnoid and suggestible state in even the most recalcitrant subjects.

"Within the next generation I believe that the world's rulers will discover that infant conditioning and narco-hypnosis are more efficient, as instruments of government, than clubs and prisons, and that the lust for power can be just as completely satisfied by suggesting people into loving their servitude as by flogging and kicking them into obedience."

Take Charge

Despite all we're up against I'll wrap this up with one final point. That any thinking being on this planet can put up with all of this and not be screaming from the rooftops about what is truly going on escapes me.

I honestly wonder, who stole humanity's guts? Where's the courage to speak out and do everything we can to fight this insanity? Why don't people make their lives a statement to the truth they've learned?

It befuddles me. But I'm not giving up, nor are many others.

Be it slickly sold religious claptrap, media insanity, geopolitical maneuvers or whatever, amongst the awakened our sails are set.

I hope yours is too. Meet you at the sunset. Or is it sunrise? Or both?

Fight on in love and truth…and beware the darkness disguised as light.

Personal Notes:

Anger Games

We're all pissed off in some form or another. No question. No one can sit idly by with any level of consciousness and not be ticked off by the insanity, inequities and atrocities going on around us. That's sacred anger and there's nothing wrong with it.

But we must keep anger in its place. The general populace is being set up and baited for violent response.

All they're waiting for is a justification to herd the unsuspecting flock right into their tightfisted fascist paradigm as the police state takes shape around us.

Don't fall for the trap.

Don't you think Obama's "crotch salutes" to fallen vets don't piss off middle "patriotic" Americans? All his actions are scripted and designed to induce compliance, or else to make people's blood boil.

Divide and conquer is intrinsic to their game plan.

An Old Trick at Work

Induced passions make people easily manipulated. When we fear or act in anger we are not fully conscious nor fully empowered. Our vision is impaired and our reasoning seriously tainted. Blind anger is akin to fear, and the ability to manipulate those acting in anger and fear is very similar.

Dr. William Sargant, a psychiatrist with the illuminist Tavistock Institute, wrote in his 1957 book, The Battle For The Mind:

"Various types of belief can be implanted in people after brain function has been deliberately disturbed by accidentally or deliberately induced fear, anger, or excitement. Of the results caused by such disturbances the most common one is temporarily impaired judgment and heightened suggestibility. Its various group manifestations are sometimes classed under the heading of "herd instinct", and appear most spectacularly in wartime, during severe epidemics, and all similar periods of common danger, which increase anxiety and so individual and mass suggestibility."

So while people get aroused and decide to become active within the framework they've been handed by the manipulators we're often walking right into their paradigm that grips like a Chinese handcuff–strengthening the enemy's hold on us by fighting them on their level and on their terms.

History proves this. One system toppled by the same tactics used by the oppressor becomes a replacement system, and the Masonic pattern continues.

Amerika – Born and Bred in Violence

The Boston tea party was thrown by dressed up Freemasons to provoke exactly what they planned all along. Another violent stronghold obtained by violence, built on violence, and that has since executed nothing but violence on the world since its inception, whether culturally, economically or militarily. Just ask the millions of exterminated and incarcerated native Americans about the "freedom of religion" excuse these invaders used to go there in the first place.

If the old adage is true that "they that live by the sword shall die by the sword", what America is about to reap is not going to be pretty.

Why should the "innocent" Amerikans suffer this causal reflex, you say? Because by and large Americans not only did nothing to stop the pillaging and atrocities being carried out by its corporo-fascist government and those they support such as insane genocidal Israel, but they de facto supported these programs and ever more importantly, luxuriated in the profits and delicacies of an over-indulgent, resource-pillaging machine, sucking the very life blood out of the poor of the world.

And yes, the U.S. isn't the only player in this. These selfish parasites are internationalists stationed around the globe, but the US is its primary arm of oppression and exemplifies all of these characteristics.

The Deliberate Piss-Off

The breakdown our world is undergoing is deliberate – and people are catching on faster and faster. It's getting to where almost anyone can see the banksters deliberately pulled the financial plug for their periodic harvest. The media disinformation and obfuscation of truth as well has become outright Orwellian as the migration into alternative news sources continues to accelerate.

Granted, much of the public still takes the disempowering soma-swill of the never ending promise of "hope and change", but the matrix mirage is rapidly evaporating for all to see.

That's the vibrational change we're talking about. Inside and out.

It's now obvious to a vast swathe of humanity that our social fabric has been dissolved by anti-moral, anti-human doctrines of seemingly satanic self-indulgence and death worship. Our food, air and water supplies are deliberately poisoned. Our leadership is clearly dishonest, shallow and inept. Even disasters, very many man-made consequences of deliberate tinkering with mother nature, are manipulated for profit and strategic control of populations, as well as downright depopulation.

Major political, economic and social changes in society don't just happen–they're engineered. And with guaranteed outcomes.

Either way they win. But their time is almost up.

Watch for Provocations...and Pre-Programming the Solution

False Flag operations have been the most successful hoodwinks to date. The relatively recent big ones like 9/11, 7/7 in

London, the clearly staged Paris event, and other staged incidences such as the many shootings and bombings like Sandy Hook and the Boston Bombing, were carefully led up to by the Oklahoma City, USS Cole, US Embassy and other similar bombings to give the "official" explanations credibility.

Much like the many military "exercises" being carried out around the county, the Occupy movement was treated as a test run on handling a larger scale street fight in the US. A fight they are preparing for at an astounding speed, buying guns and ammunition to arm not just police, virtually all US government agencies and even postal workers, but now military battalions being stationed in US cities while armed drones are dispatched overhead. Talk about a preemptive strike.

And the latest trigger pins?

Try the new black vs white racist provocations the press is fanning such as the deliberately sparked race riots, or the induced Islamophobia and migration madness now metastasizing in western society, or the revival of the cold war and WW3 fear syndrome against Russia. How about the NSA revelations and "re-education camps" now in the public information domain? Or the insane actions of the TSA or local police, or the inflammatory rhetoric regarding anything anti-government, resorting to labeling anything contrary to the status quo or mainstream propaganda as "home grown terrorism"?

It's sick, it's staged, and it's designed to provoke a response... and is dutifully bilked for every media minute they can get to create the problem-reaction-solution scenario they so love and thrive on.

What Do We Do?

Our conscious confrontation needs to be at a deeper level of awareness. While we need to make our voices known, relegating all apparent public expression to some angry demonstration will not just go practically nowhere, but play right into the Controllers' hands.

We need to express, but smartly. We need to first of all be fully aware of what we're up against, its full dimensions and implications, but then infiltrate at the grass roots level in any way we're called and be consciously disciplined about it.

A good singular example of this is "Food Sovereignty Activism" that perfectly encapsulates what one person's actions can do. And this is just one of many thousands of examples. But I dare say confronting a police battalion in public and getting your head bashed in by those robots might not do much more than piss people off more, thanks to a twisted complicit media.

Demonstrating is not all bad and there's clearly a time for it. This is especially true within public governmental chambers and places of local decision making or bringing attention to issues such as GMOs, fracking infringements and people losing their homes. Just don't play into one of their traps, usually fueled via controlled opposition.

Hit the Matrix Where It Hurts

Motivation comes in all forms, but we must behave smartly. We need to hit where it hurts the matrix the most and empowers as many as possible. Some ideas:

#1. Inform. True information clears the deck. It neutralizes the effects of the enemy's propaganda. That has to be done first.

#2. Live in alignment with your convictions. We can't speak truth to the lie while living within its bondage. Break free, in any and every way we can. Screw the consequences if it's matrix stuff, it's not worth worrying about. "Lead, follow, or get out of the way" as they say.

#3. Persist. As we follow on in a conviction of the power of truth and love it will lead each of us on to more ways of having a greater effect. People respond to courage and conviction.

#4. Teach others. Mainly by example. If you live a committed life and have paid the price of giving up a cozy life of security for one of spiritual and interactive fulfillment and are helping to change the world, others will be prodded to do more themselves. We don't want to cram anything down anyone's throats. We live by the example of commitment the enlightening love of the truth displays for itself.

#5. Act locally. Find or create local communities of active and awake people. Whether it's a food co-op or meet up groups to discuss how to change your town or city for the better, this is where we need to operate from. With the world crashing around us we need to find each other and work and build together on every front. (See FullCircleProject.net for ways to get started.)

All the while continuing to broadcast the truth in any way we can.

After all, what else is there to live for?

The Pernicious Power of Partial Truth

Here's the problem. It's not the awakened and informed that get ensnared by partial truths. It's those that have yet to find full awareness and gain a real conscious perspective. It thwarts real investigation and shunts the unwary up the garden path to Numbsville.

This is what politics and social engineering thrive on.

Do you think people would go along with complete frontal lies continually? While it seems our Orwellian society has degraded to something pretty close to that, there has to be something that appears to relate to people's everyday experience, no matter how engineered that is as well. It may be a relative truth within an entire fabricated system, but still it's something someone can relate to.

The Alternative Dilemma

What has been labelled the alternative community, alternative research community or truth community is in a bit of a quandary. It's nothing new. Whenever you have an implied or perceived polarity this kind of lumping together by the mind happens. Strangely enough almost every time our low level thinking does this polarized perception it's wrong and a false choice.

Same with this mainstream vs alternative polarity. Very lumpy thinking but deal with the concept we must.

The right/left political paradigm is a good, obvious example. A totally false premise yet a whole fabricated system is built around it making it appear legitimate. You're allowed two choices, neither of which is in the least bit viable. How many things in this life are like that. "You're either with us or you're with the terrorists." Really?

When you realize all this is a holographic projection based on intention and participation you can work backwards and see how pervasive and restrictive that limited mind thinking really is and understand why it falls for all these tricks.

With the alternative news media concept it's a little more clear the dichotomy people face with respect to where they get their information. From a mainstream perspective, the alternative press is anything outside of their accepted realm and "trusted" sources. They don't look at the details much except to accept the mainstream definition and have total disdain for anything so-called "alternative". This is why they've turned the word conspiracy into a broad brushing pejorative, when in fact it's the best, most concise, truth telling term one could use.

Why? Because this is exactly what it is.

Within the alternative news community there is obviously a lot more diversity than the flatfooted mainstreamer could ever imagine. They won't touch it, or if they do it's a couple of accidental hits or doubt-filled super skeptical queries they venture to look into. There are those that get an eye opener and it leads to new worlds of information, but I'm describing the general perception.

Amongst the overall "alternative" or non-mainstream community there are loads of dynamics at work. Which is wonderful. The truly enlightened can tell what's what and understand there are many ideas and theories and approaches and they learn from anything they can. There's no fear because they're grounded in truth and not jumping on any bandwagon that happens to roll by just because it's so called "alternative".

Moles, Cling-Ons and Psyops

Of course this ugly stuff goes on. There's also controlled opposition like the mainstream co-opting partial truthers like Glenn Beck who apparently thinks he's a radical or something. Just look at the employers, paychecks and big egos of these types if nothing else. Wittingly or not, so many are manipulated not just by selfish interests but by Zionist interests, big banks, corporate and political influences, secret societies and occult powers. That's the name of the game. That's who's running the external show. So by definition if someone isn't fully conscious and free from all that, they are being tooled around by them in some fashion.

Especially people in the media where the projected illusion is so all important.

But in the alternative world it can get pretty tricky. The labyrinth of the rabbit hole is practically endless so just about anything goes when you really get into the big picture and are trying to excavate the truth from the rubble of lies and sealed off compartments you find. So most of us are willing to consider most anything and at least take a look at it. You eventually develop an intuitive sense about things, but even that stretches and changes as more becomes apparent and your consciousness grows.

We realize we relatively know less and less in the grand scheme of things, and that's a good, wise attitude.

The Spaghetti Test – Observe and Stay Detached

As I've often said, I use what I call the spaghetti test when processing information. Not the perfect analogy, but it demonstrates several truths. You know when you first learned to make spaghetti and the test was to see if it stuck to the wall or not? If it did it was done. Messy but effective.

That's one way to approach it. If it sticks, OK, leave it there for now. Sometimes things fall away later on. The main point is to sort of leave it out there and just keep going. Something later may confirm or contradict it, or it's just lower level information that's leading you to somewhere Universe is taking you. That's the fun part, watching synchronicity lead the way.

The number one lesson I'd say is to stay the observer when it comes to information. Detachment is the key. The mind is working along with your consciousness to process whatever you're coming across so beware of getting attached to ideas and concepts and the allure of "sexy" information. It's whenever we get attached we get ourselves in trouble – whether it be to a what could become a dogmatic concept, belief or an outcome, we need to constantly let go; it's a matter of conscious awareness survival.

As Aristotle aptly said, "It is the mark of an educated mind to be able to entertain a thought without accepting it."

Look at the billions who've been sidetracked and hijacked and joined these confining mind controlled religions or belief systems or the like. We've all been in some form of a belief system or another even if just school or the overall system. The good news is the struggling to get free from that chrysalis, or a series of them, is what pushes the blood into the wings of the conscious, liberated butterfly to-be.

Snakes and Rats in the Labyrinth

We have enemies. Truth has enemies. Humanity has enemies. Just as you see the alphabet agencies infiltrate militia groups or persuade patsies to participate in some false flag scheme, the same is true in the truth community. That's a given. We see the trolls and phony social media perps all the time and we each have those sites we're wary of. Expect even more.

Information is the name of the game and if they can't shut us down, they'll try to trip up, divert and divide us.

Or discredit us. But you know what? I'm not that worried about that. While some want to be watchdogs and stop people from firing off their theories as happened with the Sandy Hook reaction for example, people need to decide for themselves and feel free to express themselves if they're sincere. It's like that insane criticism of the Occupy movement. "What's your message? You have no united voice or clear agenda..." blah blah. Yeah, so they could sculpt one for us and divert it into one of their controlled arms. Such is collectivism.

Besides, nothing would have satisfied the critics.

At least it was an expression of life, as well as protest. Sure, Soros and his dirty ilk are always up to no good and there we all kinds of plants and agents provocateur, but something else also happened– an energizing and coming to real realizations of what we're all up against from people of all walks of life. The political stuff all missed the real issues and there was a lot of short sighted frustration, but instead of listening to what people were saying and learning what people were upset about, all the major media could do was belittle and mock and criticize. That says it all right there.

But muzzle ourselves? OK, admonitions are good and needed at times, but freedom of expression needs to be exactly that. And we're not here to impress or win over the mainstream. Anyone with that idea is headed for frustration and disaster. They will not listen, but we are affecting them despite that.

But individuals will listen. Let's be sure to address people and not the illusion.

The Half-Truthers Are the Most Dangerous

There are a few things I think are important to look for in an information source. Assuming it's not already coming from one of the major media outlets I evaluate along these lines:

1. Is the information fundamentally on the right track?

2. Is the source more interested in notoriety and self promotion than the issues, or is heavily weighed down by those egoic influences?

3. Are there any obvious compromises, or glaring omissions that could be intentional?

4. Are they loving? Is the message one of love, for the good of mankind and its freedom, even if it blasts away at the lies of the matrix?

5. Are they really fully awake and conscious? Or at least on their way to "getting it" and humble and sincere in their quest?

6. Are they heart led more than mind? Can you sense the passion behind the information and ideas?

7. Does yours or a trusted associate's bullshit detector go off repeatedly regarding that source?

Big egos are a dead giveaway. That's why for all the good Jesse Ventura might do in getting some truths out there, he's anchored in trying the impress the system and be accepted. That's why he's the go-to guy for the Piers Morgan types and he gets away with what he puts in his show. I have the same askance take on Ancient Aliens and those History and Nat Geo channel productions and these Michio Kaku type spokespeople no matter how much good info is presented.

And I think that's a healthy attitude.

A lot of truth perhaps but they are always busy shoving some serious agenda down your throat sideways and most people have no idea it's happening to them. You can't lead a sheep down the path with stuff that smells like poison. There's gotta be something that gets their trust and attention that appears to be real food.

Partial or manipulated truths inoculate the masses against the full truth. Partial truth is fine with them–it doesn't shake anyone up, and it doesn't concertedly challenge their precious matrix.

Whereas whole fully conscious truth blows their whole frikking control system to smithereens.

Perceived "Truth" Can Be A Control System - Or Diversion

We should know our sources as best we can, and take from them what truths we can glean. None of us has everything figured out or are so supra-conscious we can discern or understand it all. We learn as we go.

The problem arises in the direction the spirit of some information takes us. There can be lots of truth head to toe but if it's being used to manipulate you into some controllable viewpoint or belief system or some sycophantic all-trusting relationship that stunts your growth and ensnares you, that's wrong.

Supposed whistleblowers who enjoy high profile publicity like Edward Snowden or Wikileaks are examples of diversion. While much of what they've been given to "leak" is true, it diverts attention from much more profound revelations the controllers would rather not have come to light.

In addition, carefully gauged leaks work to condition the public mind to accept programs long under way so the next stages won't be too much of a leap.

Truth As Bait

People are baited with the truth all the time. They're led down pathways that seem to have all the fixings, but they meet frustration and futility and get waylaid into a sort of stillborn mode. It's very sad as many were really looking but unwittingly took one of these engineered detours.

That's all the matrix does. It's a lie and leads you round and round to nowhere, spinning your wheels as they vamp off your energy, getting you to support and feed the system. If it takes a few truths to get you to comply and stay sedated, so be it.

Besides, sometimes they're just pulling a release valve maneuver, letting it appear they're getting it and we're having an effect to satisfy the general angst. That can stop people dead in their tracks from the hot pursuit they were on.

If we get deceived into thinking they're listening and believe this type of fake remorse or hopey changey bullshit or whatever false promise they make, we cool our jets and lose momentum.

They're liars and we cannot stop short and compromise. Conscious awareness knows no compromise.

Conclusion

Controlled opposition specializes in half truths and buses to nowhere, so it pays to exercise extreme caution in this world of mines and booby traps. There's nothing to fear. Lies don't hold any real weight except to the swallower.

The truth can take care of itself.

We don't need to censor or protect the "truth community", the truth does that. There is no political collective, only consciousness and our underlying connectivity to each other and the entire Universe. That's a force to reckon with–and tap into and utilize as much as we can.

Staying detached is imperative. When we get invested in static or defined collective notions we're limiting consciousness. Who knows what's at hand? Or what magnificent twist Universe will come up with? Maybe it's already under way and about to manifest. Where will these heavily attached designs be then?

Stay free. And have a good laugh about it all. That's a good place to start. And finish.

"Enlightenment is a destructive process. It has nothing to do with becoming better or being happier. Enlightenment is the crumbling away of untruth. It's seeing through the facade of pretense. It's the complete eradication of everything we imagined to be true." -Osho

The Manu-fractured Modern Mind

This phenomenon can seem apparent but it's quite profound when you break it down. If you watch any mainstream propaganda with an alert viewpoint it appears clear at the outset, but the underlying mechanics may be surprising. Not only are American minds in particular being targeted for total subversion and coercion, but this systematic method of indoctrination via fragmentation is shockingly powerful.

"Altered" or fractured thinking is their modus operandi. Divide and Conquer from the get go, right inside the mind.

An alter is another identity, another persona (ancient Latin for mask). This strange, implanted assumption we've subconsciously assimilated is that we have and operate from several personas and that we have to deal with all of them sequentially somehow. Not in an integrated manner but in a fractured manner, where everything operates as independently as possible, set off by societal triggers.

It works much like Pavlov's dog drooling at the sound of the bell, similar to the system of school alarms between classes and a host of stimulus-response mechanisms in society.

Coincidence, or deliberate programming and entrainment?

Normal Is Not Normal

Being one person in one situation and another in another is fundamentally wrong and unconscious. People today have work personas and home personas, sports personas and party personas, sex personas and church personas. And on and on… and it's accepted. It's fundamentally fractured from the get go.

But that's just on the surface. Many other deeper, psychologically fractured levels are being manipulated.

Living a lie isn't that hard now, is it?

You may say that's just human nature, it's always been like that. Well, sadly it has been like that quite a bit, but that doesn't make it right. Why is it people are always trying to find themselves or are looking for unity in the world?

They have serious psychological schisms and disorders, and the social fabric is so regimented yet so confusing. Should we take this compartmentalization as routine as we're chopped into bite sized portions in their demographic charts?

Where does this programming have its roots?

Isn't there such a thing as natural self expression?

Born At War and Kept At War

There's a lot of discussion in psychology, philosophy and spiritual teachings about the fundamental conflict we seem to have been born into. The right brain/left brain studies and similar research are notable in this respect. We hear about the creative side vs the logical fight or flight side, the higher self vs the baser survival self.

We've all experienced some element of this basic fundamental conflict. Is there something to be learned or are we determined to be who we are?

When lower level instincts get aroused and we lash out in anger or violence only to regret it later is quite an experience. This cold and analytical viewpoint vs the loving, warm and creative impulse is something we've all experienced.

Now think about modern society, specifically the media and mass entertainment outlets. What are they playing on? Have you ever played sports with good friends but became this competitive animal that got so wrapped up in winning you became super combative over some foul or bad call? Especially if it was an intentional foul in your viewpoint? Someone else steps in to your existence.

It's the other wolf, and he gets fed a nice piece of psychic red meat.

The Two Wolves - A Cherokee Legend

An old Cherokee is teaching his grandson about life. "A fight is going on inside me," he said to the boy.

"It is a terrible fight and it is between two wolves. One is evil - he is anger, envy, sorrow, regret, greed, arrogance, self-pity, guilt, resentment, inferiority, lies, false pride, superiority, and ego." He continued, "The other is good - he is joy, peace, love, hope, serenity, humility, kindness, benevolence, empathy, generosity, truth, compassion, and faith. The same fight is going on inside you - and inside every other person, too."

The grandson thought about it for a minute and then asked his grandfather, "Which wolf will win?"

The old Cherokee simply replied, "The one you feed."

The point here is the base duality that can be emphasized and played upon, which can then be divided over and over into further fractioning of the mind and spirit.

The Psycho Sexual Indoctrination Process

Here's a perfect example. It's still implied that sex is wrong and evil and something to be ashamed of and to hide. Yet sex is heavily promoted and used in every possible way to lure and hypnotize and entice into seemingly dark places of guilty pleasure for all types of reasons.

Then it's either internal guilt, or sexual harassment if you stare or dare to touch what's being flagrantly flaunted.

Which voice are you to believe? Which response is the right one? Dress like a tart or stay clear of the subject...when you know you can't? Sex is a natural thing. It's humanly impossible to avoid as it's a wonderful fact of life. What are you going to believe? Just look at the erotic visuals you're bombarded with all day long and how they're designed to twist your gut.

Appealing to man's most basic instincts with manipulative abandon.

And this is just one example.

The Fear Agenda

This too seems to be quite apparent but let's see how they fragment the mass mind with this.

First there is the secure citizen. "Yeah, I am a proud individual in the land of the free and home of the brave." Really? While the patriot flags wave and music plays and sports gladiators celebrate the combat society, another split in society's structure roars on.

Brazenly promoted team loyalties that people will die for are oppositional programming. And the backdrop? A massively induced "fear of enemies" to their precious prison, both outside and now inside. The possibility of random terrorist attacks anywhere at anytime sure gives a nice sense of security. What does that drive you to? Support anything supposedly protecting you from having this freedom taken.

What a set up.

It's constant insecurity as people vacillate between feeling so free to a sense of being under attack. Apply this to the banking situation–save your money but then they take it. Get a job but you lose it or there aren't any. Stay healthy yet they feed us toxic waste; be prepared for an emergency but if you move off grid or have more than 5 days of food you're a suspected domestic terrorist.

Divide and rule, from the mind on through the fabric of society. Why? A united people would sober up and recognize how they're being diddled by self serving psychopathic elitist dirtbags.

How about that classic of all dividers, religion. Talk about us vs them indoctrination. Add some religious zeal to your schizophrenic paranoia and let the wars begin.

But what does this all come from? Let's look at the Hegelian Dialectic and Cognitive Dissonance again.

How Does This Side-Taking Affect Us?

The Hegelian Dialectic – More subversive than you can imagine: (from the Crossroad website)

"The Hegelian dialectic is the framework for guiding our thoughts and actions into conflicts that lead us to a predetermined solution. If we do not understand how the Hegelian dialectic shapes our perceptions of the world, then we do not know how we are helping to implement the vision. When we remain locked into dialectical thinking, we cannot see out of the box.

"Hegel's dialectic is the tool which manipulates us into a frenzied circular pattern of thought and action. Every time we fight for or defend against an ideology we are playing a necessary role in Marx and Engels' grand design to advance humanity into a dictatorship of the proletariat. The synthetic Hegelian solution to all these conflicts can't be introduced unless we all take a side that will advance the agenda. The Marxist's global agenda is moving along at breakneck speed. The only way to completely stop the privacy invasions, expanding domestic police powers, land grabs, insane wars against inanimate objects (and transient verbs), covert actions, and outright assaults on individual liberty, is to step outside the dialectic. This releases us from the limitations of controlled and guided thought.

"Today the dialectic is active in every political issue that encourages taking sides. We can see it in environmentalists instigating conflicts against private property owners, in democrats against republicans, in greens against libertarians, in communists against socialists, in neo-cons against traditional conservatives, in community activists against individuals, in pro-choice versus pro-life, in Christians against Muslims, in isolationists versus interventionists, in peace activists against war hawks. No matter what the issue, the invisible dialectic aims to control both the conflict and the resolution of differences, and leads everyone involved into a new cycle of conflicts."

Cognitive Dissonance

It's well known now that mind control techniques have been at work on humanity for some time. From crude early experiments to electronic and otherwise mass mind manipulation, it's the manipulators' control weapon of choice.

It takes many forms, including electromagnetic and even scalar augmentation, but its groundwork has been laid by decades of social engineering. Another of those known behavioral attributes for mental manipulation and easy exploitation is cognitive dissonance. (from MasqueradeBehindtheMask)

"The theory of cognitive dissonance in social psychology proposes that people have a motivational drive to reduce dissonance by altering existing cognitions, adding new ones to create a consistent belief system, or alternatively by reducing the importance of any one of the dissonant elements.It is the distressing mental state that people feel when they "find themselves doing things that don't fit with what they know, or having opinions that do not fit with other opinions they hold." A key assumption is that people want their expectations to meet reality, creating a sense of equilibrium.Likewise, another assumption is that a person will avoid situations or information sources that give rise to feelings of uneasiness, or dissonance.

"Cognitive dissonance theory explains human behavior by positing that people have a bias to seek consonance between their expectations and reality. According to Festinger, people engage in a process he termed "dissonance reduction", which can be achieved in one of three ways: lowering the importance of one of the discordant factors, adding consonant elements, or changing one of the dissonant factors.This bias sheds light on otherwise puzzling, irrational, and even destructive behavior."

Now imagine having that behavioral knowledge while executing massive false flag events such as Oklahoma City or 9/11 and how effective it could be with the right "guiding" of a carefully groomed mass mind.

Piece of cake.

Central Drain or True Unity?

What's again ironic in all this and again deliberately mind-bending is the incessant mantra for a "united world", a "one world government" as the controllers keep fragmenting every aspect of our lives. Why is this? Besides being another cognitive dissonant signal bringing the unwary to their mind-numbed knees, it gives a false centralized goal much like the spiraled ploy of the snake oil hypnotist or a whirlpool twisting to take down its prey.

In fact humanity is looking for true unity, but in truth and love and honesty. The world we are being slammed with by these corrupt controllers has none of that in mind, only control and exploitation.

Therein lies the problem. It is not "mankind" being corrupt. It is not "human nature" run amok. It is the craven efforts of a few to exert their dominion over the masses. It is an invasive, aggressive parasitic minority attempting to hijack the majority.

And this is just one aspect of their assault.

Let's keep exposing these sick bastards.

Personal Notes:

Anesthesia - Queen of Cryptocracy

Sounds exotic, but it's true. The system's gone nuts, things have cut loose. And while an ever widening swathe of humanity is rippling into various levels of awakening, those still under the spell of the matrix' hypnotic sirens are falling ever deeper into a drugged slumber.

And it's all by design.

Humanity's been carefully anesthetized. Things are moving so fast and crazy and in so many weird directions now it's tantamount to mass insanity.

Yet despite the awakened people screaming and pointing out the in-your-face lies and affronts to humanity, most still don't even notice, and that's the weirdest thing of all.

That polarization is what compounds the problem, and that's why the cryptos love to try to divide us in every way they can.

Beware. False flags and media circus events are carefully placed and timed psycho-spiritual detonation devices with clear intentions at many levels.

The biggest division you won't hear a peep about in the mainstream is between those who dare to wake up to reality vs. those who continue on within the projected mind frame. That would be a clear admission that their reality ain't necessarily so, so they have to mock, demonize and ignore our very existence.

But we won't be ignored any longer.

As Gandhi aptly said, "First they ignore you, then they ridicule you, then they fight you, and then you win."

Medication and Conditioning, Bread and Circus, Omission and Denial

And that is where the great schism lies. The awake and aware have snapped out of the control system. Those who haven't are being tooled around like puppets on a million nano strings. When you don't know, you don't know that you don't know...and are very easy to keep being fooled.

When you've woken up, the world is completely reversed from everything you were told and once believed. You now know that you now know. And everything rights itself and all is clear.

It takes some cobweb clearing to get a handle on the real picture but it happens, and in a relative hurry. truth drives itself.

It always does.

How do they maintain this illusion? Mental conditioning is the name of the game for the designers and propagators of the matrix. Once the pattern is established in its captive subjects, the more you can pour the lies on without them being noticed. Also disguised is the fact that their every intention for humanity is for control and exploitation....at any cost or consequence to these expendable "human resources". Us.

Oh, how their attitude says it all. And stinks in the nostrils of loving truth.

To achieve this conditioning requires quite an effort on their part, because we are ultimately irrepressible and they know that. It's like chemtrails. If they don't keep spraying the required concentration of their toxic soup the effects start to wane, like the fluoride dosing and the rest. They have to maintain it or it wears off. To keep the vast majority sleep walking they every method possible and it's really quite mind boggling when it all comes together.

But it's also inspiring...because no matter what they do to us they can't put us out of commission. Unless they kill us off entirely but then they'd lose their work force. Besides, that's just a promotion to the next level.

Tools that Numb

But what specifically do they control us by? They flood our bodies with drugs delivered by any means possible; deprivation of nutrition, sunlight and clean air water and food; dumbed down education and a fully controlled media; mind numbing false news and so-called entertainment; electromagnetic smog blasting on the human nervous system wavelength; violence and oppressive fear and terror tactics, and on and on.

They do this with impunity. Imagine the world is a massive internment camp where the captors give the illusion the inmates are free by letting them have a few choices within this massive, worldwide facility, and disguise the barbed wire fence as gorgeous murals, and the control devices as modern marvels for their advancement.

Think wars—there's a perfect example. All for our "defense, safety and security", when it's the exact opposite.

Basic Simple Questions

Some fundamental questions that beg answers that are evident before any clear thinking individual:

–How can a government usurping monstrosity like the United Snakes Corporation and its affiliate thugs gang rape a planet and make it look benevolent?

–How can obviously lying elitist politicians bought off by the highest bidder be taken as serious representatives in governing institutions?

–How can known secretive government sponsored agencies pull off assassinations and staged shootings in plain sight?

–How can the most murderous, supremacist, fascist, arrogant, racist people on earth be called "the chosen ones" and given title to anything they want including their own sanctioned Zionist territory and ravenous agenda and be given complete religious, social and political immunity along with massive financial support?

–How can sweeping freedom destroying measures be instituted by "executive order" in a representative republic?

–How can the food, water and air be deliberately poisoned in public knowledge and in plain sight?

–How can electro-surveillance, mental manipulation and genetic tampering be known and accepted as legitimate human altering science and be in full implementation for mass control?

….And on and on…why wouldn't people of such an abused group not go on a full on rampage against its rulers and their minions?

The Hypnotic Rhythm of Anesthesia

Every day I'm just amazed how few seem to notice what's going on. The business as usual behavior, shallow chatter about nothing and the complete dependence on routine behavior for money and phony goals is just mind-boggling.

While the wake up is showing real promise, clearly there won't be a world in which to live those goals if things aren't changed drastically.

The day we hope our children and grandchildren to grow up in is quickly becoming not just night, but a literal nightmare if the current course isn't derailed.

In the movie *Time Machine* from one of globalist insider H.G. Wells' predictive programming pieces, when the siren sounds the humans grazing on the surface of the earth hypnotically walk into the maw of that archonic image whereupon they are devoured by the hellish beasts that live in the earth.

Despite this meme of being fodder for other beings shown to mankind for eons via literature or inside messengers, humanity doesn't get it. It's another great way to hide the truth; sci-fi or story-fy it. Turn the real direction of the controllers into a fiction, a fantasy, entertainment, while subconsciously conditioning these subjects to accept such a fate.

"A tale told by an idiot full of sound and fury, signifying nothing" as Shakespeare famously said through Macbeth.

Who's Behind This?

I'm convinced there's something very occult and spiritual that is ultimately behind all of this, and these described techniques are just to augment the signal from the bowels of the matrix. It's same as the way chemtrails enable the EMFs and scalar devices to manipulate weather patterns, earth changes and mind manipulation. These occult influences provide an enhanced medium for their designs to take effect.

That a manipulative signal is being broadcast attempting to make us subjects of another realm there is no doubt.

And that just reminds me that I'm not part of it and how free I am. Extremely free. And that has power. Wonderful, conscious, awakening power that reverberates throughout the morphic field.

That is called having a good day. You have one too.

And keep on resonating. Powerfully.

Personal Notes:

Part 4 - Taking Action

Personal Notes:

Taking Action -
The Shortcut to Now

I'm the first to admit it seems to be tough to get off our butts sometimes and do or be what's right. It's a continual struggle. We're all human and have the same battles, trials, tests and temptations.

The really ironic thing is that when we're struggling we're missing the point right out of the gate.

When we're struggling it's time to transcend what's going on around us and get conscious. When we respond consciously it immediately gets easier. While being fully here and Now is the objective and this realization is complete unto itself, there's a very practical daily path that leads to fully living this realization and all the life changes it implicates.

And it should rock your world – or you may not be getting the full message. The last thing I want to do is over-spiritualize our situation. We need to take action and now.

Always More Than Meets the Eye

Obviously there's a lot we're not consciously aware of. And while it's good to learn more continually, it's not what should be our main motivation. Our driving force is spiritual breath and existing and acting responsibly according to consciousness. Being as fully awake and aware as possible and experiencing the infinite cosmos to its deepest depth one day at a time is our enlightened life.

All else will be fulfilled in its time, but nothing is important enough to postpone living consciously.

What that means to each of us individually is our unique experience. Especially when we find out the radical changes and responsibilities that come with it and we have to make some serious decisions. Hence the challenge to find that out for ourselves, which then needs to be accompanied by a full willingness to go with wherever the awakening takes our souls.

Up to it? Sorry, you're stuck with it.

Overcome Inertia by Conscious Awareness – and Action

Some more irony to keep in mind. We're already where we're supposed to be. Getting to Now is simply realizing you're already in it and expanding within the moment. The answers we seek are within us. When it comes to necessary actions such as disentangling from contracts with the matrix be they spiritual, economic, legal, social or literal, the action is made when the decision is reached. The rest just follows.

It's getting fully in the Now where we'll find the clarity to make conscious assessments and decisions and maintain our daily being where we are.

We've been actively full time disengaging for many years, getting every little tentacle and spider's web detached from the existence that is our lives. But it all happened when we made the decision to fully disengage. The rest just followed. Getting rid of wrong attachments does take time in most cases, since we're so flipping registered and seemingly bound with all their damned paperwork and the stuff we accumulate, never mind the social contracts.

But do it we must.

In reality it's all a form of "make-believe" that we brought into existence. But cutting the ties does need to be done, stuff needs to be jettisoned, and your new more mobile "backpack" has to be carefully planned and packed with what you do need in order to carry on.

And it's way better to have it done now than have to do it under duress...or even worse perhaps not being able to do it at all nor able to escape the snare of the matrix when it starts constricting on you.

The wonderful thing is we've been having a blast during the whole process, already doing what we love to do without waiting for some future set up, and knowing each step we're right where we're supposed to be. Part of that for us is staying on the move, enjoying new sights and meeting new, wonderful people. But most of all it's been sharing what we're learning as far and wide as we can, and learning from others as we go.

Welcome–or Beware–the Accountability Factor

One of the biggest factors to me is accountability. When anyone has been confronted with any real truth they are now put on notice. This is especially true when the truth is made so screamingly clear with the passion and love and commitment of so many of today's truth warriors.

Will people really respond to the call to activate, or put it off? Once the truth has been laid out so plainly Universe moves in. For those who respond in greater commitment and action there is greater power and synchronicity. For those who don't, there will be confusion, doubt, false justification and spiritual impotence.

What we're witnessing now in society is this very polarization. Those who've let the light of truth in and are making the needed changes versus those who resist it. It will be interesting to monitor how this continues to play out. We do know that as empires became more and more barbaric it's always been the sign of the end of that civilization. The truth of the inhumanity of the tyrants of the day became plain to see and this accountability factor kicked into high gear and people took action out of necessity.

The power of the information revolution we are all a part of is just this. Creating awareness precipitates a crisis. A good one. If we can bring on this dynamic the power structure will crumble under its own false weight as the infinite power of loving consciousness in growing numbers of awakened individuals shreds the fabric of the illusory matrix before it can do further damage.

Cutting Ties Cannot Wait

As the expression goes, "The difficult can be done immediately, the impossible takes a little longer."

This applies to moving according to consciousness. Some ties to compromising situations are pretty tough to break. It depends on people's level of commitment, but these ties eventually will fall away if you simply keep the flame alive and are true to consciousness. What you don't want to happen is that you compromise your convictions in order to co-exist in a lower vibration. That's the very definition of the world's claim to humanity's enslavement.

Fight that with everything in you.

Activation is a vibrational experience and needs to be fed and amplified in every possible way. Hang around the right people, not the dead heads and naysayers. Spend more time researching and getting charged up by true information and uplifting sources. Find your people, even if only on line as is the case with many of us. Then go see them. There are meet-up groups you can find on line as well and inspiring conferences and events to attend.

Light keeps the darkness away, and the greater the light we carry, the further we can see and less encumbered we are by daily nagging downers, be they personal interactions or spiritual affronts from darker realms that would like to hold us down. I realize many cannot fully break free just yet, but any and every way you can "loose the bands" in your daily life, the more juice you'll have for the next challenge towards greater and greater activism and effectiveness.

Come Anytime from Anywhere – Just Come

The coolest thing about waking up is finding yourself standing in the Now. It's as if you've always been there and just didn't know it. It doesn't matter when you entered the "Now", you're just there now and nothing else matters. Those who've been there a long "time" welcome you accordingly, we're all just there, that's all that matters. And the need to "stimulate the plasma" and activate and attract others into the Now field is all the more prevalent.

It's really that simple.

The point is clear: to reflect and transpond this energetic consciousness in a loving manner to help others do the same, and so contribute to Universe discovering itself, or however you want to conceptualize it. Love is kind, generous, caring and most of all responsive to the inherent need. It's the complete opposite of the selfish dog eat dog get-ahead competitive meme bullshit we've been handed.

It's all to keep us from discovering the magnificence of who we truly are. That's why the awake and aware go the exact opposite way of the world system.

Crunch Time – What Are You Waiting For?

If we don't respond to the need before us we're done. We've become dead spiritually. We've closed ourselves off and become part of the problem. You will suffer, and others will suffer. On the contrary, when we do respond consciously we bring light and love and it expands exponentially.

It takes guts to be conscious. Nothing big really, just an awakened conscience, but in this day and age you have to buck a lot of crap to do the right thing. These intimidating perpetrators of the big lie and their converts desperately need standing up to.

You're just meeting a need, as am I.

Be happy, and laugh in their programmed faces when they try to stop you. Never be daunted by the naysayers. Somewhere inside of them is a spark that knows you're right and inherently carries the same answer to everything that just may awaken in them one day. Once you've earnestly tried and they still reject it may be time to move on and head for greener pastures.

And when you do they might just sit up and take notice.

It's crunch time for responding to truth and consciousness. We're slipping into an increasingly "now or never" scenario. Responding to consciousness is something that cannot be put off lest the illusory wheels of time grind past the precious portals of opportunity.

Now is all that matters.

Let's be in it, and do the conscious thing.

"At the center of your being you have the answer; you know who you are and you know what you want." – Lao Tzu

Personal Notes:

Waking Up, Speaking Up and Stepping Out

I often pose the question why more people aren't voicing their outrage and concerns about what's going on in the world regarding the many programs being executed upon humanity in plain sight to all. I know this isn't always easy to present to others, especially in certain circumstances, the most challenging of which is amongst close friends and loved ones who haven't woken up to these realities yet.

As many of you know I've talked about this challenge many times. Many of the commenters on the ZenGardner.com website are extremely helpful to others who bring up this topic, usually regarding a mate who just doesn't get it yet, although this often involves siblings, children and close friends as well.

I face the same challenges. This is an extremely common phenomenon and completely understandable. After all, awakening to a monumental shift in consciousness and perception is a very personal and ultimately individual experience, as it should be. However it's not necessarily a shared one. What compounds the issue is that those who do wake up and become aware of what's really going on usually become quite passionate researchers, only to find more and more evidence confirming the magnitude and wonder of this paradigm shift, including both horrific as well as empowering realities never perceived before.

Stepping Out to Share the Truth

I received the following email including a suggestion to cover this topic more thoroughly which prompted this article;

"I recently attended a metaphysical fair where I had the opportunity to talk to a young lady and an older man. Each had their own booth at this fair.

For the first time since my awakening, I admitted out loud that I am a conspiracy theorist.

It felt really good. Sort of like coming out of the closet. Perhaps the reason we are not shouting it from the rooftops is that we haven't been able to admit it to very many people.

What was really surprising was that the young lady said oh, my husband is one too but I'm not and the older man said yes, I am one too but my wife is not.

That got me thinking how difficult it must be to keep their relationship together.

I bet there are many couples in this same predicament. This may be a good topic for an article. Thanks for being there for all of us "conspiracy theorists."

What she did in this simple act of stepping out is extremely important. As she put it, she "came out." That's when the ball starts to roll. Of course we should be as loving and considerate and wise as we possibly can, but to muzzle the truth is never the answer. The wonderful dynamic that kicks in as we exercise this new found "muscle" is that we gain the necessary tools and insights to know how to proceed.

Some will hear some of the information gladly, most will dismiss it, and many more will file it away while pretending it's just "conspiracy talk", only to hear it confirmed from someone else they talk to which starts taking it to deeper and deeper levels.

Lose the Fear – Declare Yourself, Wisely and in Love

I never stopped doing what I do since the time I fully woke up. I see no alternative. I don't bash my kids and grandkids or family and friends over the head with it, especially when it's during one of our family get togethers that aren't that frequent, although I have overdone it on occasion. But they know exactly where I stand. Thankfully after many years now it's they who tell me how bad the chemtrails have been, or bring up some issue that is getting more mainstream coverage like GMOs or the militarized police crack down and even obvious false flags now. But it's a slow process.

Always remember, the plant can't begin to grow if the seed was never planted.

Only recently my son found out the father of my oldest daughter's husband has gotten deep into alternative research so my son turned him on to my site. I never thought that would happen as he's always considered me "out there." But that's another of those types of indicators I often talk about that show how the awakening is not a pipe dream but very real and reaching new circles of people every minute.

Another phenomenon is that some people will accept some things but go off like a bomb when you touch something they just won't let go of, like Zionism. That's a big one, especially in the U.S. The programming has been so strong for so long it takes some doing for people to open up to that issue, never mind that WW2 and the holocaust were a massively engineered scam to justify the state of Israel and play the guilt and pity card for the century to come, amongst other designs. These are tough to swallow.

In those cases just feel out what it appears people are ready for, maybe softly introducing or mentioning other areas they might be interested in reconsidering. Once something takes hold and gets some traction they're engines will start and they'll begin searching the net on their own as well as asking questions to those they know.

The 9/11 Hurdle – A Golden Opportunity

9/11 is probably the biggest gateway hurdle of all when it comes to people really waking up. I'll bet there is a very high percentage of those awakened and now active who were jolted out of their hypnotic trance by coming to the startling realization that that entire hoax was executed by the very people who capitalized on it. Everything else quickly cascades from there.

Waking up to the massive aerosol geoengineering program is another such gateway to realizing all is not as it seems.

But again it all depends on how much people are willing to let go of their old paradigms, and it's not easy, as they just found out basically that it's all a lie – or soon will.

Each situation is unique but our backs are against the wall now and our very lives and those of our loved ones and people everywhere are at stake.

We can't remain silent or let ourselves be muzzled by those who don't get it and refuse to even consider any of this, never mind the scorn and ridicule that often gets showered on us as we speak up.

When it comes to couples and family members this is particularly challenging. Most people have serious doubts and loneliness and isolation issues when trapped in these seeming dead end relationships with loved ones and friends.

My advice is to judge the situation you are in by its effect on you, especially regarding yourself as an instrument of the truth the world so desperately needs to hear.

That to me is the bottom line. But you'll need to reach that conclusion on your own. Don't let any one else tell you what to do. Know your convictions and then act on them. Every situation is unique.

Loved ones do wake up over time, but some don't. It's up to each of us to judge for ourselves what our course of action is.

In the meantime, do not let anything or anyone muzzle the truth. The rest will become manifest.

Keep Moving, Reach the Receptive and Find Kindred Souls

The answer to handling that kind of constant resistance is to move on. Go where you're received. Find kindred souls locally or even on line as fast as you can to help bolster your convictions and widen your horizons. We each need that positive feedback and confirmation of our feelings and findings and sense of camaraderie, and thanks to the internet this is readily available at any time.

I moved on. And keep moving on. And I've made the dearest friends of my life in the process and never cease to be amazed at the depth and breadth of the wondrous "truth community," if you will. It's alive and growing at an astounding rate. Sure there are pitfalls, booby traps and trip-offs along the way, but that's how we learn.

We were forced to learn in a completely wrong way so as far as I'm concerned I like to see people re-learn how to learn and let them alone while they find their way. This is what strengthens us and attunes our discernment capabilities, even if we get misled now and again.

As long as we keep on with open and sincere hearts we'll each find our true way and come to realms of truth, conviction, love and empowerment that confirm our direction.

That we can be confident of.

Lose the fear. Keep learning, keep growing and keep sharing what you learn to be true in complete fearless confidence, no matter what reactions you encounter.

That's not your business. Yours and mine is to get the message out there in love and courageous peace and certainty.

Our very example of fearless confidence and loving, selfless motivation speaks the loudest.

Personal Notes:

Thinking Outside the Hourglass

This imposed artificial time constraint is a very subtle one, especially when you realize everything depends on perspective. We're clearly experiencing a manipulated, illusory cycle of time with parameters that make us feel contained, limited. And that's the intent. Closing in on your prey is an ingrained predatory behavior. If the subjects feel there's no escape, compliant behavior will eventually follow.

That's pretty clever on the part of the controllers, but it's only effective when you're not awake to what's going on.

Perceived containment has been proven time and again in even popular science to produce certain behaviors. Time is only one factor, but an important one as it is one of the more subtle ways they exert control and amplify fear. We cannot succumb to any of these false paradigms. Humanity is running to and fro in an effort to find solutions, but only within the confines they've been cleverly restricted to. It's a closed system with clearly defined limitations.

We look within their constructed time-framed and otherwise controlled system for solutions when there are none to be found.

The only true solution lies in conscious, transcendent awareness of the true big picture.

Playing By the Rules

Herein lies the big "catch." Similar to the obvious political right-left paradigm, we've been injected into a much more complex set of confining rules and regulations. They are adopted by assumption from the parameters we've been given. It's not possible to objectively discern our condition when we think we have all the information we need to make right decisions... when in reality we don't.

We have to find out for ourselves what the real facts and truths are. And even those need constant re-examination and regular conscious, aware assessment.

These same self-imposed authorities dictate our limitations within which we're to find solutions, when they very well know there are no solutions but theirs within those confines, whichever directed "side" people choose. To snap out of this hypnotic, severely limiting mind set is our first priority.

So Where Are We?

It's hard to say exactly. We can only describe the conditions and our awakened understandings as they surface. When we put those realizations into effect in our lives a wonderful spiritual detachment takes place and we see more clearly by the day.

Taking living action on these realizations precipitates the most radical transformations in our own lives as well as in those we influence. Those who don't take action are missing out, and that is the biggest travesty of mankind.

All while the imposed hourglass lets its ticking sands of time drop into a mirrored, carefully contained paradigm.

Our solution is really quite simple. Disengage, disconnect, and stop listening to their sirens of propaganda. It's much like getting off of a mind-numbing medication to where you can think clearly again. It takes time and some simple commitment. Your resolution becomes wanting to wake up, so you do what needs to be done, come what may.

Our current condition appears quite tenuous. We can go with the flow of lies and hunker down and just take it, or we can rise to the occasion. Rising means becoming individually what each of us is meant to be. Alive, awake, aware, conscious and activated and no longer stupefied by circumstances and false information. That may sound simplistic or ethereal but without that break each of us is doomed to repeat after them and their dictates. We'll follow, react, or as so many have done just give up and acquiesce in confusion and despair.

The world condition continues to deteriorate so rapidly that it's forcing just such unconscious decisions. Like it or not, imposed circumstances are herding the hive mindset into various corners of defensiveness – the patriots, the libertarians, the anarchists, the survivalists, and on and on, and most of all the clinging system adherents.

Don't get caught up in their game of false paradigms.

Our Opposition Is Spiritual

It's more important than ever to choose our battles wisely. Our challenge is spiritual first and foremost. What we're up against manifests and lives in the minds of men as an implanted psychotropic manipulative mindset. It's ugly, it's completely controller-serving and it's artificial.

Yet it grows as if it's organic.

It's not. Clearly all of creation is some kind of vibrational wave-form or another, but what we call evil apparently is a very conscious anti-organic life form. It seems to exist to destroy and manipulate to its own satisfaction for whatever anti-creative reason. Granted, an all-wonderful Universe has certainly taken all of this into consideration. A good example is the human body with its anti-bodies, white blood cells and amazing immune system. A microcosm of the macrocosm.

The nano and genetic manipulations, and the techno, geo-engineering and mind control technologies are further evidence of this invasive force. These are mind derived, howbeit composed of Universal components. Recognizing what we're up against is most of the problem.

It's Time for No Paradigm

There's no pat, blanket answer for everyone when it comes to knowing what to do. The matrix gives itself away by offering "group plans" and locked-in behavioral boxes to resort to for comfort and security. Awakening souls naturally rebel against such confines on our spirits but this engineered "group option plan" is pretty well bought by most of humanity, sad to say.

I've seen a lot of proposals for new world systems, and to be honest none of them appeal to me. They all smack of the same old control paradigm, but with new people and rehashed religiously inclined belief systems in charge. Some of these might seem nice in the short term but where would they lead us? My inclination is to believe it will be more of the same. Just like the encroaching new world order "big idea," they generally smell like more "hope and change" solutions that only signify more sophisticated control. This is especially true regarding the technologically based future worlds I've seen portrayed as the solution.

I can't even say what exactly it is I do champion except empowering individuals and community action. That's why my conviction has always been along the lines of personal awakening. When we get there we'll understand. Right now, people are generally fighting in the dark. And it makes no sense to make unconscious decisions without the full light of truth.

Get Active, Get Local

As I see it, information sharing and strengthening local community are our best bet. Creating this evolving revolution of loving interaction from the ground up is the manifestation of our new reality. Literally. Get back to the land and communication. Work locally in not just community gardening and cooperation, but to change minds and structural mindsets around us. It's the solution at hand.

That, and continuing to dissolve this world of lies via passionate dissemination of enlightened information. And that I'm happy to report is happening at an accelerating rate, as is the growth of indigenous, caring communities.

As the old dissolves, truth based reality evolves.

Let go of the old and be part of the new emergence.

We truly are the solution we've been waiting for.

Minesweeping for Truthers

"Being the change we want to see in the world" is first and foremost. Our lifestyles, disengagement from the matrix and raising of consciousness being paramount.

But with that comes activity. We cannot be consciously aware of what's truly going around us without being prompted and moved to tell others what's going on and doing something about what's set before us.

And you never know just what wonderful energy you might be releasing into the fray when someone you affect joins the Awakening.

No Stone Unturned or Tunnel Unexplored – The Passion for Truth

This expression, "don't leave one stone unturned" is a true searcher's motto. Whether it be forensics, detective work, investigative journalism or literal archeology. This clearly also applies to the passionate alternative researcher's methodology. Leave no part of the rabbit hole labyrinth unexplored.

Those who experience a genuine wake up go on a personal campaign of truth finding and have their lives so fundamentally altered they'll never be the same.

And many run with it. I was one, I went ballistic. How could you not try to scream from the housetops what you've found out when it's so vastly profound and all encompassing? Especially when the very lives of those you love and everything on the planet is at stake.

However, many get muzzled. Mostly by themselves, and worries about what others will think, i.e. fear of rejection or humiliation. The beauty of a true wake up though is you no longer care what others think in that regard. In fact, you don't want to convince others so much as get them looking for themselves. But there has to be something that gets them started.

It Just Takes One Spark to Ignite a Bonfire

You never know who you are influencing. At all times. Someone may be watching you from a distance, knowing what you're about to some degree, and is watching your life transform and whether you live up to what you claim is the truth. Some may be people who argue in your face, even close friends, who appear to reject everything you even start to say. In many cases they may be just testing you while actually thinking a whole lot more about what you're saying than it appears.

Many are at the end of a mind-blowing email with an eye-opening article or YouTube video that puts them over the top. Some visit a blog that leads to another that leads another and whamo! It hits home.

You never know.

It may be someone you discreetly stop and point out a heavily criss-crossed chemtrail sky to and the scales fall off their eyes, at least about that subject. I've seen it happen. A website and a few key words may set them into a massively changed and charged life of activism.

We never know.

If You Don't Tell Them, Who Will?

What if the person you get the pull to talk to is getting as close as they'll get to an awakened person at the time you happen across their path? It happens. There are always ways people can find the truth for themselves, but what if? What if the comment or gesture you would have made was the nudge that would have caused their life to veer in a completely different direction at a point that was just perfectly laid out by Universe?

Sure, there will be other chances, but when?

Especially with a world rushing headlong into a totalitarian clampdown. Then what chance will we have? The only way to respond is to respond in any way we can. I promise, if you get the boat in motion, the rudder will take effect.

Where's Waldo?

They're out there. You and I were out there. Now we're Here. Home at last in the eternal Now. Others are either still looking, or under a spell. I just want people to know that if you look with the eyes of expectancy and yield to that inner voice, you might just help wake up some amazing movers and shakers in addition to the other dear souls that will be ever grateful, each of whom will have a ripple effect as well.

We preach to ourselves a lot in this alternative media, but there's nothing wrong with it. We get inspired, educated and hence armed for battle, if you will. It's empowering and we need all the juice we each can get during these times. And it will be increasingly so in the days to come.

The wonderful thing is, better than solar or nuclear power, consciousness is infinite and always accessible.

As we learn to tap into the True resources more and more we're going to be seeing some amazing things in the days to come. When darkness falls, the light of truth appears to shine all the brighter.

But we need to reach out of our confines and bring this opportunity to awaken to many, many others.

Spontaneous Combustion

The wake up has its own wonderful dynamics which we can't begin to fully fathom. But we can each do our part to facilitate changes in situations we encounter, or find ways to broadcast the awakening and its loving, enlivening and enlightening vibrations for greater and greater availability.

Seeing someone catch fire with the truth and the passion of conscious, responsible awareness it engenders is perhaps the most gratifying experience anyone could encounter.

I had 3 one hour conversations with someone staying in the same accommodations I was at and she could not get enough. She works in one of, if not the biggest defense contractor firms in the world. She's down to earth and knew something was up, but when we embarked on the journey through the maze, one thing leading to another, there was not one place she couldn't see how what she had been told "ain't necessarily so." A few days later I overheard her on her phone to her daughter, who was at one of our long conversations, telling her daughter to "look up at the sky, the chemtrails are massive today".

A week earlier she never noticed them.

That's how it works. Where she goes with what she's now been introduced to, I do not know. But I sure like to imagine.

Keep the Awakening rolling. Look for openings and listen to the nudges.

Minesweeping for Truthers – it's a blast. Literally.

Personal Notes:

Being the Change, Tipping Points and Monkeys on the Loose

So many are asking, "What can I do? How can I make a difference? How do I go about helping to effect the changes the world so direly needs?"

Good questions.

I repeatedly say to people to get conscious and you'll know what to do. What does that mean? Gain empowering knowledge and information for one. And if someone's asking those questions they obviously know just where to find it. The exponentially growing body of information available on the internet is an opportunity of the ages.

Just look, read and learn.

Admittedly, growing up in a truly enlightened culture one wouldn't have to do all this searching and have so many lies and so much disinformation to get past. It is time and energy consuming, especially for young minds.

But it's our task to learn, and here we are, so let's do it. And commit to it. Stop spending any unnecessary time giving the matrix our attention and energy. It's bad enough if you have a job you don't particularly like, especially if it's helping to prop up this dying, vampiric system.

But don't cry about what you can or cannot do and sit in front of the TV all day, or stay muzzled in your life of conformity when you have an opportunity to speak up with what you already know.

Getting Conscious

When the information comes flooding in you will eventually develop a deep spirituality. The only way this vast Universe can possibly operate is by forces and powers outside our sensory perception. Call it what you will and religions have done a great job at trying to keep it in a box, but Something is behind all this and is way powerful and wonderful.

One long look at a clear night sky says it all.

Then develop that spirituality. As you venture into the worlds of esoteric knowledge the dots begin to connect, same as they do while you investigate what's really behind the scenes running the show here on earth as far as manipulated society goes. Then act on it. Meditate if that's an avenue that appears to have some validity for greater consciousness and awareness. Pray if you're so inclined. Chant, dance, sing, laugh, cry, scream....but act on it.

I remember reading a proverb, "The desire of a lazy man kills him, because his hands refuse to work." Hit home? It has for me many times.

Don't worry, we've all been there. But now's the time to act. And as your consciousness grows and changes start to take place, the next step(s) will always make themselves manifest; be it writing a blog and networking on the internet, attending or talking at gatherings, passing out flyers, hanging posters, talking to people you meet, joining or organizing meaningful, effective demonstrations, starting a youtube channel or blog or radio show, printing stickers or T-shirts, or just hugging and smiling and sharing love....or all of the above.

And help those already doing what you know is effective.

I'm sure you'll think of more. It's getting started that's important. The boat has to be in motion for the rudder to take effect.

It Matters – Every Bit Matters

Insignificance is a matrix illusion. Each of us is infinite potential and possibility. Each of us is the Universe. Each of us is eternal consciousness. Each of us is connected to everything... everything. When we change, everything changes. A perfect illustration of this is the idea of the Morphic Field I've written about. [See Change the Morphic Field...Change the World]

Quantum physics has made this idea a virtually accepted fact. The inter-connectivity and creative ability of consciousness is profound...and needs to be implemented in our thinking and way of life. Once we know how powerful we each are and what a profound effect we each have gets you off your duff and doing everything you can.

The Tipping Point

This is another empowering bit of information that conveys the power of change. It came out of a technical University study last year and was an encouraging discovery for those who were listening. According to this study, if just 10% of the population wake up (or what they call "committed opinion holders" have a change) it would turn society upside-down.

I've included the entire article as it's quite profound:

"In this visualization, we see the tipping point where minority opinion (shown in red) quickly becomes majority opinion. Over time, the minority opinion grows. Once the minority opinion reached 10 percent of the population, the network quickly changes as the minority opinion takes over the original majority opinion (shown in green). Credit: SCNARC/Rensselaer Polytechnic Institute

"Scientists at Rensselaer Polytechnic Institute have found that when just 10 percent of the population holds an unshakable belief, their belief will always be adopted by the majority of the society. The scientists, who are members of the Social Cognitive Networks Academic Research Center (SCNARC) at Rensselaer, used computational and analytical methods to discover the tipping point where a minority belief becomes the majority opinion. The finding has implications for the study and influence of societal interactions ranging from the spread of innovations to the movement of political ideals.

"When the number of committed opinion holders is below 10 percent, there is no visible progress in the spread of ideas. It would literally take the amount of time comparable to the age of the universe for this size group to reach the majority," said SCNARC Director Boleslaw Szymanski, the Claire and Roland Schmitt Distinguished Professor at Rensselaer. "Once that number grows above 10 percent, the idea spreads like a flame."

"As an example, the ongoing events in Tunisia and Egypt appear to exhibit a similar process, according to Szymanski. "In those countries, dictators who were in power for decades were suddenly overthrown in just a few weeks."

"The findings were published in the July 22, 2011, early online edition of the journal Physical Review E in an article titled "Social consensus through the influence of committed minorities."

"An important aspect of the finding is that the percent of committed opinion holders required to shift majority opinion does not change significantly regardless of the type of network in which the opinion holders are working. In other words, the percentage of committed opinion holders required to influence a society remains at approximately 10 percent, regardless of how or where that opinion starts and spreads in the society.

"To reach their conclusion, the scientists developed computer models of various types of social networks. One of the networks had each person connect to every other person in the network. The second model included certain individuals who were connected to a large number of people, making them opinion hubs or leaders. The final model gave every person in the model roughly the same number of connections. The initial state of each of the models was a sea of traditional-view holders. Each of these individuals held a view, but were also, importantly, open minded to other views.

"Once the networks were built, the scientists then 'sprinkled' in some true believers throughout each of the networks. These people were completely set in their views and unflappable in modifying those beliefs. As those true believers began to converse with those who held the traditional belief system, the tides gradually and then very abruptly began to shift.

"In general, people do not like to have an unpopular opinion and are always seeking to try locally to come to consensus. We set up this dynamic in each of our models," said SCNARC Research Associate and corresponding paper author Sameet Sreenivasan. To accomplish this, each of the individuals in the models "talked" to each other about their opinion. If the listener held the same opinions as the speaker, it reinforced the listener's belief. If the opinion was different, the listener considered it and moved on to talk to another person. If that person also held this new belief, the listener then adopted that belief.

"As agents of change start to convince more and more people, the situation begins to change," Sreenivasan said. "People begin to question their own views at first and then completely adopt the new view to spread it even further. If the true believers just influenced their neighbors, that wouldn't change anything within the larger system, as we saw with percentages less than 10."

"The research has broad implications for understanding how opinion spreads. There are clearly situations in which it helps to know how to efficiently spread some opinion or how to suppress a developing opinion," said Associate Professor of Physics and co-author of the paper Gyorgy Korniss. "Some examples might be the need to quickly convince a town to move before a hurricane or spread new information on the prevention of disease in a rural village.

"The researchers are now looking for partners within the social sciences and other fields to compare their computational models to historical examples. They are also looking to study how the percentage might change when input into a model where the society is polarized. Instead of simply holding one traditional view, the society would instead hold two opposing viewpoints. An example of this polarization would be Democrat versus Republican. (Provided by Rensselaer Polytechnic Institute.)"

The Awakening Point is Here and Now

Interestingly, as mentioned above about feeling insignificant, when the number of "different opinion holders" is below 10% there's this innate sense of futility because the fact is, as they say, it would take virtually next to forever for the ideas to move against those of the majority, mathematically speaking.

However, by simply breaking that 10% barrier some dynamic takes place, a type of critical mass is reached, and it takes on a life of its own.

A lot of this has to do with the perceived "popularity" of beliefs. Which makes sense. But let's play along, shall we?

What we do know is people are swayed by these pressures. No doubt.

The 100th monkey phenomenon is another such example. Wikipedia notes:

"The hundredth monkey effect is a studied phenomenon in which a new behavior or idea is claimed to spread rapidly by unexplained means from one group to all related groups once a critical number of members of one group exhibit the new behavior or acknowledge the new idea. The theory behind this phenomenon originated with Lawrence Blair and Lyall Watson in the mid-to-late 1970s, who claimed that it was the observation of Japanese scientists."

"Researchers observed that once a critical number of monkeys was reached, e.g., the hundredth monkey, a previously learned behavior instantly spread across the water to monkeys on nearby islands."

The Consciousness Factor and the Tipping Point

What's even more exciting is the parallel consciousness factor as well as the vibrational change aspect we're undergoing.

While these study parameters are social pressures and societal mechanisms as they've identified them, in reality we're talking multi-level and multi-dimensional influences at play to help effect these vast and unlimited consciousness changes.

In other words, we're moving fast towards that tipping point as we speak. I can't give you any numbers or percentages, but it's happening. And ironically enough the more the powers that shouldn't be try to suppress it the faster it's growing.

I mean even the planets, stars and whole Milky Way are lining up as part of this changeover as we literally pass into a new epoch of human history.

Glorious, isn't it? What more could we ask?

Now get busy. The sooner this thing ignites into a blaze of wondrous glory the better. And you don't have to worry about the overall, just you and your part.

Personal Notes:

Change the Morphic Field, Change the World

There was an interesting article recently about researchers who found within the computer informational field what appears to be proof of foreknowledge of 9/11. The huge spike in chatter regarding the events immediately prior to the strikes is completely anomalous. In other words, it goes on to say, for it to be just a coincidence is next to impossible.

No big surprise. But what about this informational field?

They call this computer information world a type of "morphic field" or "information field" and it seems to be a virtual manifestation of the global mind. Not all of it of course, but the informational global mind, which at this point in history is a massive amount of generated information that's accelerating by the hour.

Research in this field is also being investigated by other visionaries. By tracing trends in language using webbots that crawl the internet reading data with assigned values to various words, they've been able to often predict not only major events, trends and changes, but the specific nature and sometimes locations of future phenomena.

It's not an exact science by any means, but this whole field starts to show the power of the literal electromagnetic informational mind as evidence or a reflection of human consciousness, and we should pay close attention.

Language as a Manifestation of Consciousness

Language shared is clearly consciousness at work. This is our current fundamental method of communication. Perhaps general telepathy is on the horizon, but for now words backed by intention and no doubt other influences is how we understand communication.

Whichever, it only stands to reason that the greater the body of consciousness manifested, the greater the effect on the present, and hence the future.

In the words of Roger Nelson, founder of the Global Consciousness Project (GCP) from his book Quantum Mind p. 57;

"My own 'model' is that consciousness or mind is the source or seat of a non-local, active information field (this is not a standard, well defined physical construct). Such fields interact, usually with random phase relationship and no detectable product. When some or many consciousness (information) fields are driven in common, or for whatever reason become coherent and resonant, they interact in phase, and create a new, highly structured information field... that becomes the source of the effects we measure."

Pretty profound. When the accumulated consciousness fields are driven in common or show coherency or resonance, they create a new information field.

Sound interactive? That's the whole point...we need to get busy manifesting truth and love within this resonant field.

Morphic Resonance and Quantum Physics

Taking this field changing empowerment even further, morphic field theory is the "discovery" (coming into consciousness) that there's a dynamic at work akin to the concept of non-separability and total connectivity that quantum physics has discovered. Reminiscent of Plato's Theory of Forms, these interactive force fields give form to not just plants, animals, crystals, planets and the like, but to behavioral and social patterns. This is similar to the evolving informational field concept described above but even more profound. It is much like Carl Jung's collective unconscious understanding, but even broader while on a somewhat more so-called "scientific" footing.

It is touching on the effect of Universal Consciousness coming into our experiential realm and our interaction with it. But again, morphic field study is the attempt to pursue this intuitive knowledge scientifically, so called, in a quantifiable way.

It's all part of the continued awakening of mankind, despite the manipulations, masking and withholding of knowledge by the controllers. Now you can see why so much is hidden from us – it's fuel for our flux capacitors.

No worries, we're getting our own fuel.

The "Hypothesis" of Morphic Fields
(excerpt from Rupert Sheldrake, Ph.D.)

"All self-organizing systems are wholes made up of parts, which are themselves wholes at a lower level, such as atoms in molecules and molecules in crystals. The same is true of organelles in cells, cells in tissues, tissues in organs, organs in organisms, organisms in social groups. At each level, the morphic field gives each whole its characteristic properties and interconnects and coordinates the constituent parts.

"The fields responsible for the development and maintenance of bodily form in plants and animals are called morphogenetic fields. In animals, the organization of behavior and mental activity depends on behavioral and mental fields. The organization of societies and cultures depends on social and cultural fields. All these kinds of organizing fields are morphic fields.

"Morphic fields are located within and around the systems they organize. Like quantum fields, they work probabilistically. They restrict, or impose order upon, the inherent indeterminism of the systems under their influence. Thus, for example, a protein field organizes the way in which the chain of amino acids (the "primary structure" determined by the genes) coils and folds up to give the characteristic three-dimensional form of the protein, "choosing" from among many possible structures, all equally possible from an energetic point of view. Social fields coordinate the behavior of individuals within social groups, for example, the behavior of fish in schools or birds in flocks.

Pretty amazing..

"The most controversial feature of this hypothesis is that the structure of morphic fields depends on what has happened before. They contain a kind of memory. Through repetition, the patterns they organize become increasingly probable, increasingly habitual. The force that these fields exert is the force of habit.

"Whatever the explanation of its origin, once a new morphic field – a new pattern of organization – has come into being, its field becomes stronger through repetition. The same pattern becomes more likely to happen again. The more often patterns are repeated, the more probable they become. The fields contain a kind of cumulative memory and become increasingly habitual. Fields evolve in time and form the basis of habits. From this point of view, nature is essentially habitual. Even the so-called laws of nature may be more like habits."

This Is How The Lying Matrix Thrives

Social engineers for eons have known this underlying dynamic in their own terms. The latest rash of modern psychopathic societal designers identified these causal and potentially liberating or captivating trends at whatever level of understanding, and set in place educational and society-modifying mechanisms to keep humanity from spontaneous, self-supporting growth centuries ago.

Left to our own we would naturally be drawing from consciousness new and beneficial "memes" or morphic fields to develop and help humanity, and not extinguish or control it like our current overlords of darkness.

Never forget that.

In other words: we've been sterilized, castrated, knee-capped, lobotomized and asphyxiated from the truth and Knowledge of who we truly are and our incredible power to manifest and shape a loving, conscious world around us.

Yet we thrive.

But as long as we let them fill the airwaves, ground waves and mind waves with their limiting, manipulative, oppressive and distracting propaganda and electromagnetic crap and don't retaliate in kind in order to reverse the trend, society is literally being pushed off the map of human awareness into the maw of a mental and social meat grinder.

It's Up to Us

It's entirely up to each of us what we do with this amazing energetic system. We can harm or we can heal. We can go along with the status quo or we change it.

It will simply reflect whatever is put into it in its own fascinating way, and is doing its job at all times whether we acknowledge it or not.

And it's there for conscious use if you choose. We're eternal consciousness connected to everything, yet we're free agents to choose good and truth and love, or darkness, evil, fear and hate.

The beauty of this knowledge is the realization that every letter you write, every item you blog, every word you speak, every thought you think, every prayer or intention you utter, every loving or non-loving deed, every decision to do the right thing or not…everything….is forming the world in which we live..societal, informational and the underlying morphic world which we all share.

Every time someone watches mindless TV, gets spellbound by things like Hollywood or war programming, or entertains the Matrix meme in any way, they are supporting and perpetrating the death-dealing, humanity perverting lie. Period.

While on the contrary…

The Internet Highway of Information and Transformation

Every time you blog with good and helpful information, forward an inspiring or truth-revealing article, post an idea or heart-warming picture or uplifting message, encourage or support a fellow activist in their efforts, do a kind or loving deed or reach out and shake someone up…every time…you are changing the morphic field…for the better. All while subtracting a negative imprint, first your own and then by extension the accumulated negativity of everyone involved.

Which will it be?

Will we contribute to the wake up, or be part of the problem? It's a continual choice. There's no standing still. Either way we all affect it.

Put Your Shoulder to the Shift

Hopefully this awareness of how pervasive the dynamics of intention, attraction, information, communication and consciousness are will spur you on. It has me. I've known this dynamic was at work but to see it in this light was empowering.

Participating and really making a difference that matters couldn't be any easier than it is today. You can do gobs of damage to the oppressors' constructs and help establish the righteous rule of truth, love and consciousness by just putting it out there. Manifest it in the morphic field any and every way you can and it goes to work immediately and affects everything.

Even according to nerdy quantum physics, intelligent life on this planet now knows everything you do affects everywhere in mind-blowing, non-linear or spatially limited ways. We are all interconnected with everything. What more empowering information could there be?

As we change these informational morphic fields we'll also immediately set a better precedent for future change as these fields replicate themselves in whatever state they're in. This is why we have to keep the fields morphing towards more and more truth and a loving reality continually. And as we resonate together with the truth vibes being amplified around us anything false will crack and crumble into ruins.

Now you see why they try to keep us drugged, distracted and asleep? It's time to take spaceship earth back.

Take action, in word, deed and spirit. Be a resonant voice however you can. Just do it, and if you're already doing it, turn it up. It's working even if you can't see the full extent of it yet. And as you do you'll get such a rush of confirmation and satisfaction you'll do even more, as well as get others on board.

Power to the people? It's been there all along. But you gotta throw the switch.

Personal Notes:

Deaf Ears, Foot Dragging and Moving to the Next Level

It's reality check time. When you realize the person or persons you're delivering an important message to doesn't want to hear it nor do anything about it, and in fact vehemently rejects it and humiliates and even punishes you for bringing it up, it's time to take the hint.

The so-called rulers have no interest in our petitions, protests and even demonstrations of disapproval. While supposedly being elected to represent our interests, those concerns we have are clearly the last thing they have in mind. It couldn't possibly be any clearer than it is today.

Oh they'll do a little sidestep or pretend to make some slight adjustment to calm the masses down and allay a few fears or grievances, but their overall program generally goes on. At least in this current paradigm of control.

Delayed and partial reactions are fundamentally non-reactions.

The real point or core of the issue is very rarely being addressed. They aren't serving us. In their minds we are serving them and do it best when we think we're free. So this kind of foot dragging lip service is just part of keeping the illusion of freedom up.

The Turning Point

What's unique about this particular turning point is that it's now gotten to where they're not even concerned about keeping up the smokescreen of giving a damn and or even trying to relate to our ability to participate according to their rules. They're rapidly outright removing these freedoms they've so graciously "granted" us, and they're doing it with abject impunity.

Peaceful demonstrations are met with brutality. Even freedom of assembly is slowly being prohibited. Journalists, political dissidents and even active students are being conveniently clustered as "threats" by the new buzzword "radicalized" to imply potential ISIS or otherwise terrorist associations which are being liberally applied to anyone they deem unsavory to the status quo.

This is a serious situation.

Act Fast, Act Now

Despite the unresponsive nature of the powers that shouldn't be, redress still matters. Raising our voices should never cease but we need to think beyond the box of action-reaction they've herded humanity into.

The key is hitting it hardest on a local scale. The instruments of mass information are under their tight control so whatever inroads we do make won't even be reported, or just minimally. Seeing a sway in public opinion will be marginalized, twisted, ridiculed or in most cases completely sidestepped and ignored as if it isn't even happening.

Insist on complete change – firstly in your own life. Disengage from participating. Boycott banks and matrix enforcing commercial outlets. Turn off your mind control idiot box televisor that people still think is their innocuous friend and open news and entertainment source. Free your mind and heart and fill your life with love and empowering information and interactions.

It starts there.

Then apply it at your local level. Move from the nearest influences that are working against humanity right up through your local administrators. When enough communities do this, even winning over their judicial and law enforcement officials who are from their own communities, independent hubs of full on resistance spread far and wide will be impossible for them to stop. With enough impetus this kind of grassroots community based action will eventually supplant their influence altogether.

This is why they move law enforcement personnel from neighboring areas into "trouble spots" and why the US is importing foreign and UN troops to do their dirty work on American soil. It's to break these heartfelt ties where common sense and compassion bind hearts and create conscious, empathic responses. Divide and conquer is their credo.

Therefore, it's clear their fear is that we will unite and stand together.

The Importance of Banding Together

The beauty of our grassroots revolt and affirmation of our humanity is our connectivity. We realize we're not in the least bit alone in our perception, frustration and even desperation to stop today's insanities. We have a common purpose and goal which is extremely simple: the betterment of humanity's condition through the simple allowance to get on with our lives without interference. Anyone half awake can see that is completely contrary to the role of government and globalist mandates, all working toward indifferent, mechanized one world central control.

It's extremely Orwellian in nature which has been pointed out countless times, yet we keep petitioning these psychopaths as if these megalomaniacs can possibly be "addressed" with our grievances and needs.

Let's wake up. It's time for Plan B.

A Full on Frontal Assault

There's a degree of hope for addressing local officials. There's also a degree of hope for further exposure of their wickedness and abject depravity, never mind their neglect of duty to the populations they claim to serve. At the higher levels

I'm not holding my breath for change, but true information is empowering constituents with more fuel for indignation and a desire to take action, most of all locally.

We can take a stand and turn the tide, if we want to.

Conscious awareness based in love must be our foundation. But don't think your sacred indignation isn't part of that. The point is to turn the power on, and up. If you're into intending the vibrational change then do so – but turn it up. If you're into community activism on any level, from seeding crystals to meditation to community gardening to approaching officials, turn it up. If you're into information dissemination using exposure and empowerment, turn it up.

Do it all with increased intentionally aware acumen. We have an opportunity to turn the tide but the hour is crucial. The vibrations are high and rising on the side of love and truth but the oppressors are busy making their last moves to put their building blocks in place. It's a formidable foe of destructive entropic energy but charge their bastions of lies we must.

Take Heart, and Take Action

It's hard to say what is the full on solution in this soup-like milieu of confusion we're living in. All I can say it that it's time to take your personal calling seriously and act on it. I don't care what it is, Universe is wondrous and we are all so different, but the cry of the heart is the same in each of us.

Promote love and harmony, protect the vulnerable, and expose the perpetrators of abuse, manipulative control and exploitation. Now.

It's not that complicated. But people need to wake up out of their induced (and too often readily accepted I might add) stupor to respond accordingly.

If you care, act out. Change your life into a statement. Be responsible and respond as if you mean it. Every man and woman counts.

If that isn't clear to you yet I don't know what else to say.

Just respond. Consciously and with determination.

Is the Truth Toxic?

The truth is only toxic to some. Namely those it exposes. It sure can knock just about anyone for a loop, but it shouldn't be discouraging.

I'm seeing somewhat desperate reactions more and more lately via comments, correspondence and internet postings and it's a concern worth addressing. People really do need to get a handle on what's going on both externally and even more importantly internally. This has been addressed many times and we've been warning this challenge was coming and going to continue to grow, so now it's time to put what we know to be true into action.

It's not a time to withdraw, whatever we do. We have to face this head on and not pull back into a bunker mentality, although wise personal preparations are certainly in order. I agree it's lousy "out there" and it gets all of us down at times, but we can't stay there. The longer we do the more it envelops and disempowers us.

Granted it's disturbing information coming at us incessantly, from mass surveillance and artificial intelligence being given the reigns by psychopaths to our deliberately degraded environment and encroaching police state, it's certainly not pretty on that level.

But despite all of this, being aware of what's going on doesn't have to mean dwelling on the negative. It's ours to choose how we perceive our surroundings as well as how we spend our time and what we give our energy and attention to.

As world conditions continue to close in, remaining vigilant is simply necessary, but we have to see through and past it as well as practically deal with the consequences of these social, economical and geophysical machinations being waged on humanity.

Like Swimming – We Have To Keep Paddling

Once we take the bait and fall for their isolation and dark agenda tricks it can all be downhill from there, but only if we let it. Staying above it is imperative for spiritual as well as physical well being.

When swimming you can't just stop. Perhaps you can float for a while but eventually you have to head where you are going and get back to terra firma to rest up. But once we embark into the sea of change, whether swimming or by boat, there's work to be done to keep things afloat and moving in the right direction.

That may sound moot but it's that reality of the struggle we need to get a grip on in new and more conscious ways. This is a very tumultuous time with a lot coming at us. The temptation to drop and fold our hands in despair is strong when the battle rages on seemingly indefinitely, but these surges always pass and we find respite intervals from the storm eventually. We've all experienced this.

Being mindful that "what we knew in the light should not be forgotten in the dark" is crucial during these episodes. One of the simplest solutions is to simply unplug from the information that is distressing you as necessary. Get out in nature, change the channel, create. This often brings the breather we immediately need.

Gravity Pulls Down – Eject Baggage in Body, Mind and Spirit

It feels like increased gravity (interesting word) comes over us. If we're carrying a lot of baggage of any sort that can add to our problem. This is why detachment, both physically and spiritually, to those things that can be affected by these lower level vibrations is so essential. It's simply practical.

If you're going into a race or battle, you don't want to carry anything that isn't essential, of any sort.

The more subtle applications have to do with personal hang-ups (another interesting term) that cause us those kinds of attachments to either negative sounding news, personal circumstances or mental and spiritual proclivities. If we're prone to debilitating unconscious mindsets, these can hang us up big time during stormy conditions where the assailing winds will catch anything and everything superfluous to a vessel, swimmer or truth warrior, and cause hindering as well as potentially dangerous conditions.

Develop Your Intuitive Capabilities

One place of peaceful and constructive refuge during times like these is spiritual strengthening and creativity. This can come in the form of meditation, art and music, being with those you love and like to hang out with or having extended time in nature. Let yourself follow your passion and spiritual hunger.

It's my conviction that the next frontier, in addition to connecting locally, is developing our intuitive and spiritual capabilities.

We're in a warfare, and our weapons are spiritual, not only for our personal survival and spreading of the truth, but allowing ourselves to become equipped more fully with the gifts and capabilities we each inherently have but have not been fully developed yet that are needed in these increasingly challenging times.

So many of us have woken up to the reality of the vast infinite resources available to us. It's time to tap into them and discover how to utilize these untapped capabilities at this crossroads of ages. It's clearly part of our progressing development and something we all sense and know to be right at our fingertips.

I don't have any shortcuts for finding these, but they're shared in our connectivity while also being individual to each one of us. To tap into these vast resources at our disposal at this juncture is imperative, be they healing technologies, psychic capabilities or simply manifesting more fully our light body, if you will.

Taking Positive Action Cures Confusion and the Blues

When we take initiative to confront any situation it puts us in charge. While the playing field is clearly being manipulated and we often have to operate within certain confines, we need to make the effort to participate in realms that inspire and empower us as much as possible.

This is done by helping others and being proactive in the information and community action arenas. Those fainting in their minds are often those who aren't active in any way to help expose the reality of our situation nor actively promoting the power of conscious awareness that is available to all, least of all transmitting or participating in it in their local communities. At least to a sufficient degree.

As so many wise teachers and examples have said, making others happy and sharing caring words and deeds bring happiness right back. It's the law of love.

I know this is easy to say, and we all have our moments when it gets us down, but we can't stay there and wallow in our self pity and get further overwhelmed by the lower vibrational barrage that's besetting the planet at this time. We need to constantly realize this disabling and deliberately disempowering spectacle of world events and the accompanying fear and hopelessness propaganda barrage are designed to do just that.

Coming Into Focus

Uniting in common cause is also tremendously empowering. So many of us have been doing so and quite wonderfully using the internet which has served as such an amazing catalyst to our awakening age.

We're making new friends traversing the same path, discovering wonderful realities and seeing what true information and communication can accomplish in strengthening and encouraging humanity.

But it's time to come out from our "behind the screen" lifestyles and meet up. The human touch has been neglected to a large degree as we're witnessing in epidemic proportions with social media and portable devices completely disrupting normal human to human interactions.

The human touch has not entirely been neglected, as wonderful gatherings, conferences and community action events have been happening across the earth. But there needs to be much more. Millions are looking for the next step and it's time we took it and helped others to do the same.

But it's all up to each of us to do what we can.

Wrap Up

Taking the next steps will clear the cobwebs. Don't let the information overload and machinations of the dark agenda immobilize you and make you a target instead of an agent of change. There's plenty for any and all of us to do.

Let's take this to the next level, in any way we are called. Activation cures personal problems by focusing our energy on what really matters for the greater good of all. Our personal happiness easily follows without even looking for it.

As I like to say, the rudder (steering your life's purpose and direction) cannot take effect unless the boat is in motion.

Paddle on – and see you upriver.

Personal Notes:

In the Trenches of Battlefield Earth

Have you ever wondered why you feel so all alone during this crucial time in history? Why the sense of isolation yet at the same time you feel so connected to the information field and those waking up? And all while you still appear to be living all alone?

Quite the conundrum. Yet the reality of it gets louder by the day.

This is war. An all out war on a very individual level. We're in a battle for our planet and its peoples and you're part of it. The more integral and awake you are the more isolated you may feel, I venture to say. And by design, as strange as that may seem, though we do need to connect at this crucial time.

It's a time of immense warfare, between the forces of good and the forces of evil, to put it in its most basic terms. Clearly a lot is happening on many levels but essentially this is a fight for our survival – not just geopolitically, but even physically and most of all spiritually.

We're under attack and the awakening soldiers have been relegated to their fighting positions – what you might call our trenches.

So don't fight it. Fight the enemy and stop thinking too much about your own damn issues. You've been called to battle. That's pretty much how I'm currently seeing it. However you see all of what's going on, it's a time to let personal issues go for the sake of the greater good and make whatever sacrifices need to made.

Stay Outside Yourself

There's so much more at stake than any of us individually. Selflessness is the sign of a true warrior; one who fights for a noble cause and the survival of righteous principles and the lives of all those they love and care for. This includes all of humanity and every living thing on this planet. It's a driving compassion that surpasses all of the confines of social structure or so called reason.

Passion supersedes everything. It is born out of spirit and will not cease until its purpose is fulfilled to the best of its ability. The destructive tendencies we witness today are shortsighted and of very limited lifespans. They're a different vibration altogether and basically a counterfeit impulse born out of entropic forces countering the creative design.

Hence the warfare.

Why this has been set in place and at play I don't really know. I do know it's here. The fact remains that it boils down to personal survival and that of all living things once you realize the agenda of these destructive forces. Life is clearly a struggle on many levels but today's world is unfolding an awareness of many more dimensions of this struggle as occult forces surface and come to increasingly bear on humanity.

Selfish, self centered orientation is anathema to truth and love and is the most disempowering motivation anyone can possibly have. It may seem satisfactory for survival reasons in the short term within this matrix of deceit, but anyone with any heartfelt compassion and empathy will recognize it falls flat in the real scheme of things.

The true realm of empowerment is unselfish, heartfelt motivation for the common good. Completely contrary to the self oriented societal complex, but nonetheless a fact.

Standing Strong

This concept is contrary to everything we've been taught. Bravery in the face of a storm, conscious awareness in a mind-numbed world, it's all the same. We're standing against an onslaught of abject hate, disinformation, deliberate confusion and very clever mind bending propaganda.

The issue I'm addressing is this very stance. Having the courage to be who you truly are, in heart, mind, soul and spirit. This is what withstands the destructive matrix and creates the new paradigm.

Is it futile? Can we change the tide? These are no doubt questions we each battle on a daily basis. But such is the nature of warfare.

Diametrically opposed sides endeavor to not just withstand but take an offensive approach to their declared enemy.

We didn't set up this paradigm. It was brought on by outside influences into our otherwise peaceful, cooperative communitarian nature. But again, deal with it we must. With fortitude and the courage of our convictions.

Learning and Responding

I don't mind thinking that this life is a learning ground. It makes a lot of sense. But that's at best linear, logical thinking when you come down to it. Survival in our current environment has a much more real ring to it.

Act or be acted upon makes much more sense to me as far as spurring us on to simply responding to what is transpiring around us. That's how nature works.

Any way you look at it, how will we react or respond? What will individuals do in the face of such obviously parasitic forces out for our very destruction?

These are big questions, but essentially only answered individually. One by one.

Will you react, respond, take the offensive? Or duck for cover and self-preservation, and on and on. There are a lot of options to choose from.

The reality remains – what we choose will determine our outcome.

Conclusion

There are a lot of choices before us, but the nature of our current situation is what it is. A very real engagement with both good and detrimental influences over which we have control.

It's ours to choose.

Once you've chosen, you will find yourself in a struggle against those forces that seek to eliminate your freedom of choice as well as your very right to exist.

That's a pretty strong reality. When you get it you'll understand why you're in the trenches of Battlefield Earth.

Personal Notes:

Kicking Stones

I've had a habit for many years, as I'm sure many others have, of clearing paths that I travel. I can't help it. I kick stones out of the way, clear branches, whatever I happen upon. It only makes sense and I've never thought anything of it. I was thinking today what a perfect metaphor for life that is. We don't have to take the whole world on at once, just deal consciously with what's in front of us.

Just imagine if everyone cleared the path for others in whatever way they could, even just a little at a time.

It doesn't take much. A little kick here, a toss there as obstacles appear. Some are not as easy as others. Some need chainsaws and bulldozers, heavy equipment a team will need to provide in some form. But we can each do what we can do. Many "rock kickers" have joined into teams of "earth movers" and I'm blessed to know many of them. Either way, even with the seemingly small stuff, just kick it aside and keep on.

We each make a huge difference in spite of what we've been told. It's the activation of that conscious impulse that matters, and our response to the immediate need.

Responding

It's really instinctive, or rather it should be. Unfortunately simple conscious responding has become less and less the case. The wonderful underlying reality is that many make this a way of life – whether for their children's safety or future, or even their own survival. In more advanced tribal and cultural societies this was ingrained in their way of life. In today's world, extending that impulse for the sake of the whole is seriously discouraged.

That is easily overcome.

Life is a series of interactions within ourselves, as well as between ourselves and the world around us. Our behavior is based on how awake and aware and responsive we are, and to what we are responding. Since birth we've been programmed with guidelines and rules for behavior. Having the simple courage to overcome that selfish, fear based training and allowing our own personal awakening from this programming to flourish determines how much we're letting our true essence come to life.

It's clearly a process but most of all it's a continual choice. Will I let my true convictions show and play out? Or will I cave in to conformity with a clearly dysfunctional world and stifle those conscious promptings?

It's hard to fathom the mass of decisions we're faced with every day. The underlying important ones get buried in the daily hubbub of thinking, experiences and external input. The truly conscious questions have to do with why we're here, where am I going, what is behind this apparent illusion, and what do I do about it. Once we start to grasp these essential basics we'll know how to respond consciously. The problem is these underlying questions are deliberately suppressed, discouraged and glazed over.

The beauty of it is that this latent lower level programming is almost immediately overcome when a personal awakening takes place. Whole new worlds of dynamics affect our response mechanisms and everything drastically changes.

How Does This Translate?

A smile, a helping hand, a word of encouragement, a wise word of advice, a hug, or even shared information and artistic expression, however you can get it out. It comes in all forms.

As each of us adopt and commit to this simple way of life the world will continue to change for the better. Love is affirmed, sympathetic vibrations radiate, and the social and spiritual fabric changes.

Change the world by manifesting the mystic morphic field, I like to say.

As synchronicity would have it, as I walked home from a local park thinking about this I turned up a street to see a young father and his daughter walking ahead of me. And what was he doing? Kicking gravel and rocks to the side of the road, just as I was, here and there. It was picture perfect synchronicity as I mulled writing about this lifelong habit. He seemed to be a local tourist and may not even walk that way again but he felt responsible.

That's what I'm talking about. Caring enough to at least do something whenever we get the opportunity.

No matter how seemingly small or insignificant, we each make a huge difference. And our accumulated effect is something we can derive huge inspiration from. Keeping proactive in all of these small ways has a much greater impact than can be calibrated. Have you ever watched a column of leaf cutter ants work their way back and forth from a nearby crop of leaves they're harvesting? Talk about focus, teamwork and determination…one responsible ant at a time.

The beautiful thing is it's happening with humanity. It's not new by any means, but in an increasingly callous world it is a radical act to be unselfish. It's very similar to Orwell's adage on speaking the truth in an oppressively deceptive climate such as we're seeing today:

"In a time of universal deceit – telling the truth is a revolutionary act." - George Orwell

So is behaving lovingly and responsibly in a world seriously infected with selfishness and fear.

Keep On Kicking

Each of us have our own obstacles. We can succumb to them or we can intelligently learn from these challenges and either bypass, overcome or transcend them. When it comes to common sense in-your-face issues that need immediate addressing we cannot falter. Some of these are pretty huge, such as the on-going Palestinian extermination which the world will not even acknowledge, but tackle them we must by responding consciously and not going on business as usual. As humanity arises from its slumber and learns to spontaneously care for each other and our environment, the changes for the betterment and reawakening of our planet will accelerate with blinding speed.

If the rock's in the way, kick it aside.

Others will travel "the road less followed" with fewer mishaps and obstacles, and take the awakening even further down the road. We don't need to see the results to know this, it just is.

Keep kicking and and keep on loving in every way possible.

Personal Notes:

Scattered Seedlings Restoring the Earth

Every day more people connect and learn they are not alone. While the manipulated matrix makes it difficult for the awake and aware to be physically together, the great world wide grid of love and consciously awakened individuals continues to spread like "weeds".

As we sow and grow we're coming closer together continually. In fact, we're probably bumping into each other and don't even realize it.

That's why it's important to keep communicating. We know the same central truth, we know the heart of man is the same the world over, and we know it only awaits awakening to come to full fruition.

Look for it, expect it.

What you already know in your heart to be true you'll see manifest in wondrous and wonderful ways.

Wild Seeds Will Cover the Earth

We have to get radical, truly radical in our propagation of truth. No longer are there movements to try to attach to. They are all dead in the water. It's a barren landscape compared to the rich culture it once was of vocal, active groups. No doubt real folks are fighting in their carefully sectored quadrants with various wonderful efforts, but it's all being thwarted from being allowed into public awareness, and what does appear is systematically marginalized in everyone's eyes.

Remember the full on protests? Remember the indignant opposition to a false government and its horrific wars? It's non existent now, being squelched even before it can hit the conscious awareness of the individual that there's something wrong. You have no avenue to speak of. As a result, many give up, thinking that it's no use.

College students are stupefied. Interest groups are bought off. The rest sit back in frustration.

But not all.

One encouraging arrival on the scene are Indigo children and Crystal kids that rise up. While it appears the younger generation is virtually shot, take a look at the potential of awakened kids when activated which you'll find more and more evidence of.

We Are Coming Together

In spirit, the awakened collective is always pulling together. It's spiritually natural. We may be separated in physical space and time but in reality we are together. Nothing stops us. We are united. We communicate naturally and often, as in the case of the internet and personal interactions. But even these connections are under attack. We are up against serious opposition.

The fact is, we communicate in the language of the heart, and it tells us many things, including the fact that time is short.

Knowing underground communication avenues is key to our survival for as long as we need to be here. Technology wise, network wise and consciousness wise.

The Language of the Heart

Here is a proposition that may resonate with some. I can't fully endorse the source, but the concepts appear sound enough for consideration. It comes from Nonviolent Communication - The Language of the Heart by Stuart Watson.

"The belief that people are naturally compassionate is a central awareness of Nonviolent Communication, otherwise known as NVC, or "the language of the heart." NVC provides a toolbox of insights and communication tools that reveal and nurture this state of natural compassion.

"For over 35 years, Dr. Marshall Rosenberg has traveled the world sharing NVC, contributing to a shift in consciousness from violence, alienation and oppression to a new paradigm of interconnectedness. From helping people improve the quality of personal and professional relationships to being on the front line mediating in some of the hottest conflict areas around the world, Rosenberg's radical work subverts our whole status quo system of power by identifying the type of awareness and corresponding language that disconnects us from each other.

"The NVC process is distinctly different from many models of communication and conflict resolution in that the objective is never to get our way, but to "create the quality of connection that will allow for everybody's needs to be fulfilled." The process guides us in fully and honestly expressing ourselves, while empathetically receiving the communication and actions of others; without using or hearing blame, criticism, or judgement. By focusing on the quality of the connection rather than on the strategies and outcomes, solutions can be obtained that satisfy everybody's needs more completely, without compromising their values. As Dr. Rosenberg asserts, "we each have an incredible, awesome power to make life wonderful, and that there is nothing that is more joyful than exercising that power by enriching our own and other's lives."

Take a Lesson from our Elders....

Native American Prayer
Honor the sacred.
Honor the Earth, our Mother.
Honor the Elders.
Honor all with whom we
share the Earth:-
Four-leggeds, two-leggeds,
winged ones,
Swimmers, crawlers,
plant and rock people.
Walk in balance and beauty.
-Native American Elder
Unite in spirit and in deed.

Into the Breach

What happened recently in response to the Syrian gambit of the globalist elite is profound. Besides the geopolitical upheaval it caused and subsequent dizzying effects, even more intriguing is the ensuing rise of conscious connecting of issues it seems to have spawned. It's as if a layer of the false holographic onion peeled off and exposed not just the next layer, but the more fundamental and profound realization that this phony thing we've been witnessing truly is an illusion and that it has layers to be peeled.

That's called awakening.

And it's a big deal. Especially when it cuts into the support base of hypocritical, hypnotic puppets like America's Obama and sycophantic cronies like the laughable robotic John Kerry and bumbling idiot John McCain types. Who's kidding who for goodness' sake.

And the good thing? Everyone can see it. That's a major statement in itself.

Where Are We?

In the grand scheme of things this is a very interesting time. I think the contriving controllers are regrouping. They knew we were waking up but this acceleration that's manifesting has taken them by surprise. They have plans in place to cut our communication lifeline but until then they are being forced to scramble.

It's obvious and they are humiliated. But don't let your guard down.

Besides the ongoing engineered onslaught on our minds and health, these maniacs have many weapons they can unleash at any time.

What's remarkable is to note how they treat us with a certain amount of literal fear and respect. We outnumber them by vast proportions and they know it.

Posturing is their game, a culmination of centuries of social engineering and mind control. If we get too smart they get draconian, as we see they are clearly doing in the US and other western countries.

But right now the awakening is blowing their minds. It's accelerating at a rate they did not and could not anticipate. They are of another weaker dimension.

We must remember that. While they operate well in the dullard-like long term control aspect, we can overwhelm them in the present. That's our domain, the now in which we live.

The Smell of Freedom

When the oppressed smell freedom you'd better look out. That's what's happening here – a spiritual revolution. We will jump the wall given the opportunity, and it is now.

Remember the historical lessons of famous battles. When a breach in the wall of a city or castle being attacked opened up, it was all in.

That was the chance, the opportunity–everything they treasured, committed to, and decided to fight and die for lay before them to perform for their freedom.

In that moment the golden opportunity presented itself.

Passionate, reckless abandon overwhelmed their spirits. It was time to charge.

We are there. We've always been there, but our troops have swelled and the signal is being heard. Enormously.

And this is an extremely prescient time with all that is being exposed to a massive swathe of humanity, giving credence to the mounting undercurrent of alternative forces that have been affirming these realities for some time.

We can now attack with more conviction than ever. It's time to aggressively expose their phony corrupt politics and baseless warmongering; their ecological, medical and corporate fascism; the banking control, scientific fraudulence, media propaganda and on and on….more than ever.

Take Action Yourself

Act. Approach your skeptical relatives again. Talk to strangers. Participate in blogs and marches and campaigns. Get involved in your local community. Write local papers and mainstream outlets. Make a mark. This is a real opening that we cannot ignore or bypass.

Activate. Please.

Serious media clampdown attempts are in the works. Time is of the essence. These freaks have been preparing and using anti-humanity devices for ages, from debilitating disinformation to chemical poisoning to killing our food and environment. They're sick, and will resort to anything they can get their hands on to control, subdue and vampirize humanity.

Our job is to respond accordingly. With resolve.

Will you stand by and watch your children and/or grandchildren be poisoned to death? Do you want them altered genetically so that their offspring are some sort of transhuman modification for use by abusive global usurpers?

If you don't stand up, who will stand up for them? Or you?

Take action.

How Much Evidence
Do We Need
To Take Action?

The news pouring in daily about how we're being scammed, poisoned and domineered by big food, big pharma, big oil, big corporations and big brother is almost overwhelming.

It's past time to draw some conclusions from all of the obvious evidence.

This is where the rubber meets the road. There comes a time we need to crystallize all that's being plainly revealed into a very clear picture that brings personal action and a conscious response. The global engineers are enacting a full spectrum attack on humanity, to not just subdue, control and transform the world's populations, but to drastically reduce it by slowly maiming and killing it off.

The common awareness of these programs extends to such arenas as weather and electromagnetic warfare, radiation contamination and a full on global fracking agenda, full spectrum geopolitical hegemony, invasive medical and pharmaceutical fascism, and the tightening economic vice grip on people's supply lines and their very survival.

Everything we read daily points in the same direction.

The question before us is, what will we do in the face of such an onslaught? Are we first of all willing to draw some conscious conclusions?

Or are we afraid to, due to the implications of what our personal involvement might entail? And all while our race is clearly being adulterated and exterminated.

Serious personal questions indeed. Courage is the absence of letting fear rule our lives. Doing the conscious and responsible thing is the duty of every living creature, not just "activists", another term used pejoratively to keep people from doing the obvious.

Eugenics – The Openly Declared Usurping Elitist Agenda

Elitism runs on fundamental tenets. Thinking they are superior and knowing what's best for the world, they have funded and operated think tanks, foundations, institutions, universities and secret organizations for centuries in one form or another to formulate and hone their plans.

The scale is massive with these internationalists and we are the subjects of their experimental implementations. That their aim is to modify as well as reduce our numbers is a repeatedly documented goal of these psychopaths.

All for control and arrogantly assumed domination of those they consider inferior. And after all is said and done, they're not sure of anything, despite their hubris.

We are a race with qualities they cannot fathom due to their abject lack of empathy and true conscious awareness, despite their metastasized left-brained so-called intelligence and other intimidating dark machinations and engineered influences.

Recent decades have seen a massive proliferation of such elite planning organizations, many operating openly with benign names like the Rand Corporation, the Stanford Institute, the Rockefeller Foundation, the Carnegie Institute, the Red Cross, the Council on Foreign Relations, the Institute for the Advancement of the Sciences, the Ford Foundation, the Sierra Club, the Society of Jesus and many many more.

Most hypno-zombies don't think anything of such organizations. After all, like the "Patriot Act", they must be for out collective good. More profoundly, media manipulation through language sorcery and meme repetition has been extremely successful.

Most would never even stop to question anything sounding like an "authority" on some issue, hence the worship of men in white coats with strings of degrees after their names, trusting "talking heads", institutions like these and anything sounding credible.

To the News

Which brings me to the news. Almost hourly we're reading of new exposés regarding critical health issues, from the disastrous effects of vaccines and pharmaceutical drugs to the cover up of what is actually in our adulterated and genetically modified food which they themselves won't touch, as well as our drinking water and the very air we breathe.

Not new, but bubbling up more and more in the mass consciousness.

The world militarization and mass surveillance agenda is another major factor happening concurrently as an obvious manifestation of this globalist agenda. Media complicity is clear and their influence is waning rapidly as alternative news sources become the go-to source for information and grass roots community actions proliferate.

Just the fact that the realistic, awake and aware perspective of seeing these realities for what they are has been portrayed as "conspiratorial" puts the control issue way over the top, not just in Orwellian incredulity, but exactly where they want it in the mass mind, safely ensconced in frozen compartmentalized suspended animation.

In plain reality of course it's a very real conspiracy, and they're clearly executing a stated agenda, one we're fully aware of. Naturally they have to decry anything that exposes or opposes it.

What an obvious sham. But again, who's looking?

What We're Up Against

It's a disinformation machine, spouting out whatever toxic spew it deems necessary at any given time. Keeping people in the dark is their number one job. Once you catch on to that you're on your way to mental and spiritual freedom, but it takes some doing, and takes guts to openly see past the green screen projection we're being fed.

As someone wisely said, "The truth will set you free, but first it will piss you off."

Very true words indeed. Get past that stage and start to activate. Every one of us counts.

Conclusion

If we don't respond consciously to this invasion on our kind we're not worth our salt. Doing what we can restores confidence and an innate sense of who we are, and spurs many others on to do the same.

Pass it on. And on and on. Passionate communication is the key to empowerment at this point. Never downplay or delay that.

All of this is just for starters. The rest is up to you, and me. There are massively powerful spiritual weapons of mass construction at our disposal such as localized community activism. Use them, and discover new avenues continually. We're swimming in an ocean of possibility waiting to be tapped into and manifested.

There is nothing more empowering than that as I see it.

Hope you do too. It's a wonderful opportunity for taking the initiative and making a massive difference.

See you there.

Swarm: Backlash of Awakening Humanity

The self appointed elites are on the run. We are clearly freaking them out. The astounding rate of our awakening is not anything they were expecting nor counting on. That's not surprising, considering their arrogance, but search any subject you wish to pursue and you'll find that despite their algorithms, distorting mechanisms and surveillance they cannot stop the onslaught of truth coming from humanity itself.

This is a reality to be encouraged about. We are a tide of truth coming at them so fast they honestly do not know how to handle it. We're dismissed, minimalized, marginalized and disparaged in a host of ways, but they cannot cope with our resilience. Hence their stepped up agenda towards our physical and spiritual weakening.

The war we are in is real. It matters what you do and think. We are the embodiment of our own solution and need to come to that realization fast and furious. We are literally putting them on their heels and they simply need to keep pushing their agenda in more and more draconian ways as if everything depends upon it – because it does. That's what you're seeing in the so-called "news".

A Time To Shed

It's really about letting go when it comes to moving into this next phase. Let go of entanglements, let go of any parasitic connections they have on you. Be it banking, mortgages, soul-sucking relationships, false media addictions, bad food proclivities or the like, it's time to take a stand.

Operate according to your true convictions.

I know it's easy to say, but the cut off point will come one way or the other. Either they'll do it when you're on the defensive and powerless in dire circumstances, or you do it before they can take advantage of you. That's the situation we're in, like it or not. The dependence on their system is what needs to be shed, any and every way we can do it.

From there we take the offensive. They are bluffing. So let's march.

Dismantle the Bastards

This may seem beyond reach to most but this is exactly what needs to be done. Initiative is the key – take the battle to them. This can be done extremely simply, and very locally. Challenge so-called authority. Ask them why they pass laws allowing for the toxification of your water, your food, your air. Why are your babies being injected with known toxins, why is the educational system crushing their spirit and reducing their intelligence?...and on it goes.

These are questions to be posed with intended consequences – for them. With authority. Because what they do affects you. Your loved ones, your neighbors, your community, and your world.

If we humanity do not rise to this challenge, we will deserve what comes upon us by these dark controlling social engineers. Is that what you want? Are you going to lay down and just take it?

That's the Question

What will you do – or not do? How much do you care? Are you so asleep you can't see your very life and that of those you love is at stake?

What will it take?

I don't know what else I can say at this point. I have immense trust and faith in humanity and its consciously empowered state, but when it lets itself get overwhelmed and reduced to a whimper I can only observe with sadness and wonder.

I know all will be well in the long run in a deep esoteric sense, but I yearn for my brothers and sisters who could simply awaken and take their very lives back, and those of their loved ones.

I pray you hear me.

The hour is late. It's time to shake off the shackles and activate with all that's within each of us. Just imagine if we all swarm these bastards, one seemingly small action at a time, and move toward the head of the spider. Now that should cause quite the uproar. And what an encouragement to others to go for it.

That's all I can say. It's up to you, and to me. Let's do it.

Awakened Warriors Arise

Life is a struggle. How much more then is the spiritual life, the fight to remain conscious in an illusory world where deviant forces vie for control more than caring, battering your very body and soul day in and day out on top of your struggle to survive .

Oh, we're going peacefully downstream in the conscious dimensions. There we learn to let go and follow the flow of the Universe and synchronicity.

But in this physical, lower density world, we're fighting directly upstream.

In addition, we're living in a time of increasingly turbulent waters. Our kayaks hit all kinds of eddies and crosscurrents, never mind the rocks and rapids we have to navigate–all while idiots, enemies and doubters, prodded on by the propaganda whores, are screaming obscenities from the shore and trying to hit us with anything they can get their hands on.

But alas, grasshoppers—we have powers they know not of.

The Call to Battle

We're in a warfare, any way you look at it. Only it's not a warfare of hate, but of love. It's not a warfare of physical violence, but a spiritual one of intention and a truth directed life. The inherent cause and effect of Universal consciousness is the dissolution of the ways born of ignorance and darkness by means of the all powerful exposing and enlightening weapons of light, love and truth.

The medieval matrix, no matter how fancy and hi-tech it has become, is dissolving and losing its grip. We need to actively help it on its way to oblivion, identifying its lies and blatant agenda for control and subjugation.

Don't forget, non-compliance is a decisive action, not inaction. Inaction is going with the current of the matrix.

There is no sitting still. We're all doing one or the other. Complying, or rejecting and countering their flow.

That's the choice. That's the battle.

In A Time of Imbalance the Call to Rise is Natural

Similar to the poetic beauty of martial arts, the truth warrior uses his weapons skillfully and with great discretion. While many argue we need evil for good to exist and all that esoterica, we happen to be living in a time of great imbalance.

Do you enjoy having lords of darkness rule over you and yours, exercising more death dealing, spirit quelling control over humanity by the day?

I didn't think so. Will it collapse under its own weight? In many ways it has to. Will it do it all by itself? We have to play our parts. As long as we're here we're integral to the Great Design and clearly need to do our part.

All I know is that what I am finding out and tuning in to calls me to participate, as so many are experiencing. It's as real as the sun and water hitting a seedling and the organism responding. If it's not evident to you that our planet and civilization are under attack I do wonder how you got to this article. It couldn't be any clearer.

This is why they direct the angst people are feeling, the knowing that something is wrong, towards fabricated "outside" enemies to divert attention from the real perpetrators and agenda. Hence the daily "scare" headlines, whatever they are. Similar to how religion co-opts, steers and contains the human soul's hunger for the spiritual, the Controllers arouse, channel and misdirect humanity's sense that it is being attacked and they literally harness what they themselves have aroused, using it for their own parasitic, vampiric purposes.

Cattle prods and sheep dogs driving humanity into the slaughterhouse, mentally, spiritually and physically.

Sorry, not on our watch. It's long been time to sound the alarm and awaken as many as we possibly can. The spiritual, mental and physical arousal has way more effect than we can begin to imagine. Only your mind and low level system programming diminish its importance.

Trust your heart.

There is No "They"...They Said.

The old "tell a big enough lie" ploy is at work here. Their biggest tool is to say there is no "they." There are no dark forces according to mainstream understanding in this dumbed down world. In fact, we're told the "they" are the good guys looking out for us. It reminds me of the adage that the biggest lie Satan ever told is that he doesn't exist. Pretty clever these demons. Just laugh at them.

Yet their all usurping lie remains.

There is no negative, destructive, usurping parasitic force in the Universe other than far away safely distanced religious concepts. Most feel humanity just has other controlling humans to worry about. The powers that be are here to simply save us from each other then becomes the most believable option, and into the cattle chute they go.

After all, that's the mantra of the anti-conspiracy camp. " They? Are you crazy? You really think there's some 'secret cabal' running things from behind the scenes? How insane are you? If that were the case we'd be hearing all about it in the mainstream media. No way they could hide something that big."

Same old, same old.

A very dark time right now indeed. All the recent pandemic scares, terrorism stagings, and economic and phony political rattlings attest to it. And if those fade they'll create some new ones.

Consciousness Calling

If you feel the call to participate more it's consciousness calling, any way you slice it. Take your place on the great mandala and all that, but there's a bulldozer headed for your house. Are you just gonna sit there?

No doubt you've given all of this serious thought. And I know many of you have activated and it's absolutely beautiful. I'm proud to be associated with so many amazing, loving committed people. I think we just need to be adaptive and prepared for more. The winds are picking up and the battlefield is becoming more fluid, more challenging and more demanding.

And for those on the sidelines: It's time to choose your course of action – or let it choose you.

I'm not gonna tell anyone what to do. If people don't learn to choose for themselves, consciousness is not at work and back to the old paradigms we go. But do something. Get the boat in motion or the rudder can't take effect. Find and take your calling seriously and step it up. We all have to.

Meditate, intend, pray, affirm, that's great…but act. Change your life, change the etheric world around you by your loving actions and intentions. Try new consciousness technologies while changing your lifestyle. And perhaps move to a smarter and safer location away from this obvious steamroller coming at many of you. Why just sit there?

Meanwhile write, talk, show up, contribute, speak to groups, attend gatherings of active and motivated individuals or just get honest with your loved ones.

Find the opening and jump in. The rest will follow. Time is too short to do otherwise.

Contribute we must. Hopefully with our whole lives. It's all we have for all we're worth.

It's not a time to get frantic by any means, but take this as a loving alert, something I know many of you are also feeling. Our old views of just weeks and months ago are shifting and will continue to do so. It's subtle, but it's profoundly real. We have to step it up and yield to what consciousness is calling each of us to do and let go of the baggage holding us back.

A purely inspired and motivated heart will always find the way.

Again and again.

Step Into the Role

We're at an amazing and empowering juncture in humanity's history. For each of us individually, now is always the most profound turning point, as each decision we take directs our next step. But collectively there are extremely significant eras or epochs during our development and now is one of them.

It is during these times that a major conflux of influences takes place with which humanity is challenged to either respond according to natural instinctive and intuitive processes, or lie down and let whatever dominant forces at play take their course without resistance or conscious participation.

It is within such turbulent times we now find ourselves as conditions intensify in conjunction with an ever growing collective awareness of the realities with which we are faced. This trend towards higher vibrational realizations in the face of previous paradigms of control and subjugation now dismantling before our eyes is what we loosely term the awakening.

What is peculiar to this later stage we're experiencing is the accelerating rate of unforeseen types of change we are embarking upon. And not only are our personal perspectives changing at an exponential rate both individually and collectively, but the outside realities that influence our lives at every level are also undergoing massive shifts affecting our evolving perspective.

Quite a fluid and potentially disconcerting mix.

What does this mean for us? As old paradigms crumble before our eyes, only a higher vibrational conscious awareness observing these dynamic interactions from a detached perspective will see clearly what is truly transpiring around us. This enables us to perceive clearly as well as respond consciously to these otherwise confusing shifting sands of changing perspectives and morphing realities. This increased divergence between those awakening and an increasingly comatose majority is both a wonderful opportunity as well as potential death knell, depending on our personal response.

This may sound like a mouthful but bear with me; we're undergoing conscious fluid dynamics such as humanity has never before experienced.

The Message

For awakened psychonauts traversing this ephemeral existence and longing to fulfill our role to help manifest Universal harmony via this ongoing revelation of truth, there are very practical steps for each of us to take. This path cannot be taught, the mechanics are not set, and the personal method for navigating this maze is nothing less than experiential as well as deeply esoteric.

Yet all the while extremely practical.

This of course is all by design, as only a heart led soul can navigate its way through such a life experience and discover the many wonderful secrets patiently awaiting revelation. So called reason and mind understandings soon give way to much deeper levels of experiential knowledge that begin to direct our thoughts and actions.

Dispassionate arrows pointing the way borne out of sincere seeking appear along the path as hints to the awakening soul. Anyone or anything attempting to define the nature of what we seek is soon unmasked and eventually shunned by the awake and aware traveler who realizes the Unnamed awaits a much deeper level of realization, not a finite definition. We each find out we discover what we will by profound personal existential experience – never rote, dogmatic, hierarchical, defined or limiting categorizations and linguistic definitions.

Into this vortex of eternal knowing we march unafraid. But herein lies a major clue as to our role. If we are determined, sincere and well aware we are essentially empty vessels in this great play, within this understanding we'll surely find what we should, and meaningful and profoundly effective courses of action soon appear as we continue this noble pursuit.

One very interesting question begins to arise and crystalize at this point. Once we're locked into this search and commitment meets lifestyle and our voice becomes that of truth and change, what role do we play?

What and whom is Universe ultimately releasing in these living, confident voices actively interacting with the world around us in a continued unveiling of our true, inner truth-imbued selves?

Act – Take Authority

I'm convinced we are evolving not only into a greater awakened and empowered state, but one of tremendous release of a new sense of identity as our unlimited talents and potential manifest. Be it for the revealing of empowering truths, spiritual and physical healing, or the immediate use of etheric powers for particular situations, the awakening warriors are commissioned to imbue others with a contagious sense of empowerment and confidence.

This time of manifesting is not only at hand, but is now upon us.

It is a choice to step into these roles as those empowering this transformation. You know who you are. Should anyone seek such spiritual gifts and power for their own selfish benefit they are clearly not among those called as such. For those unawakened to the full sense of unselfish love this can be a stumbling stone, as power tempts and tests the best of us. It's a fundamental filtration and purification process we all pass through. But keep going.

These "next generations" of spiritual and even physically empowered beings are not only coming, but already amongst us. And what activates them? Knowing – some call it faith – not belief or hope or any over spiritualized distraction. It's a fact of which you are intuitively certain.

More profoundly, we are now living in an epoch of awakening where such activation is desperately needed, and to my way of understanding, it is therefore available.

The even more stark reality is that it is you and I who are next in line to step into this role. For the good of all.

It is no small thing and it will likely cost your life. But doesn't any form of living cost your life? Why not live your life to the full for something with profound meaning and importance for the good of all? As far as I'm concerned anyone with any sense of conviction that's worth their salt has already crossed that irreversible rubicon. Even more directly, giving our all towards truth and right is what is immediately needed to remedy the dire circumstances that have been foisted on humanity that threaten our very existence.

This inherent urgency makes such seemingly drastic decisions to activate and take on the role of the conscious warrior a pretty easy choice in my book.

Making the Move and the Activated Rudder

Moving into a new life is least of all physical. It is a process that begins in the heart and mind. Once the lower self is convinced by higher influences of greater realities and potential life paths, decisions naturally unfold and our ships start to turn. It takes miles for a freighter or cruise ship to come about in its course which may be the case with someone's life. What is amazing is how the rudder works on an incredibly small fulcrum, much like the switch of our personal will, which literally creates a vacuum that draws the mightiest of ships into a consciously steered course.

We're each endowed with something so seemingly small yet boundlessly powerful called the majesty of free will that can activate and steer these massive ships called our lives which embodies the magnificence of the human experience. In the shipping industry these tiny rudders that in turn move the larger ones are called "trim tabs."

This for me is perhaps the most empowering metaphor there is that encourages personal activism and dispels all the blockages the naysaying, doubting mind and all of the inhibiting social conditioning memes thrown at us over the course of our lives.

The Trimtab Phenomenon

You have a vision. As an individual or as a family, maybe you wish to communicate something about a burden you have. You care. You love. Maybe your concern is to find a cure for breast cancer. Maybe to save the whales. Or maybe it's your church and you want to see people involved with your church's mission. You want to build community around your vision with others that share that vision. And you want to see change because of this burden you carry in your heart. So you want a web site out there but you think you will be lost in all the web pages that are already out there. That isn't necessarily true.

I like the quote from Buckminster Fuller:

"Something hit me very hard once, thinking about what one little man could do. Think of the Queen Mary—the whole ship goes by and then comes the rudder. And there's a tiny thing at the edge of the rudder called a trim tab.

"It's a miniature rudder. Just moving the little trim tab builds a low pressure that pulls the rudder around. Takes almost no effort at all. So I said that the little individual can be a trim tab. Society thinks it's going right by you, that it's left you altogether. But if you're doing dynamic things mentally, the fact is that you can just put your foot out like that and the whole big ship of state is going to go. So I said, call me Trim Tab." (examiner.com)

Awakened Warriors Arise – Step into the Role

This is a very fresh and even raw revelation for me personally. Although I've known it intellectually for a very long time and it has directed my life to a massive degree over the years, it has never been as profound as this current stage of my life. I've often said, "If you're not free to follow life's signs and live in synchronicity, you're not free", and I've done my best to live by those words. As my life has unfolded this has become more and more real, profound and sometimes disconcerting as each new phase revealed itself to me as I was guided, as well as prodded, to move on to the next level.

But the switch toward activation lays with me.

This has ultimately led to the realization I'm sharing here, that this full activation is our true destination. In other words, being the warriors we were clearly called to be from birth.

I know many of you will attest to this same innate conviction. It's often labelled as a "calling" which is very interesting in itself, but it is a very apt term as it draws us, ever so gently usually but occasionally quite insistently, as I feel the case is right now for a large number of us.

In reality, it's for the taking by anyone willing to step into it.

We're at the point of a kind of insistence by Universe. I know it's not only me experiencing this compelling. And if you haven't yet sensed it and you are called, you soon will be more or less confronted in some way.

Words are like levers that open gates and doors, and this message just may be your gateway to recognizing the role you are intended to play and perhaps bolster your conviction regarding what you already know in your heart but are not yet allowing to be fully realized in your life.

It's time for us all to step up

In summary may I paraphrase,
"Let those that have ears to hear, hear....and activate."

It's time to step into the role
for which we each came into this world.

What Really Matters?

It's amazing how the big questions in life are pushed to the end of the line. Sure everyone wonders about the "big stuff" on and off, but their lives are too preoccupied with other issues that they've been told are more pressing and important – when it's nothing of the sort.

This applies directly to the on-going awakening and how to put our best foot forward in times like these. How best can we be used to effect change? What is the most productive and effective course of action in our personal lives?

With everything at stake at this crucial juncture in history these questions become profoundly important. And the answers just may surprise each of us.

The Preparation

I can guarantee that any real truth seeker is facing a lot of personal challenges at this time. It may be health issues, relationship challenges and perhaps changes, or finding a sound spiritual orientation in these rapidly shifting vibrations. A lot is going on, and this is as it should be.

We're being honed and prepared for what lay ahead of us.

If our hearts are confused, anxious, distracted or over-burdened we won't be much good to anyone. We may even be carrying baggage unknown to us that Universe is peeling away to free us for our next challenges. These can often be ingrained psychic and subconscious memes that keep playing out in our daily lives and reactions unbeknownst to us that are holding us back.

We may even be subjecting ourselves to triggers that bring on these attached, reactive behaviors while thinking these are necessary or even foundational influences in our lives. These are not easy to face up to, especially when it touches on things we consider dearest to us, but if we're to keep progressing in truly conscious awakening face them we must.

It only stands to reason then that these have to be sorted out first if we're to be the true warriors we are meant to be.

But it's not easy.

First Things First

Anyone who has awakened has had this same fundamental experience: Everything began anew. Once we see the true bigger picture of who we are and what we're here for, everything gets reset and we start on a brand new path in life.

However, we tend to emphasize part 2 of the above statement and look quickly for our role here and what we can do about this ugly matrix trying to control and close in on us. That's very important, but we can't short circuit part 1 too quickly. Who are we? This naturally continues to come up as we progress through the maze of rabbit holes and broaden our perspectives. The discovery and changes just occur, as long as we keep yielding to them and making the necessary breaks with our past programming.

But the personal challenges and realizations will get deeper and deeper, and they come with a price. It's the same one every time – letting go – sometimes even of our most cherished beliefs or personal attachments. It can be quite painful, but it's designed for our good, as well as the good of others whom we'll be freer to help and influence with a truly clear signal.

The Inner Child

I've found for myself, with the help of very loving friends with whom I could open up, that issues that have been holding me back without my even knowing it have a lot to do with primal character traits that were formed since childhood. I'm intensely aware of so many aspects of this whole realm of study in personal attributes, societal influences and our spiritual path, but seeing these things in oneself can come as a real shock.

These realizations can come at a very dear price, but it's a price worth paying. It's obviously different for everyone, but if we don't see in ourselves our reactive mechanisms that still need healing then we're going to run into problems. Attributes like deep seated insecurity stemming from years of emotional suppression, neglect and feelings of abandonment develop very strong reactive defense and sublimated cover-up mechanisms that we accept as natural or "normal" when they aren't in the least.

Most everyone raised in this world has been terribly abused at some point or other. The very nature of child and adolescent rearing in this callous world seriously wounds our spirits and forms habitual responses that can only be healed when we embrace that inner child and let it know it's OK to experience and express that trauma as we truly face ourselves.

That's when the chains fall off and the deep empowerment begins.

A Time to Draw Together

I'm no psychologist but human nature I know because I am human, and we all have profound commonalities both in this 3-D dimension and in the collective consciousness. We're interwoven, which is why the matrix of deceit endeavors so hard to break up our honest and heartfelt communing with each other in every way possible, even pitting us against each other, when our closeness and shared experience is our very strength.

But we can only come together after we come apart from the old, including our old selves. We have to first get free of our previous mindsets, habits, emotional baggage and whatever is in the way or holding us back, whether we realize it fully or not.

From there we'll see more clearly, our motives will be more pure, and we'll be much more effective in everything we say and do.

The price is everything, but the rewards and results are beyond comprehension. Those can be pretty difficult to see when you're passing through the "valley of death" of the old but they will appear. You'll get hints along the way. And the more readily we let go in full confidence that Universe is right there with us and that the experience is not a "bad" one or "wrong" at some level the easier it gets.

But it can be quite painful.

In True Unity There Is Strength

As the world turns darker people are naturally drawing closer to each other. No matter how much they fully grasp what's going on in the world, people tend to pull together in small more tightly knit groups with those they love and trust.

This is a drawing for strength and support, which we all need, and now more than ever.

For the awakened this can be more challenging to fulfill. Most of us are scattered about and connected via the internet where we can find others with the same understanding and perspective. That's our true family and fully drawing together may not be that easy.

Communities are forming across the world. We are finding each other and many of us have been developing wonderful relationships with others with whom we resonate. Now is the time to further cultivate those relationships and perhaps make some hard decisions to prepare for what's ahead.

This does not preclude ongoing activism of every sort, in fact we need that more than ever, but most everyone can feel the shift has stepped up and is earnestly moving us in new and very challenging ways.

Letting Go

I'm reminded of the famous monkey trap analogy, where a box is baited with a treat with only enough room for the monkey's hand to get into it. Once he grabs the treat he supposedly won't let go of it and is not able to pull his hand out of the box.

Trapped by his own holding on.

We all do this. The point here is a tremendous change is taking place on many levels. The vibrational shift affects everything at every level and requires adaptation, movement and innovation, even if only on a spiritual level. But the key to freedom and being and expressing our true selves is letting go, detachment.

Therein lies our primary challenge. Will we be a landscape of willfully trapped monkeys not willing to let go of whatever it may be that we think we need, are attached to or stubbornly holding on to? Or will we be a liberated army of fully free warriors ready to do battle in this last ditch fight for planet earth?

It's up to each of us to decide.

As for me, I paid admission to this a long time ago and have no intention of stopping short for any reason or cherished or coveted idea or attachment. It's all or nothing. And that's freedom, which only breeds more freedom, empowerment and alignment with Universe.

Onward. There's really nothing to lose. Our need for attachments is illusory and what's holding on to them needs to simply let go. It will probably be quite painful, but it will subside.

Just don't hurry out of the experience, that's where the real learning takes place.

Draw close to loved ones during this time,
but keep your pursuit hot and determination kindled.

Love always,
Zen

17857319R00259

Printed in Great Britain
by Amazon